Sabino's Map

Para mi abuelita y para mi mamá,
que me han ayudado mucho
con su amor y con su sabiduría.

SABINO
TRUJILLO AT
THE FARMERS
MARKET IN
SANTA FE,
1977.

Sabino's Map

Life in Chimayó's Old Plaza

Don J. Usner

Museum of New Mexico Press   Santa Fe

All poems by Don J. Usner..

Project editor: Mary Wachs
Designer: Deborah Fleig
Cartography: Deborah Reade
Typography: Set in Bauer Bodoni with Nueva display by Deborah Fleig

Manufactured in Korea
10 9 8 7 6 5 4 3 2

Library of Congress Cataloging-in-Publication Data
Usner, Donald J.
        Sabino's Map: life in Chimayo's old plaza/by Don Usner.
                p.   cm.
        ISBN 0-89013-289-5 (CB).—ISBN 0-89013-290-9 (pbk.)
        1. Chimayo (N.M.)—History. 2. Plaza del Cerro (Chimayo, N.M.)
    I. Title.
    F804.C48U86   1995
    978.9'56—dc20   95-16878
                                                                CIP

Museum of New Mexico Press
Post Office3 Box 2087
Santa Fe, New Mexico 87504

Front cover photograph: Amanda Trujillo, 1994. Photo by Nancy Cutlip.
Back cover photograph: Aerial view of the Plaza del Cerro area, 1995. Photo by Betsy Swanson, Historic Preservation Division, NM Office of Cultural Affairs.
Frontispiece: Sabino Trujillo, 1977. Photo by Rosanna Hall.

Gatefold color photographs in book sequence:
(following page 24) Barrancas south of Chimayó; Sunset over Chimayó, Looking west; Sunrise over Chimayó, looking west; The Hill of Tsi Mayoh.

(following page 232) Northwest corner of the Plaza; Northeast side of the Plaza; The Oratorio de San Buenaventura and the west side of the Plaza; Victor Ortega's General Store and Post Office, south side of the Plaza.

Contents

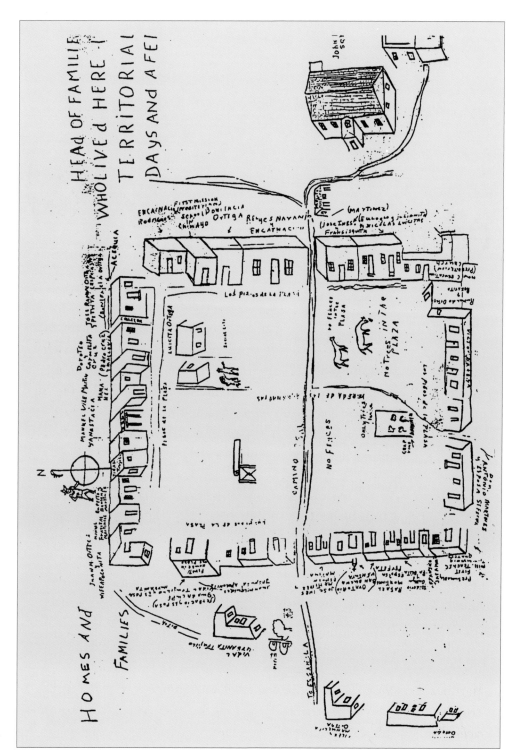

SABINO'S MAP
OF THE PLAZA
DEL CERRO.

Acknowledgments

Before I took an interest in Chimayó's past or knew of the plaza there, my grandma, Benigna Ortega Chávez, unwittingly inspired me about the rich history of the valley by telling me *cuentos* before bed each night, relating *consejos*, and by making me *tortillas*, *atole*, and other traditional foods. My mother, Stella Chávez Usner, has been no less an inspiration. She helped me sort out and translate numerous documents and also deserves recognition for taking meticulous care of original historical documents that I relied upon so heavily. My *tía*, Melita Ortega, also has been a careful guardian of many documents and photographs used in the book, including the Prudence Clark photograph collection and the poetry of El Güero Mestas.

Numerous people in Chimayó shared the stories that form the heart of this book. Besides Grandma, my mother, and Tía Melita, others have inspired me with their knowledge, insight, and sharp memories, including Amada Trujillo (whom I also thank for sharing the map produced by her late husband, Sabino Trujillo), Tila Villa, Teresita Jaramillo, Mercedes Trujillo, David Ortega, John Trujillo, Camilo and Edie Trujillo, Harold Martínez, Petronila Martínez Ortiz, Cordelia Martínez, and Gregorita Martínez. Bersabé Chávez, Benjamín Ortega, Alejandro Ortiz, and Virginia Trujillo Ortega also spoke with me before passing on to the great plaza *en el cielo*. The time I have spent interviewing these people has been richly rewarding for reasons far beyond the purposes of this book.

Many people outside of Chimayó also have helped in the process of writing the book. William deBuys, Alfonso Ortiz, Stewart Peckham, Christine Hemp, Ralph Hopkins, Dan Jaramillo, and Marc Simmons reviewed all or parts of the manuscript and provided invaluable advice and corrections. Carole Usner Hunt, Jim Sagel, and Jim Gavin assisted me with translations of the quirky local Spanish.

Among the many other people who have encouraged me in the process of writing the book are my father, Arthur Usner, Sr., Jerry Williams, Elinore Barrett, Joseph Sánchez, Aaron Martínez, David and Rosella Jardine, Michael Miller, Elizabeth Naranjo, Suzanne Forrest, Helen Lucero, Beverly Becker, Cheryle Mitchell, Roger and Frances Kennedy, Ray Medina, and Tom Horn. I've also enjoyed the support and collaboration of my fellow members of the Chimayó Cultural Preservation Association: Andrew Ortega, Dan Jaramillo, Joan Foth, Raymond Bal, Peter Malmgren, and Lucy Collier. I am grateful to Kathleen Gavey of the Menaul Historic Library for the use of the Prudence Clark collection, to Robin Gavin of the Museum of International Folk Art for access to the E. Boyd files, and to Barbara McCandless of the Amon Carter Museum for the use of the Laura Gilpin photographs.

The Eugene V. and Clare E. Thaw Charitable Trust provided a grant for travel to search photographic archives and also provided funds for the photographic reproductions used in the book. The Southwest Hispanic Research Institute at the University of New Mexico granted me financial support to complete the initial interviews and photographs used in the book.

At the Museum of New Mexico Press, I owe a special thanks to Mary Wachs, whose editorial wizardry saved many a sentence and thoroughly transformed the rough manuscript; to Deborah Fleig for the skill and imagination she brought to designing this book; and to Ron Latimer for his spirited support.

Finally, this whole production would have ground to a halt long ago had it not been for the love and support of my wife, Deborah Harris, who has endured the years of effort without a hint of wear in her enthusiasm. I couldn't ask for a finer companion.

Introduction

The word *plaza* stimulates a variety of images, from the dusty civic squares of Mexican towns to the historic centers of Spanish Colonial settlements across the Southwest. Nowadays, most New Mexicans picture the Santa Fe Plaza with its bustling tourist shops and the Pueblo-styled Palace of the Governors. Mention the word to older Hispanic natives of northern New Mexico, however, and a very different image is conjured up in their minds. These *viejitos* will envision one of the clusters of adobe houses that until recently defined the cultural landscape of the region. Strung along every waterway in the arid terrain between El Paso del Norte and San Luis, Colorado, each plaza and *placita* (little plaza) was home to its own set of extended families, and each had its own story. Most exist only in the memories of the *viejitos* now, for the old plazas have fallen down or have been swallowed up by a sprawl of new buildings, but some still retain the flavor of the old days. Among these few, the *Plaza del Cerro* in Chimayó has survived better than any other.

Ask about the Plaza del Cerro—the Plaza by the Hill—and the *viejitos* will recall a small rectangle of adjoined adobe rooms, each carefully plastered with mud, ringing an unfenced garden planted with vegetable crops. If you stay to listen long enough, they will reel off names of departed relatives and recount times spent visiting and working together, for the plaza to them comprises a community of people more than a collection of buildings. Stay a little longer still and the conversation will ramble off to include plazas distant and near, all intertwined in stories about horses and wagons and vast crops of chile.

Today, the interior fields of Chimayó's old plaza are overgrown with thickets of weedy trees and many of the adobe buildings are slowly crumbling back into earth, like teeth falling from a weathered old face. Yet in spite of its ragged edges, historians have lauded this unassuming relic as the most intact Spanish Colonial plaza in New Mexico, and not long ago it was home to a thriving community of *vecinos* with a long history in the area. Some younger people in Chimayó describe it as just another old *barrio* of the valley, but to the *viejitos* it remains the heart of Chimayó Arriba (Upper Chimayó). Many a visitor has described the plaza as "abandoned," but the plaza is far from forgotten. Several families still live there, and countless other Chimayosos cherish the plaza as an important piece of their cultural heritage.

Only a few people lived here when as a child I visited this small plaza in the morning shadow of the Sangre de Cristo Mountains. I didn't discern the rectangular arrangement of buildings or appreciate its antiquity, but the feeling of the place impressed me deeply. I remember one golden summer day in particular when my grandmother, Benigna Ortega Chávez, and I visited Prima Neria, who many years before had worked alongside her father, Victor Ortega,[1] in the family's general store on the plaza. When we came to call on cousin Neria, she no longer lived in the huge old house that she had been raised in but merely visited for a few days at a time. Old Prima Neria walked bent over and had a large hump on her back from an injury she sustained as a toddler, when they say she fell off a swing. I can still see her laboring down the steep staircase that led from the attic, hanging onto the railing and beaming her greeting to us. Her deformity— and the thought of the terrible accident that caused it—made Neria a mysterious figure, and I felt that I should pity her. But, like all of Grandma's widowed friends, Neria was a strong woman and seemed happy in that house full of spirits. Her difficult circumstances didn't diminish her smile or her generosity with *bizcochitos*.

Grandma's Tío Victor—or Don Victor, as many people in Chimayó remember him—had long since passed away, but Neria and all the old plaza residents still mentioned his name. Inside his abandoned store, I poked through leftover merchandise behind the long, low counter. There were racks of button-up shoes, bins filled with nails, and a spring scale swinging in the hollow darkness of the echoing room. Rows of empty postboxes from the era when Victor Ortega served as Chimayó's postmaster collected dust where letters once had accumulated. As Grandma and Prima Neria's chatter faded out amid the sounds of plates and cups clinking in the kitchen adjacent to the store, I listened for the voices of the people who had left the scale swinging and ran my hands over the glass case and shuffled my feet on the worn wooden floor. Half-aware of the lilting Spanish conversation of the old women, I overheard mention of names and events linked with the strangely silent enclosure of the plaza and the surrounding town. The building seemed to come alive with vibrant traces of the people who once passed through its doors, and I began to sense the close-knit community of family and friends that had gathered here for news or to purchase supplies.

I also remember visiting an abandoned adobe house that once belonged to Grandma's Tía Bonefacia. The door sagging on broken hinges was an irresistible invitation to explore. Inside, my cousins and I marveled at the worn but standing *trastero* with its dusty retinue of broken dishware and empty medicine bottles bearing the names of strange potions. Tía Bone (her nickname pronounced BONE-ay), a sister to Victor, was also long dead, but among Grandma and her peers Bone's house still bore her name as if she had just left for a walk in the *arbolera*. To these people, the house is still Tía Bone's. And so it is for me, too, for I feel that her presence is sustained in that dwelling by the stories and scattered traces of her life. I also sense Tía Bone's wizened spirit whenever Grandma tells me *cuentos* that she learned from Bonefacia, who was a keeper of much lore handed down through generations of Ortegas who lived in Chimayó. The *cuentos* and oral history are as much a part of this plaza as the buildings, and, like the buildings, much of this wisdom seems on the brink of vanishing.

Everyone who has known the old plaza—and many have spent a great deal more time there than I—relates fond memories. This place was home for many of my relatives and friends in Chimayó, *home* in a sense that few people experience anymore. For me, the plaza served merely as a place to visit in the summer when

I stayed with Grandma, an escape from "the Hill" in Los Alamos, where I lived and went to school the rest of the year. Like many people from the Río Grande Valley who lived part of their lives in Los Alamos, I became accustomed to traveling back and forth between two very different worlds. It was always a wonderful trip back in time and back to the earth to come to Chimayó, where people still grew their chiles and apples and had time to enjoy small things such as conversation over *bizcochitos* and stories about the past. I loved the sense of history and culture as much as I loved the feeling of freedom in the fields and hills around Chimayó. The web of family and community so firmly rooted by the rolling foothills tugged on a deep need I felt for a sense of place in the world. It gave me a feeling of belonging that I could not explain to my peers in Los Alamos when I returned for school in the fall. And I still have not found a place so rooted as the Plaza del Cerro.

By the time I graduated from high school, Prima Neria had died, joining the mythic ranks of the *viejitos* who had passed on, and the store that was a romping ground became a mysterious memory beyond my touch. Not long after, Tía Bone's house was renovated and transformed into a new home, and I sorely missed rummaging around through its fragments of the past. Yet in spite of my attachment and fascination with the old place, as soon as I graduated I left the plaza behind, just like so many people before me had done. Ten years away gave me the education and experience that I sought but never erased my memories of Chimayó. I eventually began to crave some solid point of reference in the world I'd found, and the plaza of Chimayó pulled on me. Finally, I came back to Chimayó, hoping to savor again the dusty silences, hear the musical Spanish, and try to understand more about this old community that so enchanted and nurtured me through childhood.

I came home to find some of the plaza buildings listing a bit and several roofs caved in, but each room was still filled with memories. And to my delight I discovered that in spite of the passing of many of the old people, my grandma and many others were still very much alive and telling stories. Just the way I remembered them, the *viejitos*, like the old buildings, still conveyed a timeworn connection to place. Their old-world mannerisms and singsong Spanish welcomed me home.

Deciding to make my fascination with Chimayó conform to the requirements for a master's degree, I enrolled in the University of New Mexico in cultural geography, intending to study the historical geography of the town. My adviser, Jerry Williams, listened to my enthusiasm and dreams and suggested that the Plaza del Cerro would provide a focus for my vaguely defined ideas. He pointed out the significance of the plaza to geographers and historians as the last relatively intact example of the defensive Spanish plazas of the region. With a little research, I realized that numerous written records from the plaza area exist, most of which are in my own family's collection. Most importantly, I recognized that the plaza—the neighborhood where my mother's family has lived for at least eight generations—is the part of Chimayó that I knew best.

With an interest deeper than curiosity, I began my research by seeking out the old people and asking them about the plaza. I had always enjoyed hearing stories about the old days, especially the long yarns my grandma spun over dinner or before bedtime, but for my research I needed to maintain a focus in the discussions. I approached the interviews with trepidation, wondering how I could maintain a feeling of spontaneity in the formal setting created by a tape recorder, a notebook, and a camera. Fortunately, my very first formal interview provided me just the tool I needed.

As Amada Trujillo and I pulled up chairs by her kitchen table and I mentioned the purpose of my visit, she responded, "Oh, I have something you might be interested in," and went off to rummage through boxes in the back room. She emerged with a large, rolled-up paper that looked like it had been around for quite a while. She unrolled it and spread it on the table, revealing a wonderful map drawn by her late husband, Sabino Trujillo, in the 1950s. Looking at the map, the old plaza community seemed to come to life, for it is more than a representation of the physical plaza. The names, drawings, and curious notations on Sabino's map form a fascinating piece of folk art. Sabino's aim was to create a picture that matched his mental image of the old plaza where he grew up in the early decades of the twentieth century. It was just the image I needed as a visual aid to my interviews.

I made copies of Sabino's map to take to every interview. Many people responded to my initial inquiries with excuses for not remembering much about the old days, but I had only to open the map to trigger a flood of stories about the plaza the way it used to be. *"Ah, que lindo*—My, how nice!"* Teresita Jaramillo exclaimed when I placed it before her. "Who drew it? There's the plaza—look, here is my Tía Bone's house. And then, there's the alleyway by 'Mana Carmen's house, and here is where Doña Anastacia lived." Grandma added, *"Sí, tenía cabeza mi primo Sabino, tenía cabeza y sesos*—He had brains, my cousin Sabino, he had a lot of brains. *Ese Sabino era muy curioso!*—That Sabino was sure an ingenious fellow! What made him think of drawing that map?"

In addition to the interviews, which formed the core of my research, I searched for written documents in archives in Santa Fe and history books in Albuquerque. I dug through old shoe boxes filled with faded papers found in attics in Chimayó and found birth and death records, documents tracing land ownership, and wills and legal settlements. But most telling were the old photographs, letters, notes, Sabino's map, and the many stories from people who lived on or near the plaza. I listened carefully to stories in order to record them before they were forgotten, and gradually, the human story of the plaza began to emerge.

My approach was to answer some basic historical questions about the Chimayó area first: What did this valley look like before the first Pueblo and Spanish settlers arrived in the area? Where and how did the Pueblo people live in this valley? Where did these native people go, and what caused them to leave? Further questions derived from my wanderings around the plaza itself: Who built this plaza, and when? How did the first settlers here manage to make a living? How did the plaza function as a community in my great-great-grandfather's time? And what happened to make some people abandon their homes here?

At the heart of my inquiry were questions that went beyond matters of historical fact. In spite of my intentions of keeping interviews short and focused on the plaza, they often drifted into hours of casual conversation. Such conversation proved as useful as the pointed question-and-answer sessions, for, through the eyes of the *viejitos*, I began to see how the residents made their livings, how they saw each other and the outside world, and I started to understand the evolution of perspective and character that came to define this small valley. This

BENIGNA
ORTEGA
CHÁVEZ AT
HER HOME
IN CHIMAYÓ,
1991.

was the kind of picture of old Chimayó I had longed to put together ever since those days when as a youth I began to pick up pieces of the puzzle.

Six years after starting my quest this story is far from complete. I am still translating and transcribing old papers and talking with people, and more intriguing questions turn up almost every day. Scarcely a week goes by that I don't hear a new story or receive a new document or photograph from someone in Chimayó.

Ironically, the plaza began to receive attention from the outside world only after its residents moved away and the place appeared "abandoned." Recognizing it as an important historical site, state and federal governmental agencies began to propose plans for "saving" or "restoring" the plaza. A great deal of controversy has erupted around these ideas, but much of the talk and debate has neglected one fact: buildings can be restored or rebuilt but memories, once lost, are gone forever. While residents have stabilized roofs, shorn up walls, and replastered old adobes, the human history of the plaza and the people who can tell us that story have largely been ignored. Without an understanding of those who inhabited the plaza, full restoration, if it ever came to pass, would create little more than a shell of lifeless buildings.

I offer this book as a starting point for unraveling the history of the plaza community, but this is no lament for the loss of things past. Rather, I pass along the stories to celebrate the people who once filled these old buildings with life and to convey the idea, expressed best by an old friend, that "those were some good times there, on the plaza." Yet I can't deny that I share a dream with my grandma and many other people that the Chimayó community will once again care for the gardens and buildings of the Plaza del Cerro and other neighborhoods. I hope that this book inspires and informs a vision of the plaza as one of the pieces that makes up the heart of Chimayó. These places deserve special care and attention so that Chimayosos can treasure them into the next century.

Chapter One: From the Hills

The Cerros of Chimayó

These are the hills that welcomed the First People
On their first walk in this world,
The hills that breathed the smell of rain
Into their sleeping bodies
And taught them how to pray.

These hills own the bones of all the
grandfathers and grandmothers,
Watching over every birth and death—
So many that no one can count them.

Every stone here is polished with memories
That only these hills remember.
The brittle red and orange rocks
Shimmer with the light of a thousand sunrises.

From the raw rock of deep canyons
These hills sing the song of life and renewal,
Played on silver strings of water—
The only song worth singing.

And these hills know every step
Of the Last Dance on the hilltop
On the Last Sunset over the valley
When finally all things are still.

Almost forgotten, overgrown with weeds and crumbling back into earth, the Plaza del Cerro seems to belong, as its name suggests, to the hills themselves. Indeed, the Plaza del Cerro is located at the very foothills of the Sangre de Cristo Mountains below the Cerro de Chimayó—a towering hill called *Tsi Mayoh* in the Tewa language of the Pueblo Indians who established settlements in the region prehistorically. Tsi Mayoh, long revered as a potent landscape feature, and the other hills loom tall and imposing over the head of the valley, defining the plaza and Chimayó in both character and name.

From my back door, these hills rise to the east, and I look up at them every day, just as my grandmother has for ninety-six years now, and just as her parents and their ancestors have, going back nearly three hundred years in this valley. I think of all my *abuelos* and wonder what they thought when they gazed at the glowing hills. Grandma tells me that she takes the time to look at the *cerros* every morning in the new sun, and she says that the sight has always made her happy. I sometimes imagine my great-grandfather Reyes Ortega looking up from his plow at the end of the day or from the door of his *dispensa* after a long night of weaving and smiling at the familiar presence of the rounded landscape.

I often walk in the hills, following the old footpath that leads up past the *camposanto* where Grandpa Reyes and two of his daughters are buried. The trail curves up a sandy arroyo and climbs over a small pass in the hills on the way to *La Cajita*, the little box canyon where Perfecto Trujillo built his gristmill. It continues on over the *cerros* to Cundiyó. In the years when my family visited Chimayó, we began most hot afternoons with the cry, "Let's go to La Cajita!" Around the turn of the century, the walk had a more practical purpose, as people from the Plaza del Cerro followed the trail laden with sacks of chile that they carried to 'Mano Perfecto's *molino*. The ditch that fed the mill is still there, tracing a faint course from the granite sluice of the streambed to the few posts that remain from the mill structure that washed away decades ago.

"I was little when we used to go up there to grind chile," Grandma tells me. "About ten years or nine. I hardly remember." "Did you walk up there alone?" I ask her, thinking of my solitary jaunts up the trail. "Oh no—we couldn't go alone! My father always went with us. It was like a desert, no people around,

nobody—only coyotes. We took the chile on our backs, or sometimes on a horse. We didn't take so much chile, just enough for the winter."

Grandma and other Chimayosos returned over the rocky path with bags of fresh ground chile, emerging from the hills at the Plaza del Cerro. Now, I walk the trail up in the hills, seeking the solitude and the coyote calls that Grandma feared, and I return down the footpath daily with my mind stilled by the peace of the hills and the comfortable feeling that generations of ancestors walked here before me.

The pink-colored, granitic bedrock of the Sangre de Cristo's core shows through a thin covering of soil on the *cerros*. These old bones of the mountains give the hills a radiant reddish color, and I know of no other place that is blessed

THE UPPER
SANTA CRUZ
VALLEY AND
THE CERRO
OF CHIMAYÓ
(TSI MAYOH),
1995.

with the kind of light that they cast over the Chimayó Valley in the evenings. The glow is augmented by soft illumination from the badlands, or *barrancas*, bordering the valley to the south and north like long, ragged arms. Their subtle light casts a luminescence over the valley long into summer twilight and even into darkness, when they catch moonlight and starlight. Wild and uninhabited, the *barrancas* and the *cerros* together embrace the verdant fields and orchards of the valley. From the hilltops, in the context of the surrounding terrain, the human landscape seems in its proper place: people belong in the valley by the water; the hills and badlands belong to the mountain spirits.

Walking in these hills, I've come to appreciate the Pueblo notion that the hilltops are powerful intermediaries between the world of people and the world of the mountain spirits. From the hilltops above town, the contrast of the two worlds stands out starkly. To the west, curving toward the Río Grande, a patchwork of fields fills the valley, seamed with the willows and cottonwoods of the *acequias* (irrigation ditches)— cultivated land where people exercise a little control over nature. To the east, the lilting, orange foothills rise through forested mountain flanks to thirteen-thousand-foot peaks—the huddled summits of the Truchas peaks, and, farther south, Santa Fe Baldy and Lake Peak. South Truchas Peak was known to the Tewa of San Juan Pueblo as Ku Sehn Pin, Stone Man Mountain, and it marked the eastern edge of their cosmos. The austere mountain summits seem perpetually bathed in ethereal, ever-changing light and appear nearly out of human reach, on the edge of the Beyond—truly the realm of the mountain spirits.

The *cerro* of Tsi Mayoh, though remote and impressive, is a little closer than the peaks and more accessible to the human world. The yaps of dogs and the whine of chain saws float up from the valley to the top of the *cerro*, blending with the staccato roar of cars racing up and down Chimayó's two highways, which intersect just outside the plaza. These sounds announce the chaotic and rapidly changing domain of people. Toward the mountains, space and silence wrap the piñón-covered hills. The cries of piñón jays and ravens or the cascading trills of canyon wrens only serve to accentuate the emptiness. The *cerro* is the pivot point, the fulcrum that balances the two contrasting realms. From there, the valley seems contained, cradled between the blue, rounded Jémez Mountains on the western horizon and the rugged, wild Sangre de Cristo Mountains to the east. What more world could a soul need?

This is the world of the northern Río Grande Valley, sometimes called the Río Arriba or the Tewa Basin—by any name one of the richest regions for human habitation in the Southwest. Here, the Rocky Mountains taper to their southern terminus, and a spreading of the earth's crust has formed the Río Grande rift, marked by deep gorges cut into black lava flows and by the wide, subsiding Española Valley, through which the Río Grande makes its course. The Santa Cruz River, which feeds most of the *acequias* of Chimayó, cuts jagged canyons through the foothills, settles to a less hurried, meandering pace along the badlands, and joins the Río Grande just below the town of Española. Three tributary streams —the Río Medio (not to be confused with the small river the Río en Medio, nearer to Santa Fe, which feeds the Pojoaque River), the Río Frijoles, and the Río Quemado—flow from the Sangre de Cristo Mountains to form the Santa Cruz River. The first two merge at Cundiyó, just upstream of Chimayó, and the third, the Río Quemado, emerges from a steep, narrow canyon to join them at Chimayó. These streams are the threads that connect the valley world to the mountains.

Grandma has always told me that the name "Chimayó" comes from an Indian word that means "the place where the third river meets." Similarly, she believes that Cundiyó means "the place where two rivers meet." This is an old story in Chimayó, and I grew up believing it, for it fits with the geographical circumstances of the valley. As I began to read books and papers about Chimayó, however, I discovered that other people have different explanations. J. P. Harrington, an anthropologist studying northern New Mexico place names in the early 1900s, concluded after interviewing some Tewa people that the name came from Tewa words meaning "good obsidian" or "flaking stone of superior quality."[1] An elderly Tewa woman I recently talked with gave the same translation, but the interpretation remains puzzling, for there is no local obsidian in the hills. Indeed, obsidian is of volcanic origin and the nearest deposits lie in the Jémez Mountains, more than twenty miles west of the Chimayó hills. Except for some layers of flaky mica here and there, there is no flaking stone of any kind around Chimayó.

Over the years, people have proposed many other stories for the origin of this valley's name. Some explain that it was a Tewa word meaning "the place where the big stones stand,"[2] and others trace it to "a Maya word for a kind of dark hardwood."[3] Perhaps the most convincing explanation was finally offered in the 1970s by anthropologist and Tewa native Alfonso Ortiz. Ortiz writes in *The Tewa World*, his exhaustive study of Tewa cosmology, that "Tsi Mayoh" in Tewa simply means "the Hill of the East," and that the summit is so named because it is one of the four sacred hills (the *Tsin*) defining the Tewa world.[4] When I asked about Harrington's work, he explained it this way: "Harrington broke up the words into the wrong components. It's not 'tsi', which means obsidian, but 'tsin', which means hill or mesa." Another Tewa historian told me, "Oh, I guess that the people that Harrington talked with back then told him whatever came into their minds first. His informants were young and didn't know the meaning of the words. Maybe they just wanted him to go away."

Ortiz's translation fits with the way people most often name places, by association with a landmark. The great hill of Tsi Mayoh marks the head of the Santa Cruz Valley and is visible for many miles in every direction. It stands as a natural beacon to anyone trying to find his way to Chimayó. To the Tewa and modern people alike, the surrounding hills and peaks also provide icons for the imagination, places where the human spirit can soar above the more mundane, domesticated realms below.

At the same time, the translation that many Chimayosos give also confirms an important geographical feature, for it is the confluence of waters that sustains this valley. The Santa Cruz River and other major tributaries of the Río Grande flood these valleys with soil-enriching sediments from the mountains that allow crops to grow well. Yet, it is more than the presence of water and fertile soil that has sustained human settlement in the region for so long. The moist uplands are also rich in plant and animal resources of great importance to people living in the region—more blessings given by the mountains.

By their elevation alone the valleys in the Río Arriba would be considered uplands in most parts of the U.S. Elevation of the Santa Cruz Valley floor increases from about 5,600 feet at the Río Grande to 6,200 feet at Upper Chimayó.

The summit of Tsi Mayoh, which modern maps name "Santa Cruz," towers at just over 7,000 feet. This *cerro* and the surrounding hills and summits are outliers —isolated masses of rock—of the hard granitic core of the Sangre de Cristo Mountains. These giant chunks of crustal rocks are over one billion years old, and all the human history of the valley pales beside their antiquity. During the immense span of time that they have existed, tortuous changes wrought by extremely high temperatures and monumental pressures have deformed the rocks, and huge blocks have moved along faults, leaving behind scars of crushed rock. Exposed rock faces bear the marks of their turbulent history in flowing bands of gneiss (a granitelike rock), twisting veins of quartzite, and sheets and folds in

SANTA FE GROUP BADLANDS (BARRANCAS) EAST OF CHIMAYÓ, 1995.

the fabric of the rock. Gouges and grooves trace the movements of rock along the many faults that dissect the foothills region. The rocks have endured so long because of their resistance to erosion, which is also the reason for the steepness and height of the foothills. Rainfall runs off the *cerros* quickly, and only very poor soils of coarse sand form a thin veneer over the bedrock. Even if more water were available on these hills, they would not sustain crops. But they have always sustained legends.

The north side of Tsi Mayoh falls to a deep chasm cut by the Río Quemado, and a *peñasco* (large rock outcrop) midway up the slope conceals a cave on the mountain side—a place that in Tewa cosmology is a place of great mystery and power. Here the Tsave Yoh, "masked supernatural whippers," watch over the Pueblo world.[5] The people in Chimayó call the cave *La Cueva del Chivato*— "the cave of the billy goat." Grandma, who visited the forbidden place in her girlhood years, long ago told me that the cave connects through subterranean passages to Black Mesa at San Ildefonso Pueblo, ten miles distant in the Río Grande Valley. Many other people in Chimayó repeat this myth, and some say that Indians from San Ildefonso once tested the veracity of the story by building fires in caves on Black Mesa and then shutting their entrances. Legend has it that smoke rising out of the cave on Tsi Mayoh confirmed the presence of the passage-way. Tewa stories also warn that tall, dark giants inhabit the subterranean passageways on both Black Mesa and Tsi Mayoh and that both landmarks are dangerous places for the uninitiated to visit. In the Tewa world, only men belong-ing to specific societies could visit Tsi Mayoh and the three other sacred hills.

I recently visited the cave, trudging up the hill through snow flurries and gusty winds, and was amazed to find a warm breeze exuding from its small entrance. I took off my jacket and sat inside, watching the blizzard blow by and trying unsuccessfully to imagine malevolence in the cave's darkness. In spite of the cold, my dog Gerónimo would not come near. He sat at a distance and whined, seeming to sense something that I could not detect. This was unsettling because I had reasoned that for the Tewa the cave was a *metaphorical* point of contact with supernatural realms—but Gerónimo knew nothing of metaphors. And neither did the Tewa, for if I understand Ortiz's thesis, in their world there was no seam between what we call myth and reality. After a time in the silence of the cave, I decided that the Tewa legends are perhaps more than quaint mythology. It is best if very few people visit this cave, only those who are willing to fast and sit quietly, as I imagine the Tewa once did, to gain understanding of the mountain spirits.

Soon after my winter visit to the *Cueva del Chivato*, I learned of someone else's experience there. Having heard that this mysterious cave connected through subterranean passages with Black Mesa, a new arrival in Chimayó recruited a group of friends to explore the cave. With backpacks full of ropes and climbing gear, they boldly assaulted Tsi Mayoh. They reached the cave and lowered themselves in, only to encounter a dead end in just a dozen or so feet. As he expressed his disappointment to me about the paltry depth of the cave, I realized that my friend had missed entirely the point of the Tewa stories. Seeking to explore, conquer, and solve the mystery of the cave, he proved only how different the worldview of the Western mind is from that of the Tewa who knew this hill over centuries of living in its shadow. For those people, the important fact was that the cave and the hill are conduits for the flow of spiritual energy, vital to the well-being of the community. It was of no importance at all whether or not the cave actually connected physically to Black Mesa. In fact, in the context of the Tewa world these kinds of questions seem ludicrous. They tested the old legend with smoky fires only after Europeans had arrived to question what they had always taken as simple fact.

Unlike the tall *cerros* of hard granite, the two arms of eroded *barrancas* to the south and north of the Santa Cruz Valley are made of sandy rocks that crumble underfoot. They confine the valley to a width of about two miles at its widest point and squeeze it to a waist only one-half mile wide. The Santa Cruz River flows against the badlands on the southern side of the valley while the *barrancas* on the north side of the valley are separated from the river by a broad, sloping plain where most houses and fields in Chimayó are located. Perhaps it is because the rugged badlands so enclose the upper Santa Cruz Valley that some early records refer to the area as the "Cañada de Chimayó"—the vale of Chimayó.

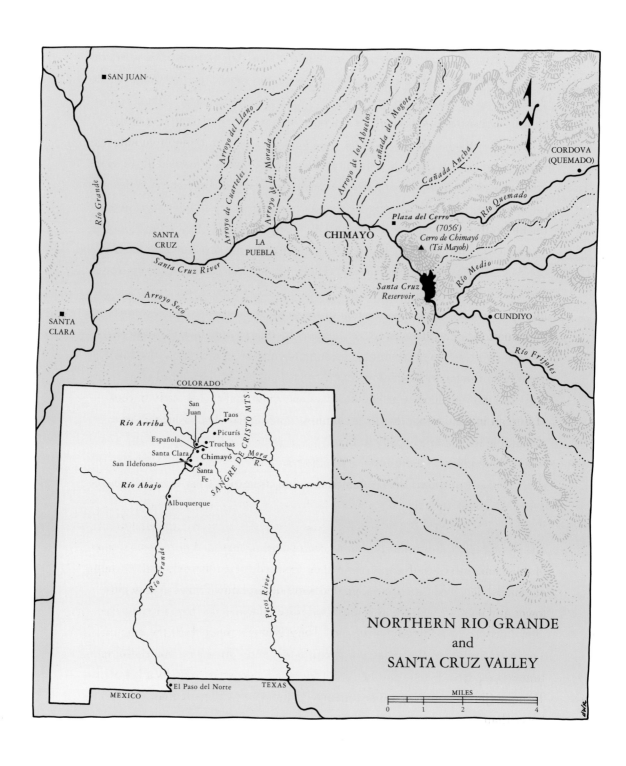

■ SAN JUAN

Río Grande

Arroyo del Llano

Arroyo de Cuarteles

Arroyo de la Morada

Arroyo de los Abuelos

Cañada del Mogote

Cañada Ancha

CORDOVA
(QUEMADO)

Río Quemado

■ *Plaza del Cerro*
(7056')
Cerro de Chimayó
▲ (*Tsi Mayoh*)

SANTA
CRUZ

LA
PUEBLA

CHIMAYO

Santa Cruz River

Río Medio

Arroyo Seco

*Santa Cruz
Reservoir*

■ SANTA
CLARA

● CUNDIYO

Río Frijoles

COLORADO

San
Juan

● Taos

Río Arriba

● Picurís

Española
● Truchas

Santa Clara

Chimayó

San Ildefonso

SANGRE DE CRISTO MTS.

Mora R.

Santa
Fe

Río Abajo

● Albuquerque

Río Grande

Pecos River

● El Paso del Norte

MEXICO

TEXAS

NORTHERN RIO GRANDE
and
SANTA CRUZ VALLEY

MILES

0   1   2   4

The steep *barrancas* are practically impenetrable and, along with the hills on the east, severely limit access to the valley. This was fortuitous for the early settlers, Pueblo and Hispanic alike, for it meant that enemies could enter easily only along the river from the west or from a few small gaps in the hills to the east.

The *barrancas* comprise huge piles of sand, gravel, and mud that long ago washed down from the mountains and piled up in rivers and lake beds. In some areas near the Río Grande, interbedded ash layers from extinct volcanoes have for centuries provided important materials for pottery makers at Santa Clara Pueblo to the west. The sandy rock formations of the *barrancas* are much younger than the granitic rocks of the foothills. These sediments are part of the Santa Fe Group, which extends from south of Santa Fe northward beyond Ojo Caliente and Abiquiú. The rocks are barely consolidated and erode easily into spectacular forms. Pinnacles and spires capping spinelike ridges remain the domain of red-tailed hawks, ravens, and eagles that nest there in the most inaccessible crannies. The badlands seem all of a uniform color from a distance, but within the labyrinth of ridges pastel shades of brown, red, gray, white, and even maroon startle the eye. It is a stark, quiet landscape, fairly devoid of human intrusion and unable to support much vegetation, which makes it unsuitable for grazing or farming.

The Santa Fe Group is in large part responsible for the glorified "magical charm" of the northern Río Grande Valley, but this geological circumstance has earned fame for more than its spectacular forms and vivid colors. In its crumbling strata lay thousands of fossils, most of them from extinct mammals, making it one of the richest sources in the world for fossilized skeletons of vertebrates. Many of these animals were of huge proportions. Paleontologists have unearthed bones of camels, deer, horses, rodents, predecessors of elephants (with tusks in both lower and upper jaws), rhinoceroses, and huge "dogs-bears" that lived in the area more than four million years ago. These animals roamed over warm and humid savanalike plains crossed by great rivers and dotted with lakes, during a time when palm trees flourished in the hills near the present-day location of Tesuque (just north of Santa Fe), where the elevation was more than 3,300 feet lower than it is today.[6] These giants revealed by modern science are no less impressive than the dark Tsave Yoh of Tewa lore.

Numerous arroyos slope down through the *barrancas* to join the Santa Cruz River along its length, cutting directly through irrigated and settled land on their way. Most of these flood channels come down from the north and provided a convenient system of access throughout the valley before the advent of road graders—albeit a system plagued by floods from every major thunderstorm. Recently, government agencies posted many of the arroyo-roads with county road signs, and some of the arroyo roadways have been paved. Giant earthen dams control the floods that used to rage down from the badland ridges. The dam builders couldn't block every arroyo, however, and the new road signs look oddly out of place when they stand in roiling floodwaters. The arroyo-roads have been named prosaically with a system of numbers, but in the past, these flood channels bore much more descriptive, if unwritten, names: Arroyo de los Abuelos, Arroyo de la Cuesta Colorada, Arroyo de los Encinos, Cañada del Mogote, Arroyo de los Alamos, Arroyo de la Cueva, Arroyo de la Cuesta de los Vaqueros, and many others, most of them today nearly forgotten.

The largest of the arroyos sweeps down the Cañada Ancha from the northeast and was long a travel route to Truchas and other mountain villages, channeling trade from the east side of the mountains and from Taos. Indeed, this canyon cuts the only route of reasonable access to the valley other than the river corridor. The Plaza del Cerro sits near this important trade road, now rerouted and christened by tourist brochures as "the High Road to Taos." Don Diego de Vargas probably rode up this sinuous arroyo when he chased the last of the Pueblo Indians from the hills of Chimayó in 1696. This was the *cañada* that my grandma and her father followed by wagon on their arduous way to tend wheat grown high on the Llano Abeyta near Truchas. The people of Picurís Pueblo also used the Cañada Ancha route when they passed through Chimayó, stopping at the Santuario before continuing on to Santa Clara for feast day. I can picture them as my neighbor John Trujillo remembers, led by a drummer and singing as they followed their wagons in a long procession down from the sandy hills.

Spectacular floods once churned in all the arroyos, and people took care to build their homes well away from the arroyo beds before earthen check dams were constructed in the 1960s. Now random arrangements of mobile homes lay boldly in the path of some of the temporarily constrained washes. None of the arroyos carries perennial water flow, but springs and seeps flow out of the *barrancas* on the northern side of the valley and disappear into the sands of the Cañada Ancha. It is surprising to come across the cottonwood trees that are tucked into folds of the stark badlands where water emerges to the ground surface, forming tiny oases where birds and other animals come to drink. The relatively gentle terrain and the presence of water historically made the Cañada Ancha the only place in the Chimayó vicinity that was suitable for grazing cattle and sheep.

The abundant sunshine and clear, dry air of the northern Río Grande region similarly grace the Santa Cruz Valley. As in all of New Mexico, moisture comes mostly in the form of summer rainfall, when humid air from the gulfs of Mexico and California is drawn toward the Río Grande Valley and billows into great thunderheads over the mountains. But the timing and intensity of the resulting moisture—often mistakenly called a "monsoon" cycle—are unpredictable, and the almost whimsical variation in precipitation year to year has frustrated New Mexico farmers for centuries. No records for annual precipitation at Chimayó are available but, because precipitation increases with elevation and proximity to the mountains, on the average Chimayó probably receives slightly more precipitation than Española, at ten and one-tenth inches annually. Higher up, over 40 inches falls in the mountains, much of it in the form of snow. The mountains' ability to intercept and precipitate moisture from passing air masses —to make rain from the heavens, the Tewa might say—is of paramount importance to lowland agriculture.

People dependent on their crops for survival watched the rain very closely in the Santa Cruz Valley, but for farmers at the Plaza del Cerro, situated comfortably at the very base of the foothills where reliable streams watered the crops, a lack of rain was often less of a worry than too much rain all at once or, worse, the curse of hail. The dirt-covered, flat-roofed buildings of the old plaza could only absorb so much water before they began to leak. Grandma remembers her family taking their dinner beneath the kitchen table, protected by a waterproof oilcloth from the interior rainstorm that was drenching the house. "I remember when my father put the tin roof on our house," she says, "because that year, it rained so much that we spent all our time under the table. And my mother couldn't cook because it was leaking on the stove. We had to put the wood to get dry in the oven. It rained so much that all the people started putting tin roofs on their houses."

In Chimayó, thunder rumbles and roars as it bounces off the steep foothills and echoes off the badlands, and the sandy earth smells sweet as the moisture percolates through the coarse soil. The sudden thundershowers of summer, often frightening in their intensity, can be both a blessing and a curse, bringing needed moisture but often causing torrential floods in the arroyos. Grandma's great-grandfather, El Güero Mestas, wrote despondently to his grandson Victor Ortega about a particularly devastating flood in 1880: "The 26th of July there fell here in Cuarteles [about five miles down the valley from the Plaza del Cerro] a down-pour that left me almost without a house. The little arroyo that comes down in front washed out my chile fields, and all my vegetables and fruits. The vegetables won't come back, although the chiles have grown back a little. It would be a long story telling you the straits I found myself in that day."[7]

The valley saw fearsome floods, especially in areas where grazing animals denuded the hills and left them vulnerable to erosion. Such experiences taught Chimayosos to respect the power of the thunderstorms and their attendant floods, although the people apparently didn't make the connection between floods and overgrazing. I remember Grandma rushing outside once when a particularly loud peal of thunder rolled, tossing a handful of salt to keep the lightning away while exclaiming "Jesús y Cruz!"—a gesture oddly reminiscent of the ceremonial propitiations that the Tewa performed to supplicate the rain spirits. Other people in Chimayó keep a small jar of holy dirt from the Santuario on the windowsill to ward off bolts of lightning.

Despite its lush appearance, it is not easy to make a living off the land of this valley. Besides the erratic rainfall, temperature and growing season are also unpredictable. Farmers in Chimayó can count on a growing season of only about 140 to 160 days. They can usually rely on the hot, clear summer weather to ripen

BARRANCAS AND
THE SANGRE DE
CRISTO MOUN-
TAINS FROM
CHIMAYÓ, 1951.

the chiles, but killing frosts frequently destroy the spring blossoms of orchard crops and make subsistence agriculture risky and commercial cultivation of fruit practically impossible. Extremely cold air masses creep down the Río Grande Valley from time to time. In the winter of 1972–73, temperatures dropped to thirty degrees below zero and killed many of the fruit trees in the valley, snapping their limbs with a sound more common to the Arctic than to sunny New Mexico. Grandma remembers cold years like this from early in the century, days when the ice on the ditch was thick and taxed the men's efforts to break it. But break it they must, because although the people could melt snow the livestock relied on the ditch for water year-round.

Prehistoric people at times were able to rely on rainfall alone to water their crops, and as recently as fifty years ago some years were wet enough for corn production without irrigation. But for most of the past several hundred years farmers have relied on irrigation to grow their chile, corn, melons, and other crops.

The increase in precipitation moving eastward from the Río Grande to the Sangre de Cristo Mountains creates a series of vegetation types, from grasslands along the lowest elevations through woodlands of piñon and juniper trees on the foothills to forests of ponderosa pine and mixed conifers above 7,000 feet and a narrow band of spruce and fir below the treeless alpine zones of the highest peaks. Vegetation that is dependent on flowing water follows the stream courses through this rugged terrain. The diverse habitats from the dry, warm valleys to the cool, moist mountains provide areas for hunting, plant gathering, grazing, and woodcutting.

Narrow ribbons of riparian vegetation—cottonwood, alder, and willow— follow the Santa Cruz River and the maze of ditches that sew the patches of fields together. A total of eighteen main ditches and numerous smaller ditches serve the Santa Cruz Valley. Two of these—the Martínez ditch and the Ortega ditch—water the Plaza del Cerro area. The first Hispanic settlers dug these old *acequias* with the crudest of tools, although in some places they may have followed the courses dug previously by Pueblo farmers. The District ditch, designed by engineers in the 1930s, flows directly across the plaza. Its water is off-limits to plaza residents.

Of these three *acequias*, only the Ortega ditch derives its water from a free-flowing stream (the Río Quemado), and its flow is virtually guaranteed even in dry years because of numerous springs just up the canyon from Chimayó. The other two ditches of the plaza area draw from the Santa Cruz River below Santa Cruz Dam. Some people say that the Río Quemado water grows better crops, for it lacks the pollution of the dammed waters and their incessant motorboat traffic. This makes me glad that my great-grandfather and other plaza residents refused to participate in the dam project nearly seventy years ago, although their reasons had nothing to do with motorboats.

Chimayó may appear to be a small town in the midst of undisturbed land, but people have altered the appearance of this valley and the hills since they first

arrived long ago. The Pueblo and later Hispanic settlers used the land in similar ways, clearing fields for farming and cutting trees for firewood and building materials. On the highest hills around town—even on the summit of Tsi Mayoh and on the steepest ridges of the badlands—old stumps of piñón trees, cut by axes before saws were available, attest to the far-ranging wood harvesting that has taken place. Hispanic people introduced livestock grazing, a more damaging land use that was to leave scars throughout the Southwest. Goats were best suited to the rugged terrain near Chimayó and foraged extensively in the hills until the early 1960s. Many of the gullies and ravines around Chimayó formed because of the terrain's natural susceptibility to erosion, but the natural processes have at times been greatly accelerated by woodcutting and grazing. Many deep gullies remain from the harsh overuse by goats, though many of these have slowly recovered in the past thirty years as plants have taken hold.

No one can say exactly how Chimayó looked to the first Spanish settlers entering the valley, but we can be sure that the dense cover of domestic and riparian trees was largely absent before settlers built the wide-ranging network of ditches that distributes water throughout the area. The relatively recent arrival of aggressive nonnative trees such as the tree of heaven, Siberian elm (often mistakenly called the Chinese elm), and Russian olive has also dramatically altered the vegetation, crowding fields and forming dense, knotty thickets along all the irrigation ditches. Some Chimayó people remember when there were few trees in the valley. Cordelia Martínez talks about a time when someone from "the government" came to Chimayó to plant trees, ostensibly for shade. Grandma saw the first Siberian elm planted in the plaza area, sometime in the 1950s: "Yes, you used to be able to see the plaza from the arroyo way down below. That was before there were all these trees everywhere—when people took care of their land. Now all the fields are so *puerco* (dirty). Before, everyone on the plaza swept their *patios* every day and hoed the fields, and they were *muy limpiecito* (very clean). There weren't so many trees dropping leaves all over the place then." Roots of the elms not only are taking over open land but are also actively tearing down abandoned adobe houses, including many on the plaza. People have been trying unsuccessfully to eradicate these trees ever since the first was planted.

Historic photographs and surveyors' notes from the early 1900s confirm that the only riparian trees in the valley were cottonwoods and willows and that these were confined to the river and ditch banks. Perhaps the Cañada Ancha and some of the other major arroyos also once supported permanent watercourses lined with cottonwoods and willows. As has been documented for many areas in the Southwest, streams there may have been transformed into dry arroyos by changes associated with overgrazing.

Ponderosa pine trees may also have grown in the vicinity of Chimayó. These trees were of great value to the first settlers for firewood and for *vigas* (roofing supports) in home construction. Because of their limited availability in the valley, they probably would have been the first trees to be eliminated.

From the hills above Chimayó the past four hundred years have revealed a slow seasonal greening of the valley, as more and more land has been cleared, irrigated, and planted with crops. Over time, the fields have been divided into smaller, narrowing pieces dotted with ever more numerous houses. The 1940s and 1950s saw an explosion of green as aggressive trees were brought in and began to overrun every field not closely tended.

In the thirtysome years that I have climbed these hills and watched, the process of change has accelerated. The expansion of land claimed by domestic trees continues as the planted fields shrink. I have seen the recent phenomenon of ribbons of blacktop slice away from the highways and through the green of the valley. Houses and trailers have appeared on top of hills, away from the life-sustaining waterways, and some of the old ditches hardly run anymore. At night, the valley is filled with lights when only fifty years ago there were no lights at all, and in the hills I find bits of trash and new footprints where for decades only my feet have trodden.

Change has been a constant in this valley and more is on the way, but the Plaza del Cerro, a tiny anachronism in the changing human landscape, is still almost completely dark at night, for the highways and the surge of house building have largely passed the old plaza by. Once an isolated outpost of civilization, the plaza has survived recent changes to remain as an isolated remnant of a less civilized time.

Chapter Two:
Donde Vivían
los Indios

Broken Pots on Sandy Hilltops

On those small hills,
Amid cholla stems and paintbrush,
Above the curving highway
Where commuters rumble past,
Coffee cups spilling—
That's the place where the Indians lived.

Their mud rooms stood there,
Where you see the fields spread like cut cloth,
Green in summer
Tan and brown in winter,
And the river snaking past cottonwoods
At the base of the small hill.

There they sat and
Drew patterns on clay,
Black-on-white stripes and scrolls and parallel lines,
And watched sunsets linger
Over these mountains,
Praying to the powers of the Earth,
And listening to the song of the creek.

The older Chimayosos all know that Native Americans once lived in the valley near their homes. Grandma refers to the local prehistoric ruins simply as the places *donde vivían los indios*—the places where the Indians lived—and she gestures to the little hilltops south of the plaza where pottery sherds lay among cholla stems and blooming Indian paintbrush. *"Tiene mucho misterio de los indios, ese lugar* —There is a lot of mystery because of the Indians in that place," she says.

Grandma is right about the evidence of Indian inhabitation in Chimayó. As in most of northern New Mexico, remains of prehistoric village sites are so common in the Santa Cruz Valley that they are practically part of the natural landscape, adding much to its haunting beauty. Several major and dozens of small ruins lie throughout the valley and surrounding hills. One Chimayoso tells me that prehistoric pottery was once so common when he was growing up that he and other boys sometimes used whole pots for slingshot practice. Such finds, now considered rare treasures, were doubtless more abundant when the first Hispanic settlers arrived four hundred years ago, even though most pueblo ruins of the Santa Cruz Valley by then had laid vacant for some two hundred years.

The people of San Juan Pueblo believe that their Tewa ancestors lived in the Santa Cruz Valley, a fact that is supported by the types of pottery found at the ruined pueblos here. However, although no one can say for certain when the first human beings wandered into this sandy valley, the evidence shows that the Tewa were not the original ones. Starting at least twelve thousand years ago— long before the Tewa came here—bands of hunters probably passed through as they followed herds of mammoths and giant bison across the cool, humid forests and grasslands of the Pleistocene landscape. These wanderers left only faint traces of their passing at camps and kill sites where they gathered to feast on meat. Archaeologists have found the stone weapons and tools of these Paleo-Indians in the northern Río Grande region, although no artifacts from this period have been unearthed anywhere near Chimayó.

A changing climate forced the large game herds to extinction, or at least away from New Mexico, about nine thousand years ago, and Paleo-Indians gave way to cultures with a more flexible life-style. These peoples, labeled as Archaic cultures, also led a wandering existence without permanent dwellings, but they hunted smaller game and gathered wild plants from the Río Grande Valley floor to the highest ridges in the mountains. Vestiges of Archaic cultures are more common than Paleo-Indian artifacts, and numerous hearths (abandoned fire pits lined with stone cobbles) and scatterings of stone artifacts lay in the hills and badlands surrounding the Santa Cruz Valley. Finely crafted spear points of obsidian distinguish Archaic artifacts from those left by other prehistoric people. I know of one Chimayoso who on his wanderings has (illegally) collected several axes and Archaic spear points. These artifacts were found in locations that hardly suggest an abundance of game, a testament, perhaps, to the gradual drying trend in the climate since the Archaic people hunted here.

A professional archaeological survey of the upper Santa Cruz River watershed in the late 1970s confirmed a substantial Archaic presence in the region. On the rolling terrain at the foothills of the mountains a few miles southeast of Chimayó, researchers found several areas where Archaic hunters sat and worked on spear points, leaving a scattering of flaked stones.[1] A survey closer to Chimayó would probably indicate a similarly intensive occupation, in spite of the fact that a large number of artifacts have been removed by novice collectors. These scattered remains hint that Archaic people passed through the area in their migrations between the mountains and the valley.

It wasn't until about A.D. 1000 that people started to settle down in the Santa Cruz Valley and build homes. The first dwellings consisted of small, semisubterranean pithouses, but eventually these same cultural groups built the numerous semipermanent villages whose ruins have made the northern New Mexico region of great interest to archaeologists. Pithouse remains are rare in the Santa Cruz Valley, but the area is replete with the remnants of a culture called the Río Grande Anasazi, ancestors of today's modern Río Grande Pueblos.

The nineteenth-century archaeologist Adolph Bandelier pioneered archaeology in the Southwest, but he apparently never visited the ruins in the Santa Cruz Valley. He mentioned in his journals that "higher up [in the Cañada de Santa Cruz] toward Chimayó there are said to be well-defined ruins on the mountain sides." He correctly surmised that one of these was the historic Tano ruin of Tsawari near La Puebla, built after the Spanish were run out of the valley in the

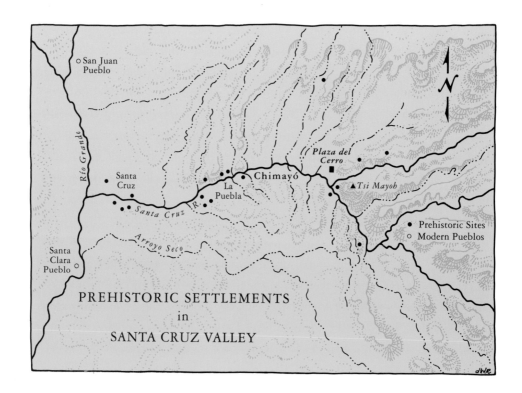

PREHISTORIC SETTLEMENTS
in
SANTA CRUZ VALLEY

Pueblo Revolt of 1680. Bandelier also noted that a second major ruin site represented the remains of San Lázaro, also built by Tanos after the revolt, and he alerted "future explorers" to the fact that the valley contained both historic and prehistoric ruins.[2]

Edgar L. Hewett, famous more for his wholesale promotion of archaeological resources than for precise methodology, came to the area in 1908 on the heels of Bandelier and may have collected some materials, but I have found no written record of his visits. The only systematic research concerning the archaeology of this ruin-filled valley was produced in the 1930s, when Harry P. Mera, a Santa Fe physician-turned-archaeologist, studied pottery sherds from seven of the larger ruins in the Santa Cruz watershed. In addition to identifying pottery types, Mera was interested in Pueblo settlement patterns and used pottery styles to trace the locations of Pueblo people over time. He noticed that over the span of a few hundred years, prehistoric Pueblo people in the Santa Cruz Valley seemed to move their villages from locations in valleys to positions on hilltops.

where they could be more easily defended. He believed this gradual migration upward was a response to increased raiding by people from outside the valley.[3]

Stephen deBorhegyi, a geographer who lived in Chimayó in the early 1950s, also visited some prehistoric sites in the Chimayó area and studied the surface pottery sherds. Since he lived near the Plaza del Cerro, deBorhegyi focused most closely on the ruins nearby. He, too, tried to reconstruct the relocations of Pueblo villages over the past few hundred years. His research also led to the conclusion that the villages on hilltops represented efforts to build defensible settlements.[4]

Since the work of Mera and deBorhegyi, few archaeologists have visited the Santa Cruz Valley ruins, and no new large ruins have been discovered. In the intervening years, a few small sites have been surveyed in highway salvage projects and as the result of construction activities. An exciting discovery came during a survey in conjunction with highway construction in 1963. About fifty feet from the roadway a researcher found a human burial near the top of a sandy hill. The skeleton lay alongside obsidian arrowheads that may have been embedded in its lower spine, hinting that this individual had met a violent end.[5]

More recently, in 1984, two pithouses containing human burials in their floors were discovered when a Chimayó family bulldozed a site for a mobile home. The family wisely alerted the Museum of New Mexico's Laboratory of Anthropology, and archaeologists arrived to recover the human remains and make quick sketches of the pithouses. This seemingly meager find is noteworthy both because of the presence of pithouses and burials and given that no pottery was found, indicating that the site may be a very old one. Estimates date the pithouses to about A.D. 400–600, which would make this site the oldest yet uncovered in the Santa Cruz Valley.

Only one ruin in the valley has been excavated—the remains of small aboveground dwellings near Santa Cruz that were encountered during a road-widening project. In one day there, archaeologist Stewart Peckham and a crew of two workers hurriedly cleared soil and debris and jotted a brief description and sketch of three surface rooms and a kiva at this small site, which already had been partially destroyed by highway construction.[6] The pottery at the site came from the west and south of the area and dated from around A.D. 1000–1100. A much larger ruin site, located near Córdova and known as Pueblo Quemado, or

Wiyo, also was destroyed by highway construction, but no excavation took place prior to the destruction.

All the documented work in the Santa Cruz Valley reveals a total of thirty-three prehistoric sites, only eighteen of which contain concentrations of pottery sherds that suggest they were lived in by Pueblo people. Two of these Pueblo ruins occupy the tops of small hills less than a mile from the Plaza del Cerro. The non-Pueblo sites in the valley consist of small scatterings of stone flakes indicative of toolmaking activity, isolated concentrations of pottery fragments, and abandoned hearths. But the valley has yet to be professionally surveyed, and there are many more large and small sites that remain unrecorded in the official archaeological register. Their scrutiny, if it ever happens, will fill one of the largest missing pieces in the archaeological survey of northern New Mexico.

Because no archaeologist has tarried long enough in the valley to study the ruins in detail, the story of prehistoric settlement here remains sketchy. Fortunately, Mera and a few others took notes on the types of pottery at some of the ruins. Mera pioneered efforts to compare design styles and firing techniques on the pottery sherds around the region, making it possible to identify cultural groups and allowing a rough guess at when people lived at each village site. Accurate assessments based on pottery alone are confounded, however, by a lack of data and because pottery types and their date of manufacture are not always precisely defined. Furthermore, even a skilled archaeologist may misidentify pottery types, and opinions and methods of identification have changed considerably over the past sixty years. However, based on meager and sometimes equivocal evidence, a story of prehistoric settlement in the Chimayó area unfolds, similar in most respects to one pieced together for other parts of the northern New Mexico region. The story begins with a struggle to survive by farming a dry land swept by episodes of drought and perhaps violence, and it concludes with abandonment of every village in the valley.

The oldest pottery found in the Chimayó area bears black designs on a plain white background. This early black-on-white pottery is fairly rare in the valley, but there is some at one of the two ruins near the plaza. According to archaeologists' notes, the general decorative style of these sherds conforms to the types known as Red Mesa Black-on-white and Chaco Black-on-white. The former, produced about A.D. 875–1050, was made, or at least traded, over a wide area centered on Chaco Canyon. Its presence in the Río Grande predates the migration of Four Corners Anasazi people eastward after the decline of Chaco canyon after about A.D. 1100. The decorative motifs on Red Mesa Black-on-white emphasize triangles, interlocking scrolls, and parallel, zigzagging lines. The types classified by early archaeologists as Chaco Black-on-white are also rare in the Chimayó area but can be found on the two ruins nearest the Plaza del Cerro. However, it is doubtful that these sherds actually represent Chaco Black-on-white, which was a highly refined type that is unusual even in the Chaco area, but they probably do indicate local varieties of an artistic tradition emanating from Chaco. This pottery style, produced for a brief period about A.D. 1000, feature hatched and solid designs.

These two types of pottery—Red Mesa Black-on-white and a variant of Chaco Black-on-white—dominate the potsherds at the two ruin sites nearest the Plaza del Cerro. People living here and elsewhere in the Santa Cruz Valley beginning in the late twelfth–early thirteenth centuries probably inhabited small clusters of pithouses with a few aboveground rooms. Nothing remains of these structures except some irregular mounds of soil capped with vegetation indicative of human disturbance. The Great House architecture that we associate with Chaco Canyon and that has been found throughout the Anasazi region west of the Río Grande was not to be repeated by the Anasazi who migrated into the northern Río Grande Valley. Instead, this region's earliest architecture reflects the fluid settlement patterns that had always characterized Anasazi culture.

The blessings of the mountains that today's Tewa Pueblo people so reverently honor may help explain the paucity of early ruins in the Santa Cruz Valley. Some archaeologists believe that the first Pueblo people in the northern Río Grande didn't organize into highly structured societies until much later (after A.D. 1300) because the moisture and rich animal and plant resources of the mountains provided a ready source of sustenance. According to this logic, these Puebloans simply didn't need to organize large-scale agricultural cooperatives and housing such as were developed in Chaco Canyon.

THE CAÑADA
ANCHA SEEN
FROM A PUEBLO
RUIN SITE,
1995.

Various ceramic sherds from the period after Chaco's collapse have been
found in the Santa Cruz Valley, and developments in pottery traditions region-
wide can be read in artifacts found here. Interestingly, ceramic wares produced
after A.D. 1400 are almost entirely absent from the valley sites, indicating that
the area was abandoned by about that time. Some archaeologists have suggested
that the area may have been used agriculturally to support growing Pueblo
populations in the nearby Río Grande villages of San Juan and Santa Clara.
Theories behind the Anasazi pattern of occupation and abandonment abound.
Some researchers find evidence that the Anasazi periodically left their homes
because they had used up all the available resources—especially firewood and

perhaps game—and had depleted the soil. Others believe that drought or in-creased pressure from raiding groups compelled them to abandon settlements. A drought descended on northern New Mexico from A.D. 1245 to 1290, which may have initiated a regional move away from upland, dry farming areas to the consistent water source of the Río Grande.

* * *

The first Europeans arriving in northern New Mexico in the early 1600s found what they understood to be permanent settlements up and down the Río Grande

Valley. They called these settled places *pueblos*, Spanish for village, but all the while the Pueblo people continued their patterns of impermanence. In the Santa Cruz Valley, the Spanish encountered emptied settlements, and facing the same formidable obstacles to settlement as those faced by the earlier people, the colonists naturally took advantage of any foothold they could find. Not surprisingly, they often built their villages upon Pueblo ruins, drawing on the experience of people long gone who had already selected good places for farming.

When an old building on the plaza collapsed in 1991, I picked through the crumbled walls and found many sherds of pottery. A neighbor remodeling a plaza home also found an abundance of large pottery fragments in the old adobes, although few bear the characteristic black-on-white patterns of early Pueblo pottery. Finding sherds in modern pueblo walls is a common experience. For generations the collapsed walls of ruined buildings have been scooped up and mixed into the mud for new adobes. Finding sherds at the plaza seems to imply that Pueblo people may also have built homes here, but there are complicating factors. Some people tell me that Chimayosos went to an abandoned Anasazi site—Pueblo Quemado, overlooking nearby Córdova—to obtain sand for plastering their homes because they preferred the light color of that local sand to the dark material available near the plaza. When they gathered the sand they no doubt also picked up sherds from that ruin, and this may be the source of the fragments we find in the plaza today. However, possible solid evidence of prehistoric habitation at the plaza appeared recently when an archaeologist found the remnants of ruined walls directly beneath the plaza's *torreón*, or watchtower. No one is certain yet if these are prehistoric wall remnants, but if they are they would indicate that the Plaza del Cerro represents only the most recent cluster of adobe rooms at a place that was settled as many as a thousand years ago.

Chapter Three: Scraps of Paper

Faded Papers

Tía Juanita lived alone by the acequia,
In the old adobe shaded by cottonwoods,
And when she slept in the back room—
The very room where her mother,
Holding herself by a rope from the vigas,
Had given birth to all eight sisters
And died birthing the only boy,
Wailing while the children covered their ears—
When she slept there, I wonder if the swirling
ditch water
Was the only voice she heard?

In the wooden chest beside her bed, my mother, Stella Chávez Usner, keeps folders full of faded papers dating back to the early eighteenth century. Written carefully in flowing longhand or scribbled in barely legible print, the papers were authored by many individuals from the Plaza del Cerro to document important transactions that took place in Chimayó. Through the decades of the past three centuries, there was always at least one person in each generation who valued these scraps of paper and passed them on. Reyes Ortega received them from his father, José Ramón, and left them to his unmarried daughter, Juanita. Tía Juanita carefully guarded these papers in a chest in her father's house in Chimayó and then gave them to my mother, who stores them faithfully in her carved box. The documents include records of land sales, wills, personal letters, minutes from meetings, and many other kinds of correspondence and legal papers. No two pieces of actual paper are the same, for paper was a scarce and precious commodity and the authors used whatever was at hand. Now these bits of paper are invaluable for a different reason—for what they can tell us about life in Chimayó over the past three hundred years.

Given the nature of life in this isolated valley, it is remarkable that people preserved these records. They at times must have seemed obscure and irrelevant to the exigencies of daily life. The fact that they have been so carefully preserved reveals something of the nature of the people who kept them—and undermines the notion that all the people here were simpleminded farmers living in primitive isolation. The early Chimayosos who left these records not only knew how to read and write, they also had a strong sense of legal propriety—always with an eye toward the future. I like to think that at least some of the people guarding these yellowed pages anticipated a day when someone like me would think to tell the history of a family, but their preservation is fortuitous not only because they shed light on family history. Now on file in the New Mexico State Records Center and Archives as part of the Borrego-Ortega Papers, the documents form one of the best collections from the Spanish Colonial period from outside of the *villas* (major towns) of the province.

DOORWAY ON THE ABANDONED CRUZ HOME, NORTH SIDE OF THE PLAZA, 1994.

Not surprisingly, the papers in the collection deal mostly with affairs of the guardians of the documents, the Ortega family. The oldest paper in this collection, though, is a petition for land in Chimayó written in 1706 by Luis López—land on which the Plaza del Cerro was eventually built. In his petition, López mentions many of the important figures and events that influenced settlement in Chimayó: the Pueblo Revolt of 1680, the King of Spain, the Governor of the Province of New Mexico, the Tano Indians, the Spanish settlers, and the old ditch that later provided water to the plaza. López's simple claim is a convenient point of departure for unraveling the complicated story of Hispanic settlement that began long before he came to the valley. Like almost all stories of European and Native American encounters, this one began with the violent domination of indigenous people, but López's claim for land is innocent of any mention of violence, for he arrived after the battles had been fought and the natives forced out of the area.

López scrawled his petition with a quill pen and presented it to Governor Cuervo y Valdez. It read, in part,

Luis López, native of this kingdom, inhabitant of [Santa Cruz de] la Cañada, married and with children, I appear before you in good faith. . . . And I state that, finding myself in this kingdom of original settlers, having been here since 1693 when it was resettled, I find myself with neither farmland nor house. And I know of a piece of land that has not been settled above the Cañada de Chimayó which has never been cultivated, and [has never had] an owner except for the King (may God keep him), and the boundaries are an arroyo that divides the property [from that of] Francisco Martín and with ditch that the Thano Indians made when they lived in San Cristóbal, which is on the south side, and another arroyo touches the north part whose boundary follows along the road to Taos.[1]

The language of the document implies that Luis had been born in New Mexico before the Pueblo Revolt, which drove all of the Spanish from the province. Confirming this suspicion, other colonial documents list Luis as a child among a number of people from the Santa Cruz Valley who survived the revolt. His father, Nicolás López, had lived in Santa Cruz de la Cañada with his wife, Ana María Bernal.

Nicolás López was probably part of the initial wave of Europeans to arrive in New Mexico in the seventeenth century, when Santa Cruz de la Cañada was the largest population center of the fledgling province. For nearly eighty years it and other small settlements existed in an uneasy peace with Pueblo neighbors, as the Spaniards exploited Indian labor and exacted tribute while usurping native lands. The weaving economy in the area had its roots in this era, and woven cotton cloth was one of the forms of tribute extracted from the Pueblos. Spanish landowners and government officials relentlessly abused Pueblo labor and demanded ever-increasing tribute, and the priests harshly repressed Pueblo religion. At the same time, Pueblo populations plummeted as the people succumbed to new European diseases. The loss of native laborers put a strain on those remaining to keep up with the Spaniards' demands. Squeezed between the competing factions of church and state and stressed to the breaking point by several years of severe drought, the Pueblos finally rose up in violent revolt against their European lords.

On August 10, 1680, by prior agreement, the natives of pueblos from Taos to Sandía attacked Spanish homes and missions. They made a sweep of the countryside, killing hundreds of settlers and clergy, and moved on to attack Santa Fe, which was the only formally organized town in all of New Mexico. After a drawn-out siege of Santa Fe, they completely evicted the Spanish from New Mexico—succeeding as no other native group in North American history in expelling Europeans from their land.

The insurgents killed every settler and priest in or near the pueblos of San Juan, Santa Clara, San Ildefonso, Jacona, Nambé, and Pojoaque, but the lives of the López family and most of the residents of Santa Cruz de la Cañada were spared in the revolt because of advance warning of the impending attack.[2] They gathered at the home of Luis de Quintana in Santa Cruz de la Cañada and on August 13 fled south to join the governor in Santa Fe to retreat to El Paso del Norte. On the journey, however, Nicolás López was killed at Santo Domingo Pueblo, leaving his wife and three sons, Carlos, Luis, and Juan, to flee south to El Paso with the rest of the Hispanic population.[3] Luis was a child of two years at the time.

Twelve years after their eviction, the Spanish, led by Don Diego de Vargas, returned to New Mexico. Many people who had lived in New Mexico before the revolt were with Vargas when he brought settlers to the reconquered province a year later, including López's widowed mother and her three sons, who came back to the family lands in Santa Cruz de la Cañada. Luis López would have been fifteen years old. Some thirteen years later, when he had children of his own, he petitioned for land.

Tradition and legal precedent would have required that López share his deceased father's land with his siblings, but the division may have left him too little land to support his new family. Perhaps it was disappointment at finding much of the Río Grande Valley and the Santa Cruz area claimed by other settlers, missions, or pueblos that drove him to explore the upper Santa Cruz Valley. In any case, López followed the Santa Cruz River up toward Chimayó, seeking land. His search was gratified by the sight of the green, well-watered valley, largely unoccupied except for a few scattered farms. The promise of land there was enough to tempt him away from the safer core of Hispanic settlement and out to the more vulnerable hinterland of Chimayó. There, at the foothills, he found the vacant land by the Tano ditch.

With the usual formality employed even on humble documents in this isolated outpost of the Spanish Empire, "Don Francisco Cuervo y Valdés, Caudillo of the Order of Santiago, Governor and Captain General of this Kingdom and Province of Nuevo Mexico" granted Luis his claim "in the name of his majesty." His flowery signature is followed by that of his secretary, Alphonso Rael de Aguilar. With the stroke of a pen, land that never before had been defined as personal property became Luis López's real estate.

The Tano Indians who had built the ditch that López mentioned may not have understood the concept of private property ownership (few native groups viewed land as a commodity that could be bought or sold), but they had been less than sanguine about giving up the land in the valley. It had taken an army to compel them to leave the acreage that López claimed in the name of the king. The story of their struggle with the Spanish government unfolds in the journals of Diego de Vargas and his lieutenant, Luis Granillo.

The trouble began soon after Vargas returned to New Mexico with settlers in late 1693. His much-lauded peaceful reconquest of the previous year faded when he met resistance from Tanos and Tewas who had claimed the Santa Fe Plaza and now were using it as a base for confronting Spanish resettlement. Vargas, with his entourage of settlers and soldiers, waited outside of town for two weeks, demanding that the Indians surrender. When finally a battle erupted, Vargas stormed the plaza and ordered seventy captive Tanos and Tewas executed. Four hundred who surrendered were taken captive and sentenced to servitude for a period of ten years. The Tanos who escaped gathered with their Tewa companions on top of Black Mesa near San Ildefonso Pueblo, nursing their hatred of the Spanish conquerors, but they soon dropped their resistance and joined the Tanos in the Santa Cruz Valley. There, they immediately began plotting a rebellion that they hoped would rid them of the Spanish as the revolt of 1680 had done—and they came perilously close to repeating that feat.[4]

Because of the presence of the angry Tanos, the Santa Cruz Valley posed particularly vexing problems for Vargas as he proceeded to oversee settlement of the reclaimed province. He knew that Tanos had claimed the valley; riding through during his campaign of reconquest in 1692, Vargas had taken pains to note that the Indians were using fields and ditches that the Spanish settlers had built before the Pueblo Revolt. In his journal, Vargas briefly described the location of two Tano pueblos, San Lázaro and San Cristóbal, in the lower Santa Cruz Valley, where a priest accompanying Vargas had baptized some 155 Indian children.[5]

That the two Santa Cruz Valley pueblos described by Vargas bore the same names as two ancient pueblos in the Galisteo Basin is no coincidence. Forced from their homeland by drought and marauding Apaches after the Pueblo Revolt, Tanos from the Galisteo pueblos of San Lázaro and San Cristóbal had settled initially near San Juan Pueblo. A few years before Vargas's reconquest, however, most of the Tanos had moved into the Santa Cruz Valley, where they took over fields abandoned by the Spanish settlers. At the time of Vargas's reconquest, there were about five hundred Indians, most of them Tanos but some of them apparently Tewas and Piros, inhabiting these two pueblos.[6]

In the fall of 1694, Vargas visited the two Santa Cruz Valley pueblos and assigned a priest to minister to both. By the next spring, Vargas faced a need to find suitable land for new settlers arriving from Mexico, but after the experience of the Pueblo Revolt he was loathe to settle near lands claimed by the Indians in the Río Grande Valley. Irrigable land outside of Pueblo ownership was scarce, and Vargas looked to the Santa Cruz Valley to absorb the new, land-hungry settlers. He announced plans to settle the entire Santa Cruz Valley, but peacefully evicting the Tanos from land that had once belonged to Spanish citizens proved to be more than Vargas could accomplish.

Vargas sent Luis Granillo, his first lieutenant and former *alcalde mayor* of Santa Cruz, to oust the Tanos from their pueblos. Granillo was to command the residents of San Lázaro to return to Yunque-Yunque, the village near San Juan Pueblo where they had first relocated after the revolt, and the residents of San Cristóbal to resettle "at the end of the canyon called Zimayo [*sic*] close to the mountains." Accompanied by Tano leaders, Fray Antonio Obregón, translators, and the majority of the natives of San Cristóbal, Granillo rode up the valley and showed the Tanos the site they were to occupy. His journal recorded this account:

At the distance of two long leagues [six miles], having gone through the Cañada and past a small rivulet which comes down from the mountain range and which borders with the farm of Captain Juan Ruiz up the river, and having gone a little farther, about half a league [one and a half miles], where there is a ruin on the left, the Indians, governors, and caciques showed me the plain which is adjacent to the said ruin which is in a cañada wide and large enough for them to build their pueblo . . . and I examined the intake for the ditch and the dam . . . and the rivulet has water sufficient and permanent . . . and returning to the plain the said Indians again proceeded to mark off and describe the place for which they had asked the Governor and Captain General, and which grant he had made and conceded to them, and they marked off the plan for the town, saying that it was to be of sixty-eight houses, in order that the people of the two pueblos might occupy the same, and adding to them the Thano Indians and captive women who had escaped from the Villa of Santa Fe, in case they should desire to come with them. [7]

Chimayó had been mentioned in documents prior to the Pueblo Revolt. Indeed, the few records that survive from the prerevolt era (1598–1680) mention twenty-three settlements within the La Cañada district, including three at Chimayó or in the Chimayó district.[8] Still, Granillo's journal gives the first solid geographic clues to the location of a place with that name. The description is anything but precise, but it indicates that the site known as "Zimayo" was on a small plain at the foot of the mountains and that it was near permanent water. The grant was adjacent to Juan Ruiz's farm and there was a ruin nearby, on the north as Granillo came up the valley. Whether the ruin was a prehistoric pueblo or a Spanish farm is unclear. There are only two large prehistoric ruins on the north side of the valley in that area that fit Granillo's description. One of these lies above the small plain at Río Chiquito, about one and a half miles up the Río Quemado from the Plaza del Cerro, and the other is above Córdova, another two miles up the Quemado. These small irrigable plains are indeed up against the mountain range, and the permanent water of the Río Quemado flows through both.

It is unclear if the Tanos ever lived on the piece of land at Chimayó. They hurriedly petitioned Vargas for permission to stay in San Cristóbal until they harvested their crops, a request that Vargas granted with the stipulation that he would settle forty-four newly arrived families from Mexico at San Cristóbal when the Tanos moved that spring. This offer, too, proved unsatisfactory. By the next spring, the Tanos complained to their mission priest, José Arbizu, that there was nothing but open land in Chimayó and no place to live. In March of 1696, Arbizu reported that the Tanos in his charge had deserted San Cristóbal to assemble in the mountains of Chimayó, where they had stockpiled most of their corn, clothing, and weapons of war (and all of Padre Arbizu's chocolate) and had set traps at the entrances to their mountain stronghold "to make themselves invincible." Arbizu had overheard mutterings of a planned major rebellion and feared for his life. In one of his letters he wrote, "I have spent a most terrifying night, at times awaiting death."[9] His pleas for soldiers to guard him and the holy sacraments conveyed his desperation.

Missionaries at several other New Mexico pueblos were also aware that an uprising was at hand, and they too begged for protection. Indians were scorning the sacraments and mocking the priests, and Arbizu wrote to Governor Vargas that all the young men of San Cristóbal supported the rebellion while only the people of San Lázaro remained friendly to the Spanish. Arbizu warned that there were rumors of a revolt on the next full moon. He signed his letter "from the devastated mission at San Cristóbal" and soon after fled to the relative safety of Santa Cruz.[10] He was convinced that the Tanos would kill him if he remained and, thoroughly demoralized, wrote that he doubted his death would make him a martyr for it would do little to advance the Catholic faith among the hopeless heathens: "What afflicts me and most preys upon my limited intellect is to consider that if I am killed, would it be true martyrdom or not?"[11]

Governor Vargas received the pleas and warnings from the mission priests but did not feel compelled or able to respond. He could spare very few of the one hundred soldiers in his charge for the protection of all of New Mexico, and he didn't believe that a full-scale rebellion was imminent. He finally did consent to assigning four soldiers to San Ildefonso, to protect a large area including the Santa Cruz Valley pueblos. Vargas also rode to the hills of Chimayó and for three days called for the Tanos to come back to San Cristóbal, but to no avail. The rebels called back to Vargas that they only wanted to fight. They must have presented a formidable enemy, for almost all of the five or six hundred residents of San Cristóbal had fled to join the rebellion.

From Santa Cruz, Arbizu fired off a scathing letter to Vargas on April 18, 1696, criticizing the governor for failing to protect the mission, and then returned to San Cristóbal. He went back "not to minister, for today there is no purpose in ministering," but to guard the unprotected, sacred vessels in the church. Arbizu was at San Cristóbal when, finally, the rebels of San Cristóbal staged their long-planned attack, joining in the Indian uprising in June of 1696. Fulfilling Padre Arbizu's worst premonitions, they murdered him and a visiting priest (Fray Antonio Carbonel) and left their disrobed bodies laying face up in front of the church at San Cristóbal. The corpses were laid across each other to form the shape of a cross—a grisly mockery of the Catholic faith they so resented. The Tanos had also killed three other priests and several settlers at other missions.[12]

46

Governor Vargas recognized the peril that the newly established colony faced and set out on a campaign, pursuing the Tanos through the mountains and confiscating their hidden food and supplies. Fortunately for the Spaniards, the Pueblo people were less unified in this rebellion than they had been in 1680. By the end of the year, Vargas and his soldiers had crushed the rebellion and the Tanos of San Cristóbal fled.

The Pueblo occupation of the Chimayó area ended with the departure of the Tanos, who by the end of their ordeal must have been reduced to a starving, ragged band—the last remnants of the once numerous Tanos of the Galisteo Basin. The fate of the survivors is not entirely clear. Some went to live with Tewas who during the Pueblo Revolt had fled to Hopi First Mesa in the village of Hano.[13] A few returned to the Galisteo area,[14] and others may have settled among their Tewa neighbors in the Río Grande Valley. Some Tanos also may have remained and assimilated into the Hispanic population.

Had the course of events been different—if the Tanos had accepted Vargas's offer of a grant of land at Zimayo or if they had succeeded in their rebellion— it might have been Tanos who built a thriving village at the base of the *cerro* of Tsi Mayoh. As it is, the Tanos are gone and are remembered in Chimayó by the barely used name for the canyon above Córdova, the Cañada del los Tanos. (That this canyon is so named may be evidence that Córdova was the site of Zimayo that Vargas described.) Some people believe that the name of a ditch that branches off of the Ortega ditch, the Acequia del Pueblo, also derived its name from its proximity to a Tano pueblo. In any case, the valley was wholly open to Spanish settlement when Vargas starved out the rebellious Tanos. Luis López was one of those settlers, filing his petition for land along a Tano ditch ten years after the Tanos had departed.

During Vargas's struggle to resolve the Tano problem, he formally founded a new *villa*, La Villa Nueva de Santa Cruz de Españoles Mexicanos del Rey Nuestro Carlos Segundo, or, more simply, Santa Cruz de la Cañada. He established the town on April 19, 1695, on or near the site of San Lázaro Pueblo, on the south side of the Santa Cruz River. (The town was later relocated to the north side of the river, where it is today.) This became the civil and ecclesiastical center for a large area that included Chimayó. In a ceremony with considerable fanfare and formality, Vargas granted the settlers land in the valley and "possession of all the ores that might be found in the mountains of Chimayó,"[15] but he made no mention of any communal grazing lands for the community—an important aspect of many other land grants in New Mexico.

Even after the experience of the Pueblo Revolt, the Spanish *pobladores* (colonists) continued to build their homes far apart and, thus, indefensibly. There was no formal founding of Chimayó, where López staked his claim and where other people were already rebuilding their prerevolt farms. After showing the Tanos where their new pueblo was to be built at Chimayó, Granillo had reconnoitered the Santa Cruz Valley. He noted the presence of at least twelve farms in the valley, including two in the Chimayó area near the head of the valley. He remarked on the Martínez *estancia* at a distance of about half of a league (one and a half miles) from the Tano grant and the Captain Juan Ruiz farm on the boundary of the Tano lands.[16]

Like the Lópezes, the Martínez family had also returned from exile in El Paso to reestablish farms in the Santa Cruz Valley. Granillo wrote in 1695 that their home consisted of standing walls only and that five families were living in the ruins. These people were Luis Martín, who had lived on the land prior to the revolt, and his married children. Granillo mentioned other similarly resettled farms in the valley but failed to mention the Hacienda de Moraga, even though it was one of the prominent prerevolt settlements in the valley and Vargas had explicitly ordered him to locate it. Granillo's descriptions, which include approximate distance from the Tano grant, give us an idea of the extent and location of seventeenth-century settlement in the Chimayó area. There was still no plaza in Chimayó at this time, but the evidence suggests that in years to come the plaza would be built on the very land that Luis López claimed in 1706.

The Tano *acequia* that López mentions is probably the waterway later called the Martínez ditch, which appears as a south boundary for López's property in land transactions that took place later in the 1700s. The road to Taos that López gave as the northern boundary of his land was an ancient travel route. It followed the arroyo in the Cañada Ancha up toward the high plateau where the village of Truchas now sits. (This old trail remained the primary route up to the mountains until a new highway was built in the 1950s.) The arroyo passes only a few hundred feet from the Plaza del Cerro. López apparently built the Ortega ditch soon after making his claim for land, and papers indicate that the ditch followed the northern boundary of his land. Thus, it appears that López's land lay between the Ortega ditch and the Martínez ditch—the two major ditches that today lay north and south of the Plaza del Cerro.

Disputes about land use started early in Chimayó's history. In 1712—just six years after he claimed his land in Chimayó—Luis López authored a complaint to the governor concerning his neighbor, Melchora de los Reyes. López complained that Melchora was causing great harm to her neighbors by prohibiting them from grazing their horses and flocks in the communal pastures. Vargas had not designated any upland communal grant to the settlers of the Santa Cruz Valley, but he did explicitly designate the pastures in the valley as communal property. It seems that controversy about these communal lands arose as soon as the valley began to fill up with settlers. The governor, the Marqués de la Peñuela, sent Roque Madrid to inform Melchora de los Reyes that she should not block entrance to the pastures.[17]

Parcels of land were actively bought and sold throughout the 1700s, and Lopéz's landholdings began to fragment as he aged. In 1758, López sold some of his land to "Grabiel" Ortega. (Throughout the historic documents, the name is consistently spelled "Grabiel" rather than "Gabriel." People in Chimayó are still named Grabiel or Grabiela.) The parcel's boundaries were: "On the east, the lands of the said seller and a graded stone [*piedra grada*] which aligns with an *acequia* which runs to the south in a straight line; on the north bounded by lands of the same seller and an *acequia* which bounds with the two [López and Ortega]; on the west by the lands of the said purchaser and on the south by the *acequia madre*."[18] The Ortega ditch flows roughly in a north-south line for some distance and is probably the first of the *acequias* mentioned in the document; the *acequia madre* was probably the old Martínez ditch. López was selling Grabiel land between the two ditches where the plaza is now located.

The fragmented record of this first subdivision of the plaza area continues in 1766 with a land division between Micaela Antonia López, Luis's only daughter, and Isidro Medina. This paper describes a boundary by "designating to them a blue stone which is on the edge of the *cerro* on the part east to west."[19]

Puzzled about the location of this blue rock, I asked people in Chimayó about it. My mother immediately associated the description with a large, greenish-blue outcrop at the base of the hills just above the plaza. This may be the same as the "graded stone" mentioned in the conveyance to Grabiel Ortega in 1758. This rock still marks the east-to-west border between two properties—one belonging to descendants of Grabiel Ortega and the other to descendants of the Martínez clan—and a benchmark at its base remains to this day.

López's daughter donated some of her father's land to his adopted orphans, Concepción and Juan Antonio, when Luis died in 1772 at the age of ninety years. (His age in the burial records was probably only an estimate; according to census records, he would actually have been ninety-four in 1772.) The document making this transfer mentions lands on its borders belonging to Grabiel Ortega.

Micaela Antonia married Francisco de Mascareñas, who later abandoned her and their child, Juan Francisco Mascareñas. In his will, Luis López had left some land to Juan Francisco to use as payment for López's funeral and burial —a common practice when money was scarce and land was plentiful. In 1776,

50

A Chimayó
adobe home
covered with
chile ristras,
ca. 1910.

long after López had passed away, Juan Francisco sold his farming lands at "San Buenaventura de Chimayó" to Grabiel Ortega for forty pesos.[20] He must have paid for Luis's funeral with other funds or deferred payment for four years.

San Buenaventura was later to become the patron saint of the Plaza del Cerro, and the mention of this saint's name is a strong indication that Grabiel's land was to become the site for the plaza. In 1796, María Antonia Mascareñas, probably a descendant of Antonia López Mascareñas (or the same person), added to the holdings of the Ortega family by selling property to Pedro Asencio Ortega, a son of Grabiel. Again, this land lay between the Martínez and Ortega *acequias*. Pedro's will lists among his possessions a home on the Plaza del Cerro, supporting the idea that the Mascareñas land was in the plaza area. Grabiel further augmented his landholdings by acquiring land from other people, including a purchase from Felipe Romero of land adjoining the Mascareñas land. [21]

Judging by these surviving land conveyances, Grabiel Ortega had acted quickly after his arrival in Chimayó to obtain land. By the end of the eighteenth century, most of the Luis López land and some surrounding land had come into the possession of the Ortega family, mostly through sales or transfers to Grabiel. (Some of the López land could have passed to Grabiel through his marriage to Ana Bartola López, who may have been a relation to Luis.) The plaza was built on these lands and possibly on adjacent lands in the Martín family. The fate of the Martín lands is less clear; Chimayó genealogist Aaron Martínez found evidence that the Martín land was inherited by the Jaramillo family, whose original landholdings are located southeast of the plaza. The reasons that the Ortegas and Martíns allowed or fostered the building of a plaza on their land are unclear. It may have been simply that they saw that their own survival depended on the mutual cooperation of all the people in the community to form a defensible structure.

Grabiel remains an enigmatic figure in terms of his origins. The elders of the Ortega family all state firmly that Grabiel was their ancestor, but genealogical research fails to confirm that he was the original and sole patriarch of the Chimayó Ortega family. (Baptismal and census records fail to show a link between Grabiel and the dominant branch of the Ortegas—the José Ramón Ortega y Vigil clan; the records do suggest, however, that he was the progenitor of the "other" Ortega family, which descended from Pedro Asencio Ortega.) No one has been able to determine where Grabiel lived prior to his arrival in Chimayó. Grandma remembers that her Tía Bonefacia Ortega said that she was a descendant of Grabiel and that he had been born in Galicia, which is a province of Spain. It also may be that Grabiel or his ancestors came from the province of Nueva Galicia, in Mexico, one of the areas where Vargas went to recruit colonists in 1691. The 1790 census lists his age as forty-eight years old; he was sixty-four in 1806, when records from the Santa Cruz church indicate he was buried. This would place his birth year as 1742.

Whatever his origins, Grabiel Ortega owned a large share of the land that the plaza was constructed on and much of the surrounding land. Some of the acreage in the plaza area was also owned by the Martín family. Residents with both of these family names to this day retain ownership of large acreage in and around the Plaza del Cerro. Continuing the process initiated by Grabiel, the Ortega offspring remained influential in the evolution of the plaza well into the twentieth century.

Chapter Four:
Para la Defensa
Otra Vez

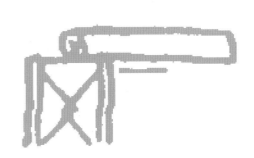

Watching for the Enemy

From the crest of the cuchilla,
The centinelas *watch for movement in the*
ribbon of sand,
Where blinding sun streaks the Cañada Ancha.

Still no smoke signal from primos *in Truchas,*
But painted faces and a glint of steel
Appear in the shadows of piñones—
¡De allí viene el enemigo!

And once again the sun sets
Blood red through the thin air,
And darkness settles cold
On callused hands gripping rosaries
Behind thick mud walls.

Not even the oldest *viejitos* in Chimayó can say when their ancestors built the Plaza del Cerro. Most simply accept that it has been here since the first Hispanic people arrived in the valley. Everyone agrees that the *vecinos* of Chimayó made this sturdy plaza to protect themselves from enemies, but there are no old stories to tell who was responsible for conceiving and erecting it. The papers in my mother's collection offer no clues, and I've had to search through sparse written records collected elsewhere to piece together answers to these questions.

Looking at the old, flat-roofed adobe buildings on the west wall of the Plaza del Cerro, it is easy to imagine this as the original townsite established by Spanish settlers in Chimayó, but in fact documents show that people lived in the area for nearly two hundred years before the plaza was built. Papers from the time of the first Hispanic settlement in New Mexico in the early 1600s refer to a place called Chimayó, but none of them mention a plaza. It seems that in this early period people conceived of Chimayó as the whole upper Santa Cruz Valley, naming the area after the *cerro* called Tsi Mayoh by the Tewa Pueblos. As far as the records tell there was no townsite called Chimayó during this time. People lived in scattered homes and maintained their farms throughout the valley.

Don Diego de Vargas seemed to have a specific place in mind when he ordered the Tano people off of their land in the Santa Cruz Valley in the late 1600s and assigned them the place called "Zimayo." The unsettled tract of land was probably up the Río Quemado from the town we call Chimayó today, and the reasons he named it Zimayo remain unclear. References to the name continue in numerous documents in the early 1700s, and the name "el paraje de Chimayó" (the site of Chimayó) comes into use in the 1740s, leading many historians to conclude that the Plaza del Cerro was founded at that time.[1] "San Buenaventura de Chimayó" appears for the first time on a 1752 will[2] and again on a marriage record of 1767 that mentions "el puesto de San Buenaventura de Chimalló."[3] A 1772 document also refers to "San Buenabentura de Chimallo."[4] San Buenaventura is the patron saint of the Plaza del Cerro, and many people have assumed that the plaza was built by the time this name came into use. But in Chimayó, as in many other places, dedication of the town to a patron saint took place well before the construction of a church or plaza.

Neither Bishop Pedro Tamarón nor Fray Francisco Atanasio Domínguez mentioned a formal plaza in Chimayó when they toured the area in 1760 and 1776, respectively, even though Domínguez did take pains to describe plazas in Truchas and Trampas at that time.[5] Although the founding of a plaza was normally preceded by a petition to the governor, no such document has been found for the Plaza del Cerro. It was not until the late 1700s that the word "plaza" appears in historical records of Chimayó, beginning with a reference to the "Plaza de San Buenaventura de Chimayó" in 1785.[6] Thereafter, there are numerous references to the Plaza de San Buenaventura and the Plaza del Cerro.

There is no precise date for its construction, but the reasons for building the plaza relate to thoroughly reported problems with nomadic Indians who plagued all of New Mexico in the eighteenth century. Relations between the Pueblos and their less sedentary neighbors varied in the centuries preceding European contact, but the acquisition of horses and firearms in the 1700s, introduced by the Spanish, tempted many traditionally nomadic Indian groups to

55

start raiding the agrarian Pueblo and Hispanic villages. Throughout the eighteenth century, Utes, Comanches, Navajos, and Apaches stole livestock and food from the unprotected colonists of New Mexico. The Comanches were particularly fierce and relentless. The raiders also routinely took captives to be sold as slaves or ransomed back to the colonists. The scattered Spanish farms and ranches lay vulnerable to attack, even though some buildings may have been fortified and some haciendas were built with *torreones*. Most Hispanic settlements made easy prey for the well-armed and mobile Indians.

Even in the larger, more affluent *villas* of Santa Fe, Santa Cruz de la Cañada, and Albuquerque, homes and farms for the most part were spread out and lacked a means of organized defense, even though plans for grid-typed towns had been specified by 1573 for Spain's New World provinces. The settlers of New Mexico ignored these regulations and built to be near their scattered fields and farms. Marauding Indians for centuries exacted a heavy toll on the pueblos as well, but their clustered, multistoried villages proved to be more defensible than the Hispanic ones. By the eighteenth century Spanish settlers began to take refuge inside the pueblos; the period became one of cooperation between the two cultures for common defense.[7]

Located on the northeastern frontier of the Spanish colony for the first half of the eighteenth century, Chimayó was especially vulnerable to the attackers. It lay in a productive valley, far from the few soldiers on hand to defend the province, and its vulnerability lured the mounted raiders. Fray Atanasio Domínguez wrote in 1776 that Chimayó, lying two leagues (six miles) to the east-northeast of Santa Cruz, was "a large settlement of many farms in good lands [with] more orchards than there are at La Villa de La Cañada [Santa Cruz]." Domínguez also noted that there were seventy-one families comprising 367 persons in Chimayó at that time and that these families were settled in many scattered *ranchos*, some in "nooks like cañadas" with different place names to the south—a reference, no doubt, to the homes and farms scattered along the Santa Cruz River and *acequias* and nestled up against the badland ridges.[8]

People in the Plaza del Cerro remember that their ancestors endured attacks by ravaging Indians and that the attackers usually rode in from the wild foothills east of the plaza. It seems ironic that centuries earlier it was the mounted

56

Spaniards who struck terror in the native people; now it was the Hispanic farmers who lacked mounts and arms with which to defend themselves. Although
the details have blurred, the name of the nearby town of Centinela, which means
"sentinel," reminds residents of the hostile world their *antepasados* faced. On
a high ridge crest above Centinela, lookouts kept watch for the wild people on
horseback whose living depended on plunder. *"De allí cuidaron por el enemigo*
—From there they watched for the enemy," Teresita Jaramillo explained to me,
adding that the sentinels would run along a long, knife-edge ridge of sandstone
to shortcut their way to the plaza and alert the villagers. Some old songs also
recount the raids from the Cañada Ancha, among them the folksong *"De allí
vienen los indios en la Cañada*—There come the Indians in the Cañada."[9]

Because Chimayó was isolated, exposed to the pillaging Indians, and
offered few of the comforts of civilization, the authorities in Santa Fe regarded
it as something of a Siberia of New Mexico, itself an isolated and lonely province.
Juan Romero was banished to Chimayó in 1734 for his "public vices" and Roque
Lobato was sent here for three years in 1765 as a punishment for crimes.[10]
These incidents no doubt started the oft-repeated story that Chimayó was a
penal colony. While it is true that criminals were banished to Chimayó and
other remote villages in the eighteenth century, the area was populated mostly
by poor farmers struggling against formidable odds to subsist off the land.

Near Chimayó, the village of Córdova, originally known as Quemado, was
even more remote than Chimayó and suffered severe and frequent attacks. The
situation became so bad that the people of Quemado abandoned their village in
1748 and moved to Chimayó for its relative safety. They returned to Quemado a
year later, although they took the precaution of leaving women and children in
Chimayó for a time while the settlement was being firmly reestablished. The situation became equally intolerable in nearby Truchas, where the villagers grew
so desperate to alleviate their losses that in 1772 they petitioned the governor for
arms (twelve firearms along with powder and munitions) and Pueblo Indian
scouts to help them defend themselves against the "Cumanche [*sic*] enemies."[11]

The Spanish government in Santa Fe could offer very little aid to the
besieged villagers. Governor Mendinueta was unable to spare even the twelve
muskets that the colonists of Truchas pleaded for. Furthermore, in an act that

must have thoroughly disheartened the colonists, he forbade the people from leaving their village. Chimayó was one of the strategic hamlets of the Spanish Empire, maintaining a precarious foothold at the very base of the *cerros* from which the enemy Comanches attacked. The Crown long regarded these small, struggling outposts as the redoubts of the northern frontier, which Spain feared losing not only to the raiding Indians but also to the French, already encroaching from the Louisiana Territory. Hence, it was illegal for settlers to abandon their settlements without the permission of the governor. After France ceded the Louisiana Territory to Spain in 1762, concern shifted to the aggressive Americans pressing on the Mississippi country from the east. Spain returned the Louisiana Territory to France in 1800, but worries about the zealous Americans redoubled in 1803 when France sold the territory to the United States.

The vulnerability of the Spanish settlements did not escape the far-seeing eye of the Spanish Crown. Because of its tenuous position on the frontier of New Spain, New Mexico had been under strict military control since its earliest settlement, but the military presence in New Mexico and the other "internal" provinces was strengthened dramatically as cries for improved defenses came from all quarters. Governor Mendinueta lamented the situation in New Mexico in a report to Viceroy Bucareli in 1772:

The pueblos of Indians are all grouped together and for this reason more defensible, while of the Spaniards there is no unified settlement. . . . Their being indefensible has caused some of the advantageous frontiers to be abandoned. . . . One of the opportune means which can be taken is to compel settlers of each region who live . . . dispersed, to join and form their pueblos in plazas or streets so that a few men could be able to defend themselves. [12]

Indeed, a map from 1779 shows more abandoned than occupied settlements in the province. In 1782, Fray Augustín de Morfí commented on the moral depravity that resulted from the haphazard settlement in New Mexico. He felt that it was because of the isolation of their homes that citizens were liable to act with independence and even insolence, to commit crimes with impunity, and to neglect the sacraments. And what was worse, the people were not ashamed to go about nude, so that lewdness was "more common among the Spanish than among the brutes." [13]

After repeated pleas for official action, the Viceroy held a council in Chihuahua in 1778 and issued orders for consolidation of the towns. When the news trickled down to New Mexico, a reorganization of settlements began. The *villas*, except for Santa Fe, whose "churlish" residents resisted all authority, were organized into plaza-type towns. Rural communities also were consolidated. [14]

The two defensive plazas of the Santa Cruz Valley—at Santa Cruz and at the foothills in Chimayó—as well as those at Trampas, Ojo Caliente, Cebolleta, Dixon, Taos, Ranchos de Taos, and elsewhere, probably had their origins in this period. Instructions for building a plaza at Truchas were laid out in the land grant establishing that town, and Domínguez described two plazas in Truchas in 1776. In 1782, Fray Morfí reported that Governor Anza, Mendinueta's successor, had reduced the settlement at Santa Cruz de la Cañada, which had been spread out along the river, to a "regular form" in 1779. These towns were the original gated communities of New Mexico.

The Chimayosos probably came together to build the Plaza del Cerro sometime in the late eighteenth century during the phase of consolidation of New Mexico settlements. The written record supports this time line. A 1785 baptismal record refers to the "Plaza de Sanbuenaventura de Chimayó," and in 1806 Grabiel Ortega filed the first written statement mentioning the plaza as an enclosed space when he complained to the governor that horses were being allowed inside the plaza and were ruining his crops.[15] In the next few decades, land transactions frequently mention the synonymous Plaza de San Buenaventura and the Plaza del Cerro.

When viewed in this historical context, the Plaza del Cerro is foremost a monument to the compelling need for defense in northern New Mexico in the eighteenth century. The Pueblo people had always recognized this need, and in many ways the plaza mimicked the consolidated villages of the neighboring pueblos. However, the plaza structure also had old-world roots. The military-minded Romans first devised the concept of centralized towns as an efficient means of defending newly claimed territory during the colonization of Spain. As Spain reclaimed the Iberian Peninsula from the Moors in the centuries preceding Columbus's voyages, the Spanish established grid-plan settlements similar to the Roman design to solidify control of regained lands. In 1573, King Philip II defined the plaza-type settlement in the New World in ordinances for establishing towns on the frontier of the expanding Spanish Empire. Embodied in a chapter of Law of the Indies, the plan called for a central plaza area with houses built continuously around it for defensive purposes.[16]

While the plazas of colonial New Mexico initially were defensive structures, they deviated greatly from their old-world antecedents. The rigid gridwork of streets and the concentration of military and religious buildings on the plaza were aspects seldom observed in the villages of northern New Mexico—primarily because there was very little military or religious presence and very few roads to speak of. Like every other old-world convention, plazas here took on a simplified, highly utilitarian form. Rather than building defensive walls or trenches, the *recinos* simply adjoined their small adobe homes into a roughly rectangular configuration. Basic function had priority over grand design, and plazas resembled small adobe forts more than the centralized towns envisioned in the Law of the Indies. The word was used in New Mexico to describe any cluster of buildings, whether or not it was organized into a defensive pattern. *Placita* described a smaller cluster of homes, and still less populous groupings of farms were referred to as *lugares*. As a result, today there are many places in northern New Mexico that people may call plazas or *placitas* that in fact were not established as fortified, rectangular settlements.

The Plaza del Cerro preserves the remnants of a fortified plaza structure better than any other plaza in New Mexico. There were originally no windows on the outside, and adobe watchtowers probably stood outside each of the plaza's walls. The two small entrances on the north and south could be easily and quickly closed to keep out attackers, and the residents could have survived for some time in the plaza interior, although enemies would have had an easy time cutting off their water supply.

The plaza probably presented a formidable fortress to raiding Indians, but, ironically, the need for defense in the Santa Cruz Valley diminished not long after the Plaza del Cerro was built. Governor Juan Bautista de Anza made peace with the Comanches in 1786, securing the frontier for settlement. Navajos and Apaches resumed their raiding in a few decades, but Chimayó apparently enjoyed its first period of relative peace soon after it was built.

The 1790 census recorded 8,895 people—the highest concentration of population in the province—in the Santa Cruz de la Cañada district, which encompassed the rural populations of the Río Arriba area, including Chimayó.[17] The population began to grow more quickly in the early nineteenth century, perhaps in part because of the introduction of a smallpox vaccine in 1805.[18] The swelling communities together with a decreased need for safety prompted the settlement of lands that were away from the newly fortified plaza towns. The emboldened *pobladores* followed creeks up to mountain valleys and spilled out onto the eastern plains. They spread out from the Río Grande, up the Chama drainage, down the Pecos, south on the Río Grande, over the mountains to the Mora River country, and west into the Río Puerco drainage, entering territory where they would not have dared venture before. New fortified Genízaro plaza towns—towns inhabited by Hispanicized Indians who had been captured or ransomed—were established at Abiquiú, Ojo Caliente, Tomé, and San Miguel del Vado late in the colonial era.

Meanwhile, in the long-settled valleys near the Río Grande, the growing

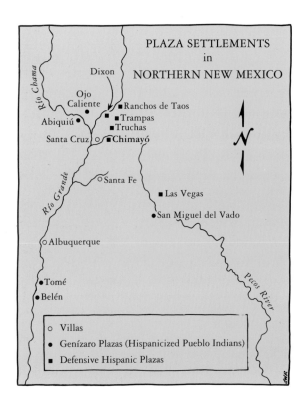

population squeezed onto every piece of land that was accessible to water. Isolated buildings, perhaps initially used seasonally by men working the fields, became permanent homesites. Children added onto their parents' homes or built nearby, and land was subdivided so that each heir had access to a ditch. This resulted in long, narrow plots of land stretching from irrigation ditches toward the dry hills and badlands—a pattern that is still strikingly apparent in northern New Mexico villages today.

In Chimayó, scattered *ranchos* gradually grew into clusters of homes belonging to extended families. These became small communities with their own names—often the surnames of families that initially settled the land. The Chimayó *placitas* of El Rincón de los Trujillos and Los Pachecos—each a cluster of houses on the Cañada Ancha

ditch—were so named. Other communities took on names that were descriptive of local geographic features. La Plaza del Potrero, where Bernardo Abeyta and his neighbors later built Chimayó's illustrious Santuario, looks over large pastures (*potreros*) along the river, and Rincón de los Trujillo's houses cluster in a small *rincón*, or corner, in the badland cliffs along the edge of the valley. La Cuchilla is the neighborhood near a narrow, knifelike ridge (*cuchilla*) of sandstone. The community west of the plaza became known as Los Ranchos because of its large farm fields. To the northeast of the plaza, Centinela took its name

from the important role the nearby ridge played as a post for sentinels watching the Cañada Ancha for raiders coming from the mountains. (Smoke signals from kin in Truchas often provided the first alert of trouble.) El Llano was situated on a flat plain of good farming land in lower Chimayó.

If it had assumed the name of its founding families, the Plaza del Cerro might have been called La Plaza de los Ortegas or La Plaza de los Martínez, but instead it is named in deference to the *cerro* of Tsi Mayoh. Older documents also refer to it as the Plaza de San Buenaventura, and some people still call it by that name. Many young people have forgotten both of the old names and refer to it as

63

simply the Plaza Vieja, in recognition of its antiquity, or the Plaza Arriba, describing its location high at the head of the valley, well above the lower Plaza Abajo.

The diversity of Chimayó's distinct *placitas* was spread out along travel routes and ditches in the area. Though there was a great deal of contact between the neighborhoods, each place developed its own history and a definite character that persists to this day. It's all Chimayó to outsiders, but Chimayosos still talk of these subcommunities as if they were distinct towns: "Oh, he had to go to Rincón to see his sister." "No, she's not from here; she came from over in Potrero." People seem especially prone to make distinctions between the Plaza del Cerro and the Plaza Abajo:

CAMILO
TRUJILLO

Those people from "down below" in the Plaza Abajo—they always talked and dressed different than the people from the Plaza del Cerro. And the people from up here didn't mingle with the "abajeños." There were very few intermarriages between those two communities.

That Plaza Abajo—that was the home of the malos. *People from Lower Chimayó they liked to fight. They used to say that the State Police could never come past that arroyo down there, way down by La Puebla [west of Chimayó]. There were quite a few killings down there. And you know, the people talked different down there. Their Spanish down there uses more slang than up here.*

Of course, the people from the Plaza del Cerro were different than those from here in Potrero, too. When they got mad over there at the plaza, they stayed mad forever. Here, they'd really cuss the hell out of each other, then the next day they'd say, "Buenos días, compadre, como está? Quiere café? Llega a café." But the people from the plaza, they'd control their tongue more. They wouldn't use profanity or anything like that.

In some respects, the Plaza del Cerro was just another of the separate neighborhoods of Chimayó. What set it apart was its fortified layout, unique in the Santa Cruz Valley but for the plaza at Santa Cruz. The Plaza del Cerro, as

Gregorita Ortega Martínez told me, was *muy mentada*—very famous or talked about. Although she speaks of the early twentieth century, when the general store and post office were located there, it seems that the plaza's reputation began well before her time.

In the early 1800s, the Chimayosos prospered in their newfound peace and began to settle in to the plaza community. This time period is beyond the horizon of the earliest memories of living residents, but glimpses into life on the Plaza del Cerro in the nineteenth century flicker between the lines of papers from the period. Most of these are tucked in the chest full of records that my mother keeps.

One document, written on March 25, 1803, declares that José Guadalupe Martín sold a house on "the Plaza of San Buena bentura" for the price of "two masses to be said for the souls of [my] parents." A house may seem a high price to pay for the promise of a good afterlife, but the price Martín asked reflects just how much people in Chimayó valued religion and how deeply they believed that a better world awaited them in *El Cielo*. Martín's bill of sale goes on to describe the house as *"bieja y despoblada"* (old and abandoned)—language that could be used to describe many of the rooms on the plaza today. Apparently, some buildings were neglected only a decade or two after the plaza was built, and renovation must have been ongoing to balance such periodic abandonments.[19]

In 1826, Antonio Meregildo Trujillo sold land in San Buenaventura for "one burrito, a bridle, some spurs, and a *sarape*," and in 1861 a tract sold for "the munificent price," as historian Myra Ellen Jenkins put it, of one burro.[20]

Another record from early in the nineteenth century shows that life on the plaza was not without conflicts. On April 9, 1806, Don Manuel García de la Mora, *alcalde mayor* and *capitán* of the Santa Cruz militia, made a written statement concerning a land-use dispute on the plaza. Grabiel Ortega had earlier petitioned Governor Fernando Chacón during a visit to Chimayó to order some of Ortega's neighbors to move their corrals "far and out of the Plaza del Cerro. . . . so his garden would not be damaged." This was done, but then the neighbors, Toribio Mascareñas and Manuel Durán, went to the governor and again requested permission to build a corral within the plaza. Chacón asked de la Mora to visit the site and settle the case. De la Mora reaffirmed the earlier deci-

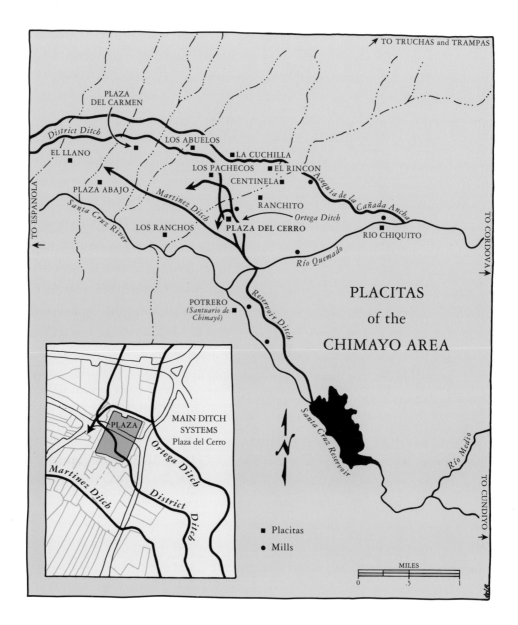

TO TRUCHAS and TRAMPAS

PLAZA
DEL CARMEN

District Ditch

LOS ABUELOS

EL LLANO

LA CUCHILLA

LOS PACHECOS
EL RINCON

CENTINELA

Acequia de la Cañada Ancha

PLAZA ABAJO

Martinez Ditch

RANCHITO

Ortega Ditch

TO ESPANOLA

Santa Cruz River

LOS RANCHOS

PLAZA DEL CERRO

RIO CHIQUITO

TO CORDOVA

Río Quemado

POTRERO
(Santuario de
Chimayó)

Reservoir Ditch

PLACITAS
of the
CHIMAYO AREA

MAIN DITCH
SYSTEMS
Plaza del Cerro

PLAZA

Ortega Ditch

Martinez Ditch

District Ditch

Santa Cruz Reservoir

Río Medio

N

TO CUNDIYO

■ Placitas
● Mills

MILES

0   .5   1

sion in favor of Grabiel Ortega and provided certification of the action for the
safekeeping of the Ortega heirs.[21]

The record of this land dispute is especially interesting for several reasons.
The fact that Ortega deferred to government authorities indicates that the final

say on management of the interior of the plaza did not lay in the hands of the plaza residents. This implies that the plaza was not privately held land; it was public or in some way communal. The paper also shows that the interior of the plaza was used primarily as a garden space, at least by Ortega but probably by other people as well. I can imagine Durán and Mascareñas testing the mettle of the local residents regarding rules about the use of the interior of the plaza and Grabiel rising to their challenge, wisely assuring that a written verification of his rights was passed on to his heirs.

Another paper from the period also seems to imply that land in the plaza was community property. In a land sale that was certified on July 7, 1827, Mariano Silva declared that he had sold a piece of property and a house to Luis Ortega. In confusing, colloquial Spanish and barely legible writing, he tried to make clear that he did not intend to include any rights within the plaza, which was *"patio comun para todos*—common grounds for all." This brief statement once again carries the implication that the land within the plaza could not be bought or sold—a situation that has not existed within the memory of living residents of Chimayó. It also shows that this communal policy was already being challenged at that time.[22]

In general, papers from the early nineteenth century sketch the plaza as a residential center for a population subsisting mostly on its own agricultural produce. Among the crops and products mentioned are fruit trees (apples, apricots, cherries), sorghum syrup (*miel*), tobacco, and cotton. Horses, burros, and cows are mentioned as trade items in land transactions. All of these commodities were very highly valued. One will divides up fruit trees as if they were gold: single fruit trees, halves of fruit trees, and even individual limbs on fruit trees are carefully documented and passed on.

The period also brought the first official attempt to develop weaving as an industry in northern New Mexico. Weaving had been a common activity in the Hispanic villages for a long time, and organized production based on native labor was a central feature of New Mexico before the Pueblo Revolt of 1680. The Ortega weavers of Chimayó, among the legendary artisans of northern New Mexico, believe that the first Ortega to arrive here, Grabiel Ortega, was a weaver and that the craft was passed down through the generations to the present. However, the census of 1790, while listing many weavers in the Río Abajo, identifies only two weavers in Santa Fe and doesn't name a single weaver in the jurisdiction of Santa Cruz de la Cañada.[23] Furthermore, there were very few large ranches in the Río Arriba area, so wool for weaving would have been scarce. If there were weavers among the families of Chimayó, they elected not to declare their livelihood when the 1790 census was taken. Soon after the turn of the century, though, Chimayó weavers probably began to produce textiles.

Seeking to expand the sheep and wool industries in the north and thereby generate some economic activity, the Spanish government in 1807 contracted with the Bazán brothers, accomplished Mexican weavers, to train northern New Mexico youth in their craft.[24] A legend in Chimayó says that the Bazán brothers (referred to as "a couple of weavers from the Saltillo tribe in Mexico") left Santa Fe "because of trouble" and lived in Chimayó for a time. The story credits the brothers with starting or revitalizing the weaving tradition, but there are no records of their coming here.[25] It is unclear what the Bazán brothers accomplished in New Mexico, although they claimed to have met their goals after only two years. They probably introduced new techniques and perhaps exposed the villages to ideas about how to organize for better production, with an eye toward developing export products. They may have had a direct or indirect role in the emergence of several weaving enterprises in Chimayó later in the century.

In the early 1800s, even as the people in the plaza clung to their habit of formally documenting transactions in accordance with Spanish law, the Spanish Empire was crumbling at its edges and revolution was in the air. The fledgling New Mexico colony entered the nineteenth century on wobbly legs, still reeling from the attacks by nomadic Indians and widespread disease that had kept population growth to a snail's pace throughout most of the 1700s. The plaza community may no longer have faced a serious threat from Native Americans but before long, turbulent political changes in distant capitals would bring hardship to the people of Chimayó. The neglect that the remote northern frontier had endured was only to increase when the Mexican Revolution gave New Mexico a new but, for all practical purposes, equally remote government.

Chapter Five: From Insurgents to Patriots

Don Pérez's Severed Head

The windows in the Villa are shuttered tight
Against the lawless longhairs from Chimayó,
Who drink by fires in the churchyard,
Boasting that they've saved us
From Don Pérez and his petty rules,
And shouting that only blood can feed their
hunger for justice,
That there will be no taxes in this land—

But in the light of the coals
Don Pérez's eyeless head is smiling.

Although the period is beyond the memory horizon of the old Chimayosos, historical documents reveal that turmoil continued as a theme in the life of Chimayó in the early nineteenth century. Curiously, few of our family papers date from this period when strife from within the Hispanic communities replaced the hostility from without. Unrest in the villages began as Spain lost its grip in the New World and New Mexicans struggled with a weak and poorly equipped government under the Mexican flag. People in the Plaza del Cerro must have felt the strains of the transition as sorely as any community in northern New Mexico.

With the Mexican Revolution in 1821, the new government brought a welcomed easing of trade for its citizens in the northern territory. Up until this time New Mexicans traded freely with their Pueblo neighbors and received imported goods from throughout the Spanish Empire by way of Mexico City. At the same time they were forbidden from conducting trade with any party outside the empire and were utterly isolated from the United States and its territories, by which they were bordered. With the opening of the Santa Fe Trail to commerce with enterprising Americans, this isolation came to an abrupt end. Trade south along the Chihuahua Trail also flourished, thanks in part to a new trade policy that allowed all citizens to trade freely rather than being restricted to state-sponsored caravans. Over 20,000 textile items were exported to Mexico from its northern province in one year alone.[1] After 1829, trade also intensified along the Old Spanish Trail, which connected New Mexico to the West with southern California.[2] Such a boom in trade must have encouraged weavers throughout the region to produce more wares, and Chimayó's weavers probably felt this surge. Some of the thousands of woven products going south on the Chihuahua Trail were no doubt produced here.

In spite of the general increase in prosperity that came with the 1821 opening of the Santa Fe Trail, New Mexico suffered under a renewed Indian menace from Navajos, Apaches, and others. The governor frequently called on residents to join campaigns against the enemy. The ragtag militia fought without the benefit of assistance from the regular military and was required to supply its own weapons, few of which included firearms. The *vecinos* wearied of this and other burdens, which they felt exceeded the benefits gained from being citizens of the Mexican nation—benefits that were, in any case, greatly diminished in the chaos as the nascent government changed hands over and over and the economy of the new nation teetered on the brink of total collapse.

The struggling farmers of the Department of New Mexico were the least of the Mexican government's worries when President Antonio López de Santa Anna revised tax laws in 1836 that would apply uniformly to all citizens in all of Mexico's departments. For decades, New Mexicans had been exempt from paying taxes because they provided their own military protection and benefited very little from federal monies, for there were few schools, hospitals, or federal roads anywhere in the north. The government managed to subsist off taxes on goods imported into New Mexico by way of the Santa Fe Trail. At about the same time that the new tax laws were to take effect, Mexico enacted a new constitution that weakened local governments throughout the young country. López de Santa Anna also appointed a new governor, Albino Pérez, to New Mexico.

Pérez quickly earned a reputation as a tyrannical leader and one excessively concerned with his personal comforts. His detractors accused him of sponsoring orgies and of spending state funds on his expensive wardrobe. He was not a native New Mexican and didn't understand the politics of the impoverished northern villagers. Although there is no evidence that he ever did so, rumors spread that Pérez was about to force without compromise the new tax structure on the citizens. The *campesinos* in the north regarded this new tax as the final straw and determined that they would resist it at all costs. A minor incident in Santa Cruz de la Cañada in July 1837 ignited smoldering resentment into a full-fledged revolt against the authorities in Santa Fe. This short-lived rebellion came to be called the Chimayó Rebellion because, allegedly, so many of the angry farmers were from that town. There is no roster of names to indicate who the rebels were, and research has shown that the rebels initially enjoyed broad support from throughout New Mexico, but nonetheless Chimayó gained notoriety for its central role in the civil unrest, just as it had during the fierce revolts of the reconquest 140 years earlier. This time, however, the insurgents were both Hispanics and northern Pueblos.[3]

The angry citizens rallied in Santa Cruz de la Cañada, where they founded a new political body (a *cantón*) and formally organized the rebellion. They claimed their insurgency was a legitimate response to the unfair new taxes (levied on woodcutters, sheepherders passing through Santa Fe, and on organizers of dances, among others), the extravagances of the new governor, and restrictions placed unfairly on the people by the Catholic church. In short, the rebels rose up against all the institutions of authority in New Mexico.

When apprised of the rebellion at Santa Cruz, Governor Pérez made the grave mistake of underestimating the strength and determination of the rebels. Thinking that the rebellion could be easily quelled, he marched for Santa Cruz de la Cañada. He met the rebels at Black Mesa and called for negotiations, but the insurgents fired without warning and quickly routed Pérez's force of two hundred men. Most of Pérez's army consisted of Indians from Santo Domingo, Cochití, and Sandía pueblos, and with the opening salvos they joined the rebels' ranks, leaving Pérez with a small contingent of presidial soldiers to fight for their lives. The rebel mob, drunk with violence, pursued Pérez and captured him near Santa Fe. They decapitated their erstwhile ruler and boldly displayed his head in their camp near the Rosario Church in Santa Fe before installing one of their *compadres* as the new governor.

The chaotic tenure of the inexperienced José Gonzales was brief, however. He proved incapable of controlling the mob that had placed him in power, and he failed to win the confidence of the New Mexico citizenry. A force led by Manuel Armijo—and funded in large part by newly established Anglo merchants from Santa Fe—ousted him and regained control of the capital for Mexico in September 1837. Gonzales conceded his authority in a peace treaty and was freed from jail to return to Taos, although four leaders of the rebellion—Juan José Esquibel, Juan Vigil, Desiderio Montoya, and Antonio Abad Montoya—were imprisoned in Santa Fe. Continuing unrest through the end of the year prompted Armijo to call for federal troops for assistance, and in January 1838 the first soldiers arrived in Santa Fe. News of more rebellious activities and the threat of a rescue attempt on his four captive rebels prompted Armijo to order the prisoners summarily decapitated. It was an ignominious defeat for the disheveled leaders of the *cantón*,

whose lofty democratic ideals had been lost in anarchy. After dispensing with
the captives, Armijo marched for Santa Cruz to crush the remaining rebel force.

Armijo engaged the rebel mob for their final defeat at a place called
Puertocito Pojoaque, some seventeen miles north of Santa Fe. After the battle,
Armijo ordered the former rebel governor, José Gonzales, executed by firing
squad in Santa Cruz. The story of the battle of Puertocito Pojoaque has been
passed down in Chimayó, only it has curiously become distorted with the passage of time and has been transformed into a tale of loyal Chimayosos defeating
confederate foes in a valorous attempt to prevent them from marching to
Colorado. In this recasting, the "confederates" encounter a motley army of
Chimayosos, armed only with farming tools and sharpened sticks, at a place
called La Cuesta de la Cruz. The heroic Chimayosos, the story goes, were led
by José Vigil from Cundiyó. The confederates followed Manuel Apontes, and
they are referred to interchangeably as confederates or *tejanos*.

A neighbor in Chimayó offered this oral account of the battle:

*In 1862, the Confederate Army, they were coming from Texas. There was a big
fight over here at the Cuesta de la Cruz—on the new highway, as you go over
the hill there, there's a big cross because there was a big fight with the* tejanos.
These people here, they didn't want the Confederate army to come in. See the
tejanos *were going to Colorado, but they never reached Colorado. All the people
from here, they went over there to wait for them at La Cuesta, because they
knew they were coming. Everybody was just standing around waiting, because
they didn't have no leader. So José Vigil from Cundiyó, he came on his horse, all
tied up with ropes for armor, and he carried his bayonet, you know. When he
got over here, he asked the people, "Who is going to be our leader?" And then
José Vigil decided to be the leader.*

*The leader of the Confederates was Manuel Apontes, from Texas. So, this José
Vigil, he went ahead and he fought with this Manuel Apontes, one-on-one, to
decide the battle. And José Vigil he got his sword and Manuel turned back, and
they chased him to Puertocito de Tesuque, over there, on the other side of*

JOHN TRUJILLO

*Pojoaque. He beat that Manuel Apontes and chased him all the way to Puerto-
cito de Tesuque. The Confederates didn't go any farther.*

*And then, later, José Vigil was called by the governor to the Plaza in Santa Fe.
And he went with his son, Antonito, the great-great-grandfather of the Antonio
who is living today. He thought they were going to kill him over there, so he
took his son Antonio with him so he could bring the horse back to Cundiyó. But
when he got over there, the governor told him that he wanted him to perform
the same action that he had done when he turned the Confederates from here.
So he went around the Plaza performing the action and they had music and
they were playing for him and everything.*

The Chimayó version of this battle is a curious distortion and amalgama-
tion of events from the rebellion. The local story, while referring to the Puertocito
Pojoaque, appears to be describing the encounter at Black Mesa. The names
recounted are nearly accurate: Manuel Apontes was among Pérez's presidial
soldiers at Black Mesa and a Juan Vigil (not José Vigil) also fought in the encounter at La Mesilla, but he was one of the most notorious of the rebels. Other
versions of the battle, taken from eyewitnesses, recall a one-on-one encounter
between Apontes and Vigil. According to these accounts, Vigil (whose nickname
was "El Quemado," suggesting that he may have been from Quemado, near
Chimayó) was wrapped in cloth and cord for armor, and both he and Apontes
suffered wounds in the struggle. Apontes fled with Pérez but hid in a house in
Santa Fe. Although the rebels discovered him and demanded that he be turned
over, they spared his life. Vigil, on the other hand, was not celebrated in the
Santa Fe Plaza but was decapitated with three other rebel leaders after Armijo
had claimed control of Santa Fe.

This local folklore of the Chimayó Rebellion informs us more about the
tellers than about the actual event. The story reveals the antagonism that
Chimayosos and most New Mexicans felt toward Texans, cast in the villain's role
in the story. All the rest of the details of the story have been changed to protect
the guilty. The fact that the story elevates the rebels to hero status tells us where

the sympathies of the Chimayosos lay. Clearly, the people who passed the story down wanted their rebellious neighbors and relatives cast in a much more positive light than the actual events would provide.

In addition to this story of the Chimayó Rebellion, some people vaguely recall being told that long ago two men from Chimayó went to Santa Fe and killed the governor because he raised taxes—a story told with little apology. Part of a ten-line folk ballad, or *décima*, from the nineteenth century also traces the heart of the rebellion to Chimayó:

> *Insurgent Chimayoses*
> *Men of plaid coats*
> *Who have abandoned the looms*
> *To rebel against the country. . .* [4]

The *décima* suggests that Chimayó people participated actively in the rebellion and accurately notes that weaving was already a common activity among the men of Chimayó. Another *décima* about the rebellion mentions the "braided hair" of the Chimayosos.[5] Apparently, these Chimayosos were somewhat different in appearance from the norm—a kind of long-haired counterculture of northern New Mexico. I've seen no roster of names to identify the rebels from Chimayó and there is no indication that anyone from the Plaza del Cerro actually took part. The rebellion nonetheless fueled Chimayó's reputation as a refuge for violent and lawless people.

The next rebellion in New Mexico, often called the Taos Rebellion, came almost on the heels of the Chimayó Rebellion, soon after the United States took over New Mexico in 1846. This insurrection once again erupted from the populace during a difficult transition to a new government, and vague memories of this uprising also survive in the stories Chimayosos tell. The rebels' actions reveal that at least some people felt a strong bond to the mother country that had neglected them for twenty-six years—and against which they had so recently revolted. The insurgents killed New Mexico's first American governor, Charles Bent, who was visiting his family in Taos, and they also murdered Anglos in Taos, Mora, and Arroyo Hondo.

Bent had married a woman from Chimayó and had friends there. John Trujillo recalls hearing the story that when Bent was assassinated, Trujillo's great-great-grandfather, whose name was Roybal, feared for his own life and came to stash his gold with his close friend, José Ramón Ortega, at the Plaza del Cerro. "This Roybal, he was a close friend to Carlos Bent, and when they killed Bent, Roybal brought his gold over here on a burro to José Ramón's and stayed there for a couple of days because he was scared they would come after him. He thought he'd be safer over there on the plaza. He waited until things cooled down a little and then he went back to La Cuchilla."

Through the upheavals and changes of the early 1800s, the population of Chimayó grew. As *placitas* filled the Santa Cruz Valley and began to expand toward each other, the number of people began to exhaust the limited agricultural resources. Farmers carved irrigable land into smaller and smaller pieces with each generation. Old-timers interviewed in the 1930s recalled that there had been "plenty of land" until about 1850, but that by 1875 the land had become overcrowded.[6] The Soil Conservation Service in 1937 reported that, in its opinion, the agricultural resources of the northern New Mexico region could support no more people than had lived there in 1850. More recently, some historians have argued that it was the loss of communal grazing areas and woodlands after the U.S. takeover in 1846, not overpopulation, that forced the Hispanic villages into a disequilibrium with the carrying capacity of the land. In the Santa Cruz Valley, however, the loss of communal grazing lands was not likely a major factor since the Spanish Crown granted no such lands in the area other than the small pastures in the valley itself.

In any case, the land was hard-used by the mid-1800s as villagers scraped for forage for their animals and extracted ever smaller crops from fragmented landholdings. The valley floor offered a very limited capacity for this expanding population, and because of poor forage and steep terrain opportunities for livestock raising were also limited in the vicinity of the Plaza del Cerro. Climatic variability and primitive farming techniques added to the increasing stress on the land—and on the people who made their living off of the land—as the decades of the nineteenth century wore on.

Weaving enterprises, on the other hand, continued to expand after the American takeover, and the Río Grande style of weaving reached its zenith. The style grew from an adaptation of the Saltillo-style *sarapes*, which were popular in Mexico after the Mexican Revolution, combined with the simple striped designs of traditional northern New Mexico use. While merchants coming from the east on the Santa Fe Trail introduced a wide assortment of machine-woven goods that undercut the demand for handwoven textiles, a local market for Hispanic weaving persisted among people who couldn't afford the fancy imports of cloth. Hispanic weaving also stayed alive as a consequence of a new kind of outlet for cheap, warm blankets—sale to the U.S. government. The American government practiced a "policy of gratification" toward pacified Plains Indians, and part of the payoff for peaceful tribes was a supply of wool blankets. Many of these were produced in northern New Mexico and were supplied to the government via contractors in Santa Fe and elsewhere. Demand for blankets increased when Kit Carson defeated the Navajos and forced their internment at Bosque Redondo in 1864. The U.S. Army bought thousands of blankets produced on Hispanic looms with the assistance of Indian slave labor, some derived from Navajos seeking sanctuary from Bosque Redondo.[7] When they were freed from Bosque Redondo in 1868, the Navajos took home with them some of the design styles that they had seen on the blankets of Hispanic manufacture. Rearranged elements of these Río Grande blanket styles—serrated diamonds, center-dominant motifs, and enclosing borders—soon came to dominate Navajo weaving.[8]

Though the American Civil War was mostly a distant affair for the Chimayosos, it nevertheless brought changes to the northern communities. Oral history has it that three men from Chimayó fought in the war—Eulogio Martínez, Concepción Trujillo, and Jesús Baca. (Eulogio lived in the Plaza del Cerro, Jesús Baca lived just to the east, and Concepción was probably raised on the plaza but in his later years lived in Río Chiquito.) Teresita Jaramillo recalls hearing how her Tío Anastacio eluded the men who came in search of recruits for the war: "They came suddenly to look for men for the war. They took my grandfather, Concepción Trujillo. But his brother, my Tío Anastacio, climbed a tree and hid himself there, and they didn't get him. Every other man who was at home was picked up and taken!"

Records show that Eulogio Martínez (who went by Martín) enlisted with the New Mexico Volunteers at the age of eighteen on July 1, 1861, at Fort Union, and that he served under Colonel E. R. Canby. People also remember that Eulogio was wounded in the war, although the muster role of Company A shows he was discharged in April 1862 and mentions no injuries. I haven't found records for the enlistment for the other two men.[9] The Bureau of Pensions issued a Survivor's Pension to Trujillo for service in the "Indian Wars."[10] His service may have included duty in the Civil War; he would have been thirty-four years old in 1861. Over three thousand New Mexicans, most of them Hispanic, signed up with the volunteers. The story in the plaza goes that the three men recruited here—with more than a little gentle persuasion, it would seem—fought in the Battle of Valverde. Grandma remembers hearing the story that Concepción Trujillo was one of the group who fought in this bloody encounter at a ford of the lower Río Grande, infamous in the annals of the Civil War in the West because the Union Army was resoundingly defeated by an inferior Confederate contingent. (The invaders were from Texas, and it makes one wonder if there might not be a bit of this story mixed up in the local account of the Chimayó Rebellion.)

Versions of the Battle of Valverde vary. The commander of the Union forces, Colonel Canby, reported that the battle, fought in February 1862, was lost in large part because the native volunteers (in this context, "native" referred to Hispanics) displayed a failure of nerve. But the tale told by Hispanic survivors differs. Colonel J. Francisco Chávez, who at the time of the battle served as a lieutenant colonel with the volunteers, recalled the battle in quite different terms. Chávez wrote that he and his comrades were engaged in battle when they received the order to withdraw because the Union regulars were in full retreat. Colonel Kit Carson, the commander of the volunteers, gave a similar account of the battle. Modern historians believe that Canby had been trying to cover up his own troops' weakness by pinning the blame on the Hispanics. In any case, the battle cost the Union Army 306 casualties and left 185 Confederate soldiers dead.[11] The Confederates marched on to meet defeat in New Mexico at Glorieta in March.

The Chimayosos who did fight in the Civil War came back changed people. Grandma remembers that Jesús Baca returned home permanently disabled. She knew him as an old man with a limp. He and other veterans received pensions for fighting in the war, which was very impressive to the Chimayosos. Some people say that it was with his sizable pension that the disabled Eulogio Martínez was able to acquire land around the plaza, making him one of the largest landowners in the area. The concept of the federal government coming to the aid of the people was novel in this remote land where those in power had always been only mildly concerned with the well-being of the citizenry.

The U.S. occupation and the Civil War altered life in New Mexico's northern communities, but a far greater impact was felt with the arrival of the Denver and Rio Grande Western (D&RGW) Railroad in Española on the last day of 1880. The railroad spurred the development of stock raising and mining and logging industries in northern New Mexico and southern Colorado, initiating the first full-scale exploitation of natural resources in the region. Some of these jobs involved labor on the railroads themselves, and northern New Mexicans traveled throughout the West to help construct the new rail lines. The Hispanics were almost always hired as menial laborers; seldom did they find employment in the higher-paying positions such as conductor, brakeman, fireman, station clerk, or the many other jobs associated with railroad development. Most of the work of laying track also went to imported laborers. A coal boom ensued with the arrival of railroads in New Mexico, but here again, all but the menial jobs were handed to Anglos from outside the region.

Lumbering, mining, agriculture, and ranching led this boom in the economy. Some of these industries were based in New Mexico. Lepidolite from Embudo and mica from Tres Piedras moved out of the northern New Mexico region on the D&RGW, and there were small gold and copper mining operations in the region as well. Harry Buckman, known for his rapacious clear-cutting on the Pajarito Plateau, shipped out millions of board feet of ponderosa pine from the Jémez Mountains, and lumber moved out from Tres Piedras and on a spur leading to La Madera. To the northeast, the Santa Barbara Tie and Pole Company operated in Peñasco, floating tens of thousands of ties down the Embudo River and from there down the Río Grande to a tie plant in Albuquerque. Cattle from southern

New Mexico and Arizona rode the so-called Chile Line north to summer grazing lands in Colorado, and hogs were also shipped out of the region to markets. Frank Bond built up his huge sheep operation out of Española, using the D&RGW to move his animals. Among the region's agricultural produce, chiles were most important, but piñón nuts also filled train cars. In good years as many as seventeen cars were required to carry the crop. Apples, too, became an export crop for a time, and in some years more than two hundred carloads shipped out, destined for markets as distant as Great Britain.[12]

Northern New Mexicans found work in these industries, but almost none participated in financing or managing the businesses. Many were swindled out of their land, on which they had always managed to survive, to make way for the entrepreneurs. However, in spite of the fact that the good jobs went to new-comers, the late-nineteenth-century boom created plentiful jobs where there were practically none before, and many men from Chimayó began to board the D&RGW in search of work throughout the West. The opportunity came none too soon, for farming the land would not have supported the increasing population for much longer. A major component of the population began to leave for a large part of the year, and Chimayó, like all communities in northern New Mexico, became precariously dependent on wage labor to meet basic subsistence needs. Thus, the railroad raised the specter both of employment and unemployment in northern New Mexico. Life in the region, once tied to the rhythm of planting and harvesting, became equally defined by an annual exodus of young men.

Railroad towns sprang up along the new tracks of New Mexico's many new railroads, often appearing where no town had existed before or grafting themselves onto existing towns. The economy of railroad towns was dominated by jobs associated with the railroad industry and the trade it engendered. Española, across the river from the old town center of Santa Cruz, was founded on the railroad economy and was, from its inception, dominated by Anglo business interests.

Melita Ortega keeps among her collection of odd historical notes a poem written by Francisco Antonio (El "Güero") Mestas, the legendary Irish great-grandfather to the Ortegas of the Plaza del Cerro. Melita's sister, Petrita, had memorized the poem as she heard it in her youth and had written it down for her sister. This bit of folklore from the mid-1880s describes the impact of the railroad on the farming families of the northern New Mexico region, conveying a potent sense of the conflicts and opportunities the "road of iron" presented:

El Ferrocarril [13]

Ya la gente se enlevó	Now the people have departed
Con el camino de hierro	On the road of iron
Y hasta la siembra dejó	With even the sowing left behind
Por irse a ganar dinero	So they can go earn money
Todo el territorio entero	Everybody in the territory
Se ocupa en este quehacer	Is busy with this task
Con la escrepa y barretero	And the scraper and the pickaxe
Y el desagüe en componer	And the ditch works are left in disrepair
Si no tienen qué comer	Even if they have nothing to eat
No les importa se van	It doesn't matter, they go
Pero no pueden saber	But there's no way to know
Si allá los desecharán	If they will be fired over there
Vienen luego a placticar	Then they come back to chat,
Cada uno como le fue	Each one telling how it went, saying
Y no hay donde trabajar	"There's no work
Y lo peor que no sembré	And worse yet, I didn't plant"
Dime tú ahora cómo haré	"Tell me now how I'll make it,"
Le dicen a su mujer	They ask their wives
De pastor me meteré	"I'll have to become a shepherd
Pa' podernos mantener	So that we can survive"

Ahora si has pensando bien	"Now, if you thought it out so well,
Haz como a ti te dé la gana	Go on and do as you please,
Pero también te diré	But I'll tell you one thing—
Yo quiero un corte de lana	I want a bolt of wool!"
Mujer, esa es una infamia	"Woman, this is blasphemy
No me empieces a moler	Don't start nagging me,
Mira, no seas tan vana	Look, don't be so vain,
Porque primero es comer	Because it's more important to eat!"
Bien te lo decía yo	"I told you so,
Al saber determinar	When I figured it out
Que para tener qué hacer	That in order to be sure of survival,
Lo seguro es el sembrar	The best thing is to plant."
Pero ahora ya no hay lugar	"But now we have no place to plant,
Y el tiempo se me pasó	And time has slipped away from me,
La plaga nos va a llegar	And the plague is going to come,
Aunque tú piensas que no	Even if you don't think so"
Eso es lo que siento yo	"This is what I regret
De pasar mis malos ratos	About going through these bad times,
Como ya ni trabajo	Since now I don't even work
No te compro ni zapatos	I can't even buy you shoes"
Eso también siento yo	"I also regret
Que ya no tiene trabajo	That you don't have work,
Y si se mete de pastor	And if you become a shepherd
Yo pesco la cuesta abajo	It will all be downhill for me"

El Güero is one of the most colorful characters in the stories people recount about the old days. No one I talked to knew him personally, for he died before most were born, but his flamboyant style earned him an enduring legacy among his numerous descendants—those from both his wife and his Native American servant. Neither lineage is shy about claiming ancestry to El Güero, for the effects of time seem to have erased any shame about his behavior. El Güero's daughter Petra married José Ramón Ortega of the Plaza del Cerro, and the light hair and freckles of El Güero still show up in the numerous descendants of this union.

I first heard of El Güero one day when I was visiting Virginia Trujillo Ortega at her house just outside the plaza. She was showing me pictures of her family when I noticed on the wall an old portrait of a blonde-haired, blue-eyed man. His intense stare was riveting. Surrounding his portrait were locks of light hair from his four daughters. Fascinated, I asked Virginia who this man was, and she told me her story of El Güero. She was 104 years of age when I last talked with her, but she still giggled when she recited the anecdotes she had heard about her husband's grandfather—my great-great-great-grandfather.

The most puzzling aspect of the El Güero legend is the story of how he came to live in the Santa Cruz Valley. According to Virginia's version of the tale, El Güero "got lost" during the Civil War and somehow ended up in Santa Cruz. A more common tale says that he was found as a child by some *ciboleros* from Santa Cruz during one of their annual trips to the plains of eastern New Mexico to hunt buffalo and trade with Indians. As the story goes, the *ciboleros* came across the smoldering remains of a wagon train on the Santa Fe Trail, the latest victim of a Indian attack. Bundled in the back of an overturned wagon was the blonde child—the sole survivor of the raid. They took the boy back to Santa Cruz and called him El Güero (the blonde one) because of his blonde hair. Tomás Mestas adopted and raised him, naming him Francisco Antonio Mestas.

Grandma tells a slightly different—more believable—version of the story:

They used to say that the men from here would go to trade. They went to kill cíbolos, *to bring meat from—What is it in English? Buffalo. They had gone to kill buffalo, and when they were coming back, they met some Indians. They were some place in the wilderness—wild country. So, they met the Indians, and the Indians were carrying a baby, that they had stole from some people out there. The baby! They stole him and the people couldn't get him back. But the* ciboleros *traded for the baby and brought him here to Santa Cruz,*

BENIGNA
O. CHÁVEZ

where one of them raised him. Actually, an Indian woman raised El Güero for the man. I don't think they killed El Güero's parents, but I don't know what happened to them. And then they named him after the people that rescued him—Mestas. Petrita Mestas was his daughter. She had a very fair complexion, and she had freckles. That's what my mother used to say. I wasn't even—I was just ten months old when mi Petrita died.

Wagon traffic carrying settlers on the Santa Fe Trail was nonexistent until after the Mexican Revolution and uncommon until after the U.S. annexed New Mexico in 1846. If the story of his origins bears any truth, El Güero would probably have arrived in Santa Cruz sometime after 1821. Census records give his birth year as 1811 and list him as one of Tomás Mestas's several natural sons. Other documents indicate that he died in 1890 after fathering eight legitimate and at least one illegitimate child. (Virginia blushed and hid her smile when in her ancient Spanish she reported his *"hijos ilegítimos."*)

The trade in captives was thriving in the mid-1800s, and although it focused primarily on Indian slaves, El Güero could well have been caught up in the exchanges taking place. Whatever his origins, El Güero established himself as a fairly prosperous and respected citizen of the valley. His brother was in the Territorial Legislature in Santa Fe, and people say that El Güero traveled regularly to Mexico on trading expeditions. His ties to the territorial government in Santa Fe may have facilitated similar connections for his son-in-law, José Ramón Ortega, and led to very direct and strong connections between the Plaza del Cerro and Santa Fe by the early 1900s.

El Güero was also very mischievous, according to Tía Virginia, and was fond of playing practical jokes on people. My mother recalls that Tía Bonefacia Ortega, who died in 1953 at the age of seventy-nine, often talked about El Güero, emphasizing his rowdy charm. Bonefacia claimed that his real name was Charles Conklin (Bone pronounced it "Char-less Cone-klin"), but she never explained how she knew.

Some writings of El Güero are among family papers kept by my mother. El Güero's neat, flowing handwriting belies a disciplined man, and his poem reveals a thoughtful perspective as the railroad arrived to change life in the Santa Cruz Valley. He seemed to be acutely aware that the change threw Chimayó, like every place in the new territory, into the sphere of the national capitalist economy. The age-old barter system began to erode as the need for cash began to permeate the region. Along with thousands of other small farming communities in the U.S., the villages of northern New Mexico entered the industrial age with suddenness. Even El Güero's insight could not have predicted the magnitude of the change that was to follow as it unfolded over decades. With new opportunities, the iron horse created new needs as well.

Tourists first began arriving in large numbers in New Mexico after the railroads were built. This was especially true in Santa Fe, which actively promoted tourism in New Mexico. A different kind of tourism appeared much earlier in Chimayó, however, as word spread throughout the area of the sacred healing earth at La Capilla de Nuestro Señor de Esquipulas,[14] the renowned Santuario of Chimayó. The Santuario, completed in 1816, attracted a small but steady stream of pilgrims, and the flow increased with the completion of the adjacent Santo Niño Church about 1860, which offered its own miraculous wonders. To date millions have visited the site and sought cures for the soul and body, perhaps more so today than at any time in its long history. This religious tourism has had a profound effect on all of Chimayó, including the Plaza del Cerro.

An inventory of the shrine in 1818 suggests that people in Chimayó began exploiting the market in religious tourism very early on. It lists a number of items—some donated for sale, others belonging to the chapel, but all of them made in New Mexico—in the *zaguán* (front room) of the chapel. Among the items is a long list of woven goods; altogether, the inventory includes twenty *sarapes*, thirty-seven *varas* of *sayal* (a coarse handwoven cloth), twenty-four *varas* of *jerga* (floor carpet), a five-*vara* length of embroidered cloth, a bedspread, a *frezada* (a small, multicolored piece of cloth), a tablecloth, and a dozen pairs of knitted wool stockings.[15] It seems that the two rooms attached to the front of the Santuario, which are not found on any other church or chapel in New Mexico, were originally built specifically as a venue for selling goods.[16] It may be that weavers from the plaza contributed to the Santuario's wares. The

VARA: A MEASURE EQUAL TO NEARLY THREE FEET

THE SANTUARIO
DE NUESTRO
SEÑOR DE
ESQUIPULAS IN
POTRERO, 1990.

plaza would have been in an ideal position for such trade, for it was nearby and on the main route to the shrine.

Don Bernardo Abeyta, who some families in the plaza area can claim as an ancestor, was the inspiring force behind the building of the Santuario de Chimayó. He was also a regional leader in the Penitente Brotherhood, the lay confraternity that performed penitential ceremonies throughout northern New Mexico beginning about 1800.[17] Stories abound describing the experience that led him to establish the Santuario, but Bernardo's own story was never recorded. The story told in the plaza area conforms in theme to many popular versions of this figure. Grandma tells this inherited version:

BENIGNA
O. CHÁVEZ

Bernardo Abeyta was the one who built the Santuario. He was out watering his fields one day when he found an image of Señor de Esquipulas in the barranco. He saw a light and went over, and there was a little crucifix with Señor de Esquipulas in a cave. He took it to his house and put it there, but in a few days,

86

it disappeared and went back to the fields again. He brought it back home, and it went out to the fields again, back to where he found it by the river there—you know, down there in those fields where they have mass now. Bernardo thought it was miraculous that that statue kept going back to the field. So he went to Mexico to get permission to make a capilla there. The bishop gave him permission, so he and his brothers started to build it. But then everyone from around there got interested in helping, and they made it a big place. Even the women helped to build that place; they did all the plastering. A special room was built on the exact spot—they call it El Pocito—where Bernardo found the image of Señor de Esquipulas.

PEOPLE GATH-
ERED AT THE
SANTUARIO
FOR THE
ARCHBISHOP'S
VISIT, 1945.

87

The common thread in all the tales of Bernardo's epiphany—the discovery of a buried statue or cross—may be easily explained: the buried object could be an artifact from Hispanic settlement of the valley before the Pueblo Revolt of 1680. Indeed, the site of Potrero matches closely with descriptions in Luis Granillo's journal for the location of the Juan Ruiz farm. Few if any people living in Potrero would have known that people occupied the area before, and as a consequence certainly would have been surprised to find an icon of the Christian faith buried in the soil. Such a reappearance of a buried artifact would not be uncommon even today—but the presence of Esquipulas on the buried crucifix remains in any case remarkable, for this explanation still leaves the question as to how this holy representation, whose origins are traced to a Latin American devotion, came to Chimayó.

The Santuario became an important religious site for people throughout northern New Mexico, but Don Bernardo's written request to build the church clearly indicates that he intended it as a small chapel for the people from Potrero. In November 1813, he petitioned Fray Sebastián Alvarez on behalf of "nineteen families of the plaza of Potrero" for permission to build a chapel to "venerate . . . Our Lord and Redeemer, in his Avocation of Esquipulas."[18] No record found to date discloses how he knew of this particular manifestation of Christ—an image with its origin in the Black Christ, Esquipulas, found in the southern Guatemalan town by the same name.[19] The fact that pilgrims historically have flocked to both sites to use the dirt for healing purposes affords further proof of the common origin of the two isolated shrines.

Research by geographer Stephen deBorhegyi shows that knowledge of the cult of Esquipulas traveled far into northern Mexico from its origins, perhaps far enough that Bernardo learned of it on one of his trips to northern Mexico. The alternate explanation that someone from Guatemala journeyed to Chimayó has also been suggested, but as yet no one finds any indication of who this might have been or when and why he came to Chimayó.

Adding further intrigue to the origins of the Santuario, Pueblo Indians have for years journeyed to the site and claim to have done so long before Hispanics arrived in the area. The hill of Tsi Mayoh—which rises directly over the valley at Potrero where the Santuario sits—held an important place in Tewa cosmology, and some Tewa legends tell of a sacred hot pool at the spot where the shrine is built. It was here, they say, that the twin War Gods killed a giant. The pool dried up long ago but the Pueblo people continued to visit the site and collect the holy dirt there. Something of this ancient myth may have played a part in Bernardo's inspiration to build a chapel on the site where he could honor Señor de Esquipulas. It seems equally plausible, however, that the Pueblo stories grew as a way to sanctify the site for Indian people after Bernardo and his neighbors built the Santuario.

The Catholic church was very enthusiastic about Abeyta's proposal to build a chapel, which it believed would serve not only Potrero but nearby communities as well. Writing in support of Abeyta in 1816, Fray Alvarez noted that people had been coming to Bernardo's shrine in Potrero for some time "to give praise to the sovereign Redeemer . . . [and to] alleviate their ailments." Because of the fame of these portents, the villagers wanted to build a chapel, he reported, and this would serve the church well, for as it was the people of the "five plazas" in the area had a very difficult time getting to mass. "They often can't come to the church on account of the snow or the frozen river, and the great distance, which prevents them from coming. . . . This chapel will be of much consolation to the Parish of this Villa [Santa Cruz], [allowing me] to take the Holy Sacrament to the sick of the plaza immediately. . . . [As it is now] many people die without the Holy Sacraments because of the distance from the church and the bad roads, so inconvenient and impassable in the winter."[20]

Soon after Don Bernardo's death in 1856, a second cult and a chapel dedicated to Santo Niño de Atocha sprang up in Potrero, and soon miraculous stories of the figure of the Holy Child eclipsed the cult of Señor de Esquipulas. Before long, the Santo Niño was credited with the cures that people experienced. In response, the heirs to the Santuario acquired their own Santo Niño and regained the flow of devout pilgrims seeking cures. Among the plaza *viejitos*, the Santuario remains the domain of Señor de Esquipulas.[21]

Bernardo Abeyta's daughter María Francisca Abeyta married Pedro Asencio Ortega, a son of Grabiel Ortega and a lifelong resident of the Plaza del

Cerro. Like his father-in-law Bernardo, Pedro maintained a small chapel, located on the plaza's west side. The style of its altar screen matches that of José Rafael Aragón, the celebrated *santero* who painted some of the *reredos* at the Santuario and in the Capilla de San Antonio de Padua in nearby Córdova.[22] Aragón resided in Potrero in 1821 and probably created the *reredos* in both places. Pedro Ortega's chapel became as important to residents of the plaza as the Santuario was to the people in Potrero, although Pedro never felt compelled to transform his modest place of worship into a large building.

The *oratorio*, as the community chapel is still known, served as a small religious center of the plaza through the 1800s and well into this century. Thanks to the careful research of Chimayó historian Daniel Jaramillo, we know that Pedro Asencio Ortega's will, written in 1837 as he lay dying after an accident, lists Don Pedro's belongings, including 324 *varas* of land, eight *casas*, fruit trees, and nine domestic animals. The will also enumerates a number of religious items inside the *oratorio* and mentions that *devotos* (devotees) had contributed some of these.[23] As with the santuario in Potrero, it seems that although the chapel originated as Pedro and María Francisca's private chapel, the plaza community also valued it greatly and contributed to its care.

Pedro's will leaves the room to his nephew, Isidro Ortega, but ownership of the *oratorio* is unclear between the time of Pedro Ortega's death in 1837 and the turn of the century. However, a paper shown to me by Melita Ortega lists some forty-four people who contributed to the upkeep of the *oratorio* on the plaza in 1878.[24] According to this *lista de limosnas* (list of alms), most people gave *dos reales* (25 cents) or ten *centavos*, using the names given by the Spanish (*real* pertaining to the Spanish royalty) in a state that had been a territory of the U.S. for thirty-one years. (Grandma and many others in Chimayó still refer to money by Spanish names.) But money was still scarce, and most people proffered more humble contributions. María Guadalupe Trujillo gave a half of a *ristra* of chile, Santos Corís and María Teodora Trujillo each offered two bunches of *punche* (homegrown tobacco) while José Ortega gave two *almures* (an archaic measure equal to about a half bushel) of garbanzo beans. The names read with a familiar sound, for descendants of these families still live in the plaza area;

eight of the contributors came from the Trujillo family, seven from the Ortegas, and five were Martínezes.

The ceiling of the *oratorio* is inscribed with many of the names of people associated with the upkeep of it and who apparently repaired the building in 1873. The signatures, some scrawled in careful longhand, some penciled in crude print, and others inked in bold, blocky letters, speak out hauntingly from the rough, hand-hewn boards. Some are accompanied by small drawings with cryptic, symbolic messages: a crucifix sprouting leaves, with the inscription *"El Arbol de la Cruz"*; a circular symbol resembling a toothed sun or a spiked shield; and a heart with swords penetrating it from two angles to form a cross.

The religious icons in the *oratorio* itemized in Don Pedro's last will and testament were typical of nineteenth-century chapels. Besides the painted altar screen, these included two *bultos* (carved figures representing holy personages) —one of San Buenaventura and one of San Antonio—an adobe altar, small mirrors, wall-mounted candle holders, cloth hanging along the walls, and handmade, wooden *arañas* (simple chandeliers). Most of these are still kept in the *oratorio* and have been supplemented by simple colored prints of holy figures framed in tin.

The details in Pedro Asencio's will and the careful attention people have given to the preservation of the *oratorio* make it possible to glimpse what the interior of that plaza room looked like in the nineteenth century. The appearance of the rest of the plaza in that period is a matter of conjecture, but other than its rectangular form, it probably differed very little in most respects from dozens of other plazas and *placitas* in northern New Mexico. Buildings were made entirely with adobe and hand-hewn lumber, and they probably adjoined on all sides to seal the plaza interior. A will from María Guadalupe Vigil de Ortega tells us that in 1890 there was a gate on the south side of the Plaza del Cerro, and a similar gate no doubt could be closed on the north side.[25] Gervacio Ortega's will identifies a *torreón* on his property on the northwest corner of the plaza, which likely was similar in appearance to that which still stands on the plaza's south side.[26] Flat roofs were the norm, and mud floors and corner fireplaces were ubiquitous.

EXTERIOR OF
THE ORATORIO
DE SAN BUENA-
VENTURA, CA.
1950s.

The floors were plastered with mud annually or else treated with ox blood, which produced a hard, durable surface. There were probably no windows on the outer walls—a vestige of the time when the structure was defensive; glass was uncommon and windows to the dark adobe interiors rare. Some of the more prosperous residents plastered the interior walls with *yeso,* a thin coating of gypsum mixed with water, and white cloth hung along the walls to protect them from scuffing. (People continued to finish walls with *yeso* in my grandma's youth. She remembers that a man in a wagon came through with the gypsum rock for trade. The *enjaradoras* [woman plasterers] baked the rock in an *horno* [outdoor oven] and then pulverized it, mixed it with water, and applied it to the walls.)

INTERIOR OF
THE ORATORIO,
1992.

REREDOS AND
BULTOS IN THE
ORATORIO,
EARLY 1950S.

95

Outside of the *oratorio* very few nineteenth-century architectural details remain in the Plaza del Cerro. New building materials brought by the railroad began to change its appearance by the end of the 1800s. Pitched roofs of tin worked much better at keeping off the rain, and plaza residents began adopting the new material as soon as they could afford it. Machine-cut lumber replaced the hand-hewn *latillas* on ceilings, and mud floors gave way to planking of milled ponderosa pine. By the century's end, wood stoves were available to those who could raise the cash, and glass for windows became both more available and affordable. Any building that was kept up eventually adopted these new materials. Those that retained the old workmanship were neglected and eventually fell into ruin.

In the textile industry the railroad had its impact as well. Commercial yarns and cotton warp, first available when the Santa Fe Trail opened, became more common, and weavers leapt at the chance to use these cheaper materials. While machine-produced textiles undercut the local market for handwoven materials, the connection of the railways to Santa Fe and Española also presented new economic opportunities for Hispanic weavers. The tourists who began using the trains to see the West soon discovered Hispanic and Navajo weaving. By the late 1800s, outlets in Santa Fe were offering Hispanic weavings in many sizes for the tourist market. Plaza weavers no doubt seized the opportunity and began crafting their products according to the taste of the tourists as interpreted by merchants in Santa Fe, particularly a well-known proprietor by the name of Jake Gold. [27]

"Mexican" blankets from northern New Mexico took their place beside Navajo weavings in Gold's "Free Museum and Curiosity Shop." After Gold left the business around the turn of the century, his shop fell into the hands of his longtime partner, Jesús Candelario, the scion of an old Santa Fe family and a German immigrant mother. Candelario took the Santa Fe tourist trade in Chimayó blankets into the twentieth century, and he was a close associate of most, if not all, Chimayó weavers. Some of the older people in Chimayó still remember "Sito" Candelario and the business he carried on with their families.

Among the weavers in Chimayó, there is a general agreement that the weaving tradition was passed down father-to-son from the first settlers in Chimayó. In the Ortega family, Grabiel is credited with being the first weaver and after him his grandson Gervacio, to whom some blankets in family collections are attributed. But curiously, Gervacio's last will and testament, while taking great pains to identify all of his many belongings, never mentions a loom or any kind of weaving equipment, casting some doubt on the veracity of the idea that he was a weaver. (Pedro Asencio Ortega's will does list one small item important in the weaving business—a carding tool—but otherwise, weaving paraphernalia are conspicuously absent from documents through most of the 1800s.) The will does mention a number of woven goods, including nineteen blankets (*sarapes*), four large carpets (*jergones*), and four sheets (*sábanas*), but it gives no information on their origins.[28]

While failing to identify him as a weaver, Gervacio's will provides a useful enumeration of the material goods of a prosperous Chimayó farmer in the mid-1800s. The account of his estate includes land in "Chimallo," Truchas, La Puebla, and Santa Cruz—nearly 1,000 *varas* in all, counting the land he owned by virtue of his marriage to María Guadalupe (who was from Santa Cruz). He claims ownership of at least five houses, ranging in size from one to five rooms, and of a working mill in La Puebla. His livestock consisted of a team of oxen, a team of bulls, sixteen cows and eleven calves, one mule, one horse, one mare, one colt, four asses, thirteen goats, and two pigs. Gervacio took care to identify each of his seventeen fruit trees (mostly apple and peach) in Chimayó and La Puebla, assigning ownership of individual trees to specific heirs. (It was his first will that parceled fruit trees out limb by limb.)

Gervacio's estate, while extensive, was that of a person subsisting off the land. It scarcely mentions money at all. By contrast papers from the late 1800s in the plaza detail a changing community with more and more contact with the outside world. Money becomes a regular feature of the documents, replacing livestock and produce as a medium of exchange. The simple paperwork of earlier eras gives way to tax bills, certifications of government officers, and ledgers detailing contracts for maintenance of schools and payment of teachers. These

THE FACADE
OF VICTOR
ORTEGA'S
GENERAL
STORE ON THE
PLAZA, 1991.

THE CRUZ
ADOBE ON THE
NORTH SIDE
OF THE PLAZA
DEL CERRO,
1991.

THE ORATORIO
AND NEARBY
BUILDINGS, 1992.

INTERIOR OF
BONEFACIA
ORTEGA'S ABAN-
DONED DISPENSA,
1990.

documents, along with miscellaneous correspondence and notes, show that Chimayó was well connected and involved with state politics as the turn of the twentieth century approached, largely because of the influence of José Ramón Ortega.

Like his father Gervacio Ortega, José Ramón was a justice of the peace.[29] Plaza people remember José Ramón and can attest that he was a weaver and that he raised sheep for their wool. He could read and write well, authoring many of the documents dealing with legal arrangements as well as the payment of public employees. He was also a strong Republican who worked locally to elect party candidates. Also like his father, José Ramón was fairly well off for his day. In 1887, he paid taxes in Río Arriba County for a house and land valued at $19,500 and personal property valued at $14,100. His taxes that year, which he paid in full, amounted to $162—no small sum of money in an era when some people could offer no more than a handful of tobacco as their dues to the chapel.[30]

The Republican Central Committee, seeking to contact potential voters in an election year, called on José Ramón in 1888 to provide them with a list of all voters who received correspondence in the Chimayó Post Office.[31] Impassioned letters also passed back and forth between José Ramón and Alejandro Read, a leading Republican and the probate clerk and recorder for Río Arriba County. In 1886, Read wrote—in perfect Spanish and elegant handwriting—to José Ramón, his "dear and esteemed friend," complaining about irregularities in the vote count that cost the Republicans a probate judge seat.[32] But the letter goes on to say that the Democrats "can say goodbye to any future hopes," and that "The Chimayocito won by 257 votes." It appears that Read referred to José Ramón as "the Chimayocito" and that José Ramón won the judgeship in Río Arriba County that year.

Another letter from Read to José Ramón talks of the election of 1892, in which Grover Cleveland beat out Benjamin Harrison for the presidency: "Our friends the Democrats are very happy that they won the presidency, but that doesn't mean much, for here in New Mexico it is of very little importance if one or the other party wins the presidency. It's the Justice of the Peace of our precinct that is most important. He is who we deal with more than the President."[33]

By the turn of the twentieth century, Chimayó had come a long way from
the rebellion of 1837. Once part of the community known for its defiant citizens,
the Plaza del Cerro had become firmly entrenched in the American political and
economic system, and it housed some potent advocates of the Republican party,
with few adversaries in the poorly represented Democrats' ranks. José Ramón
assumed the role of local *patrón*, wielding the political power for the plaza community and amassing considerable wealth in the process. The plaza still retained
many aspects of its Spanish Colonial and Mexican heritage in terms of architecture and life-style. In the next few decades, however, major changes took place
—changes that initially encouraged a flourishing of the plaza but in the long
run lead to the abandonment of many of its buildings. For the twentieth century,
the best source of information on the Plaza del Cerro is the people who lived
there and witnessed these changes.

REYES
ORTEGA
WEAVING,
1940.

Chapter Six:
A Plaza of Primos

Weaving the Threads

It's a sad story mi hijita,
And no one knows why.
The ways of God are not for us to understand;
Tiene uno que sufrir para merecer, dicen,
Pero yo no sé, yo no sé . . .

Ay, linda de mi vida,
How 'Mano Pedro fell to crying,
Hearing she was gone,
And all the vecinos mourn for our Prima so young,
Even Don Reyes stays inside at his looms all day,
And the gardens are quiet under the sun.

When she was real sick she told Pedro,
"Go get hermana *Julianita,"*
So my tía *went for her and she said,*
"I'm going to die sister
Can you take care of my little girls?"

"*Mis parientes era toda la plaza, y era muy bonito*—All the plaza was my family, and it was beautiful," the late Bersabé Chávez told me with a smile as we sat in her Potrero home and talked about the old plaza. "We were so close, everyone helped each other," Benjamín Ortega, who was also born and raised on the plaza, echoed from his Santa Fe home. "In those times, there wasn't a day when we weren't in contact with someone in the family. Maybe someone would kill a pig, and they'd call everyone to help butcher it and we'd have a big feast with the meat. Or maybe we'd just get together and eat piñón and apples in the winter, and that was such a treat. Life was very pleasant. We'd visit with our *primos* and *tíos* [cousins, uncles, and aunts]. It was really wonderful."

Amada Trujillo recalls a similar feeling of community: "Yes, it was nice. People knew each other, they knew their ups and downs and everything. Everybody cooperated and helped each other. Now it's entirely different—too many people gone and dead or something. Back then, even if you were not related, the feeling for one another was very close. I guess it started to change when people started going away. 'Well my job is here, who cares about who's there [in the old plaza] dying?' And that's the way people are now, these younger generations. You can lie dead, dying, and they think, 'It's OK, I'm having a good time. It's my day.' Not then. When an old person or a sick person needed help, they were Number One—it was that kind of a close relationship."

"People used to get along," recalled Cordelia Martínez. "We used to visit each other. Not like today. Now there's no time, on account of television. And in those times, we just had 'Vitrolas,' to listen to records. That's all we used to have—and each other."

Nearly everyone who grew up in the Plaza del Cerro in this century describes the familial sense of the community. All the residents were related in some way, for the plaza was inhabited by a few families that had been in the Chimayó area for several generations. Perhaps sixty people lived at the plaza itself in the early part of this century, and if neighbors were not related by blood, they were related by marriage. In the rare chance that no definitive familial relationship existed, people usually behaved as if they were family anyway—unless matters of politics or religion came between them, as they did when evangelical Presbyterians arrived in 1898 and when the Great Depression turned the political order upside down. But in the early decades of this century, these divisions were superficial. People in the plaza referred to each other as 'manos or 'manas (a shortening of *hermanos* and *hermanas* [brothers and sisters] that connotes a respectful familial affection but no blood relation), *primos* or *primas*, *compadres* or *vecinos*. They may have also called each other less endearing names, but they never called each other strangers.

For the plaza residents, the families formed the social fabric of the community. They were its many-colored threads, and for generations they interwove until they became as intricate as patterns on a Chimayó blanket. Kinship bonds stretched out far beyond the plaza's confines to draw neighboring *placitas* into the design. In fact, the plaza family was but a subset of the Santa Cruz Valley family, which in turn was part of the large network of distant relations comprising New Mexico's Hispanic population. By the early 1900s, the branches of the network in each village had grown distinct enough to know themselves as separate and different from each other. Among them the Plaza del Cerro was an especially distinctive community, largely because it was a landmark and a center of economic activity for Chimayó.

For someone who was not raised in the plaza community, unraveling the complex tangle of familial relationships is vexing. A typical conversation about families on the plaza might go this way: "Encarnación was Imperia's sister—she was José Ramón Ortega's daughter. Not José Ramón Ortega who lived on the plaza—the other José Ramón Ortega, Isaías's grandpa. And Francisquita was also Imperia's sister. This was a different Francisquita Ortega, not your grandma's *Tía*, who married Concepción's son and moved to Centinela (they were first cousins because, you see, they didn't go outside of their villages to marry and had to marry their first cousins—and the church approved of this because the priests understood the situation). And this Francisquita married her first cousin José Inez Martínez—the José Inez from the east side of the plaza, not the one from the west side."

The number of relationships that these old people can keep track of and recite is astonishing. They may go on for several minutes explaining an individ-

GROUP GATH-
ERED FOR THE
BAPTISM OF
AMBROSIO
ORTEGA, CA.
1915.

ual's place in the extended plaza family. Nearly every such conversation leaves me bewildered and ends with the *viejito* apologizing for his or her poor memory. The litany of names they recall makes Genesis seem simple. The pattern of family relations is further complicated by the frequent duplication of both family and given names on the plaza. As Melita Ortega was trying to explain in the conversation above, there were two José Ramón Ortegas, two Francisquita Ortegas, two men by the name of José Inez Martínez, and two Félix Ortegas—all living in or near the plaza at about the same time but only distantly related. Other people have pointed out to me that there were two contemporary Sotera Martínezes and two Concepción Trujillos. Such repetition in monikers complicates the web for a nonnative, but to those who lived here it seems that the repeated names caused no confusion at all.

Sabino Trujillo's 1950s map diagrams in a simple form the complex inter-weavings among plaza families and is a useful tool in attempting to sort out the web of family ties that defined the community. His image included no property boundaries but focused instead on plaza residents—often identified by their familiar nicknames. In contrast to Sabino's map, the first official land ownership

FROM LEFT:
GABRIELITA
AND REBECCA
MARTÍNEZ,
BERSABÉ
AND AMADA
NARANJO;
ENCARNACÍON
NARANJO IN
DOORWAY,
CA. 1915.

map, produced in conjunction with the small holdings claim survey and drawn to represent the same period of time, says nothing about plaza residents or their life-style. This technically accurate map does little to inspire the imagination but provides a useful tool for studying patterns of land ownership in and around the plaza. It makes it possible to tally up acreage and to clarify ownership of the interior plaza, which was undivided on Sabino's map. It shows patterns that never could be gleaned from Sabino's view of his world.

The differences between the maps were not without consequence for the plaza. Though Sabino took pains to draw a strip of community right-of-way around the plaza, known as the *pisos de la plaza* (the walkways of the plaza), this feature does not appear on the survey maps. It was understood by all plaza residents that a strip of land four yards wide was to be left for the *pisos*. Likewise, the surveyors failed to note the *vereda de las aguaderas*, a public pathway through the plaza and on to the Martínez and Ortega ditches. The *vereda* allowed residents a pathway through cultivated land to get their drinking water and to reach their farm fields outside the plaza. Benjamín Ortega recalled his father Victor telling him that the landowners on either side of the *vereda* were expected to grant a five-foot-wide strip to create the public right-of-way.

The people surveying small holding claims in the plaza apparently didn't grasp the significance of the *vereda* and the *pisos*. Sabino, like most plaza residents, had always accepted them as a matter of course. Perhaps a perplexed survey crew overlooked these rights-of-way because they were maintained by custom and, in the absence of fences, had no clearly defined boundaries. Consequently, the surveyors divided the *vereda* up among multiple owners, who thereafter placed fences to mark their land, forever removing the ancient path from public use. Although the *pisos* are still maintained as a roadway around the plaza, there have been disputes about their full width, and some people have moved fences to constrict the access way.

Similarly, the plaza *oratorio* lacks any indication of ownership on the small holding claims survey, probably because no one in the plaza professed to own it. (The Archdiocese of Santa Fe patented the *oratorio* in the 1950s when David Ortega pointed out that no one officially held title to it.) The *oratorio* was seen as a community resource, maintained by everyone who used it. Its omission, and those of the *pisos* and *vereda*, reflects the U.S. government's inability to recognize communal property rights, a problem that afflicted adjudication of land grant claims throughout New Mexico. Over time, the sense of community diminished as people began to claim the public access ways as their own private land.

Both maps agree on one thing: the large, extended Ortega family dominated land ownership in and around the plaza and shaped its destiny since it was first constructed. However, there are some twists in the lineage of the Ortega family since those early years and, as a result, two distinct Ortega families lived in the plaza area by the early twentieth century, each headed by a José Ramón Ortega. José Ramón Ortega y Vigil was the patriarch of the Ortega clan that lived in the plaza at the turn of the century, and his family group clearly controlled the local political scene. José Ramón Ortega y Abeyta, who made his home just west of the plaza, had considerably less status in plaza affairs. Although he was probably a distant cousin of José Ramón Ortega y Vigil, Ortega y Abeyta was not regarded as kin to the dominant clan. In fact, the stern moralist of the family, Bonefacia Ortega, made it a point to disavow any relationship whatsoever between the families. The reason for her adamant stand may have something to do with a mysterious gap in the genealogy of the Ortega y Abeyta family: José Ramón Ortega y Abeyta apparently was born after his alleged father, Pedro Asencio, had died, for Pedro did not mention a José Ramón in his will. Furthermore, no baptismal record for José Ramón has been found, although he claimed that his father was Pedro Asencio and his mother was María Francisca Ortega. An illegitimate child would create just the kind of scandal to incite Bonefacia's stand and ostracize José Ramón from the family.

Confusions in genealogy also tangle the history of the dominant Ortega clan. Bonefacia Ortega recounted the story that her father, José Ramón Ortega y Vigil, was a great-great-grandson to Grabiel Ortega, the first Ortega in Chimayó, who arrived in the mid-1700s and immediately set about acquiring large tracts of land from Luís López and other families who lived in the area. According to Bonefacia, Grabiel came from Galicia, Spain. However, baptismal records show no direct connection between Grabiel and José Ramón Ortega y Vigil. Nonetheless, Bonefacia was firm in her insistence that her family descended from Grabiel, and the connection between Grabiel and José Ramón Ortega y Vigil is held like gospel by the Ortegas of Chimayó today.

In any case, José Ramón Ortega y Vigil was the progenitor of most of the Ortegas living in Chimayó today. My grandmother and all his other surviving grandchildren refer to José Ramón as *"mi tatita,"* an endearing diminutive of *"tatarabuelo,"* or great-grandfather. (Similarly, people refer to God as *"mi tatita Dios"*—which is an indication of just how venerable José Ramón was.) In accordance with the respect he earned in Chimayó—and perhaps because his daughter Libradita married into the Chávez family, who owned the Santuario—José Ramón was buried beneath the floor of the Santuario in Potrero.

Grandma has one vivid recollection of José Ramón, who was born in 1828 when New Mexico was a department of Mexico and died in 1904 in the U.S. Territory of New Mexico when his granddaughter, my grandma, was six years old. Her fleeting image of José Ramón remains potent for me, for it is a striking visual link with the distant past: "All that I remember of him is that when I was about two or three years old, and I was there behind Tía Bone's *casita*. And *mi tatita* was lighting his pipe—he smoked a pipe, you know—with a flint and an iron *chispa*. He held the flint up to his face and cupped it like this, and then he went on. That's all I remember of my *tatita*." No photographic image of José Ramón remains.

Teresita Jaramillo also retains some memories of José Ramón, her grandfather, whom she describes as *"delgadito, y poco dobladito, como Tío Reyes* (thin, and slightly bent over, like Tío Reyes [Ortega])." Teresita was raised at José Ramón's house on the plaza and remembers a Pueblo Indian friend who came to visit him often. She was struck by this friendship because the stories of Indian attacks had taught her to fear Indians in general. She was also impressed because not many people in the community entertained Pueblo people as friends. She watched with curiosity as her grandfather chatted amicably with the dark, smiling Pueblo. "That Indian liked to pat *mi tatita* José Ramón on the back and say, 'Ah, *que amigo Ramón!*' And when that Indian died, *mi tatita* cried out loud."

MERCEDES
TRUJILLO,
FRANCISQUITA
ORTEGA
TRUJILLO,
HELEN
JARAMILLO,
SEVERO
JARAMILLO,
AND TERESITA
JARAMILLO,
CA. 1925.

José Ramón married Petra Mestas of Santa Cruz around 1852. Petra, who had inherited her father's (El Güero's) fair skin and freckles, married José Ramón when she was only thirteen, which, Grandma hastens to remind me, was not an uncommon age at which to marry in those days. Their parents had probably arranged the marriage, as was the custom. Petra was ten years younger than José Ramón, and legend has it that she was still playing with dolls when José Ramón brought her from Santa Cruz to the plaza as his new bride. At the age of fifteen, Petra gave birth to her first child; her fourteenth and last child was born some twenty-seven years later. Because of Petra's union with José Ramón, El Güero's fair hair, blue eyes, and freckles still circulate in the Upper Chimayó gene pool—as do tales of his rowdy Irish humor.

Virginia Ortega recalled, "In those days, they used to sleep outside in the summer, because it was so hot. They laid cowhide on mattresses on the ground.

One night, El Güero stole over to his sleeping parents and pulled the mattresses far away. They woke up very far from where they went to sleep. *Era muy travieso* —He was very mischievous! Another time, El Güero dressed up like an Apache Indian and snuck up on some women in the fields and scared them."

Of her great-grandfather Teresita recalls, "El Güero used to go to Mexico a lot, to trade, because around here they didn't have anything, you know. And one time when he was coming home, he stopped to rest at a house on the way and the woman there fell in love with El Güero. And then, when he was about to go, she said to him, 'Hey, why don't you leave me a piece of your hair to remember you by?' But he didn't trust her, because he was smart. He thought she was going to do something to him. He probably thought she was a witch. And so he got a hair from a cowhide with red hair. He cut the hair and gave it to her in a piece of folded paper and then he headed for home. On the way home, before they knew it there came a terrible earthquake. I don't remember if it lifted up El Güero or what, but his companion said, 'Look! No, I am not going back for him!' and he left El Güero there. I don't know if it's true, but this is one of the stories that they used to tell of *padre* Güero."

A year after El Güero died, a list was tallied of the land that he and his wife, María Petra Bustos, left each of their numerous heirs. On the north edge of a *bosque* of plums in the Cuarteles area, they left each heir "twelve yards" of land. (This probably meant twelve yards along a ditch and then back to an unspecified but commonly known boundary.) In the plum orchard, each received ten yards while "by the little lake," they left twelve yards to each. The list continues, assigning twenty-five yards to each near some little ponds, access to a house and some corrals, and rights to a woodpile in the shed. In the *barrio* of Sombrillo, each heir received twenty-four *varas*, and various pieces in the *cienegita* (marshy land) went to specific heirs, including his daughter Petra.[1]

Petra and José Ramón originally inhabited the south side of the plaza, but they lived on the north side by the late 1800s. Petra brought to the marriage the land she inherited from El Güero and added it to José Ramón's considerable estate. Petra was an accomplished seamstress, and she supplied clothing to numerous children, grandchildren, nieces, nephews, and neighbors. José Ramón's parents were Guadalupe Vigil and Gervacio Ortega (spelled "Jerbacio" on Sabino's map). José Ramón's grandchildren still remember their great-grand-mother's name, referring to her as *"mi madre Vigila,"* and they recall that she came from Cundiyó. Bonefacia Ortega claimed Gervacio was a weaver and that he was the grandson of Grabiel Ortega. He was also a justice of the peace, and was probably the first person in Chimayó to serve in that role when New Mexico became a territory of the U.S. in 1846.

Guadalupe and Gervacio's house on the northwest corner of the plaza bears the intriguing label "First House on the Plaza" on Sabino's map. This is the earliest generation to which Sabino assigned ownership of a plaza building, and although I have not found any evidence to corroborate his statement, there are enough indications that it may be true. There is an old story in the Ortega family that Gervacio Ortega had deeded land to a number of settlers from Santa Cruz so that they could build a plaza.[2] Gervacio, however, was born in 1800, about twenty years after the plaza was constructed. Documents do show that Gervacio's grandfather, Grabiel, owned much of the land in the area, and it could have been Grabiel who made the transfer to make construction of the plaza possible. This house may have belonged to Grabiel himself and it may even predate the construction of the formal plaza arrangement.[3]

José Ramón grew up at the northwest corner house, but all of his and Petra's children were born in the house on the opposite, southeast corner. The family subsequently moved to the northwest corner of the plaza; Rumaldo Ortega inherited their southeast house. Bonefacia, having never married, remained in her father's house on the north side after he died in 1904. José Ramón's children carried on a tradition of leadership along with the weaving tradition that had long been in the family.

José Ramón acted as the plaza *patrón* in the late 1800s, passing the torch to his son, Victor, who was without doubt the most influential figure in the plaza in the early twentieth century. Victor's political activities left an imprint on Chimayó and, through his participation in the first constitutional convention, on all of New Mexico. From 1906 to 1934, Don Victor was the postmaster, having taken over that position from Jacinto Ortiz, who had held the office since 1894.

Victor opened a general store on the plaza in 1907, and for many years he acted as the director of the local school (and owner of the property it stood on), probate judge, and an influential politician who often met with county officials. "Victor was a rich man," Amada Trujillo says. "He had big horses and a buggy." His son Benjamín remembered Victor as a large, forceful man with a knack for business and hard work, and he too described his father's legendary horses: "My father always had two teams of horses, and they were all big horses, because he used to go with a fellow by the name of Atencio from Española to buy horses in the southern part of Colorado. They'd bring back whatever kind of animal they needed. He always had good wagon horses." Such livestock was rare in Chimayó, where even owning a saddle horse was relatively uncommon.

In the late 1920s, Victor roused plaza residents to oppose a dam on the Santa Cruz River—a project that became a financial disaster and proved to be the ruin of many landowners in the Santa Cruz Valley.[4] I believe Victor (or perhaps his father) may have influenced the redrawing of county boundaries so that the plaza, which was in Río Arriba County throughout the 1800s, fell within Santa Fe County, where it could be better connected with Victor's cronies in the state and county government.[5] After seeing his picture and hearing about his style, I can easily imagine the way Victor's booming voice dominated the political rallies in Chimayó and for decades garnered a majority of Republican votes in the precinct. The people who remember him paint a picture of a man who bullied, browbeat, and cajoled voters to assure victory for his party. He, like his Democratic rivals, sometimes paid one dollar to every person who agreed to come out

and vote for his party. The jobs he controlled—from postmaster to schoolteacher to firewood supplier for the school—were greatly coveted, especially in the depression era, and they guaranteed him the respect and tribute of many Chimayosos —and the jealously of others. Victor's son Benjamín marveled that his father accomplished all these feats with almost no formal schooling: "When they used to call Victor for political conventions in the state or the county, he'd speak for an hour, keep his audience, tell them jokes. He was very well known all over the state. And I don't know how the heck he did it. He only had a fourth-grade education—and that was no education at all!"

Voting blocks almost always followed family lines, so Victor's political strategy often entailed persuasion of extended families. Teresita and my mother talked about Victor's powers of persuasion: "It was pure politics back then, and my Tío Victor had Severo [Teresita's husband and Victor's nephew] by the ear, and he used him to help him get votes. One time, he told Severo, 'I think that you have some sway with the Vigils, because they weave for you.' Severo said 'Yes, they weave for me, but—.' 'Well,' Victor went on, 'I think they'll go with whatever you do, so go get them early in the morning on voting day. The out-come of the election depends on their votes—whoever the Vigils vote for, he'll win.' See, they had all the votes counted, who was on each side, and Victor knew he needed those votes.

TERESITA
JARAMILLO

Bueno, so Severo went the evening before election day and told the Vigils to be ready early in the morning, and he went the next day before seven. He got up very early and said, "OK, I'm going for the Vigils." Now, the Naranjos also got up early, but Severo had gotten up earlier and he arrived at the Vigil's house and he loaded them all in the car, like sheep—it was a joke, I tell you. Then when they were coming down the road, Juan Naranjo was coming up the other way, on his way to get them to vote for the Democrats. So Juan tooted his horn at Severo to stop, but Severo didn't pay any attention and he came and handed the Vigils over to Tío Victor. By the time Juan came back, they had already voted for the Republicans. Eeeh, what a fiasco!

STELLA
CHÁVEZ
USNER AND
TERESITA
JARAMILLO

Well, that was the game of politics. I remember that politics was the pastime of the men. Before every election, the politicos used to sit there counting the votes. They'd say, "Fulano will vote for the Republicans, and this one will vote for the Democrats," and they'd make four little lines and then the fifth line across—so they'd figure pretty much who they had to get. And they'd pay the ones who didn't care which way the vote went, as long as they got paid. The ones who lost the votes they had counted on were the ones who lost the election.

CAMILO
TRUJILLO

But that time with the Vigils, Severo had to pay them for voting for him with goods from the grocery store that we owned. Victor said, "Why don't you just give those Vigils things from your store—just give them whatever they need." So they came and took a bunch of things. "And what did you get out of this," I asked Severo later. He was nothing but a gofer for Victor—but there were a lot of people like that. That's the way Victor operated sometimes, and it made some people mad. Others agree: Don Victor *was a big man, a smart man who knew what was happening. People looked up to him. Or they used to think he was a smart man. They considered him a guy that knew more about the things that went around, you know. Let's say you wanted advice for some kind of property sale or something like that, you'd go talk to Don Victor. But, in comparison to today, he wasn't that smart. A lot of people then were illiterate and hardly anyone knew how to speak English. But, like my father used to say, "Entre los ciegos, el tuerto es rey!—Among the blind, the one-eyed man is king!"*

Reflects Amada Trujillo, a staunch Republican in spite of the fact that her father, Reyes Naranjo, was a leading plaza Democrat: "In those days people took a lot of stock in politics because their jobs depended on politics. I think that was one thing. They fought and they argued, but there were both Republicans and Democrats. Now it's mostly Democrats, and it's going to become like Castro's country. I am a Republican until death do us part. I'm going to be a Republican even if I am the only one left. There has to be two parties."

Victor Ortega and his wife, Refugio Jaramillo, owned the massive, long, center building on the south side of the plaza. Refugio was part Indian, according to her son Benjamín. She was a sister to Simona Jaramillo, who married José Ramón Ortega y Abeyta—the "other" José Ramón, who lived just outside the plaza. This created a marriage link between the two José Ramón Ortega families. Refugio and Simona's sister Julianita Jaramillo married plaza resident Eulogio Martínez, forging an important familial link between the Ortegas and the large Martínez family. Indeed, the matrimony of the three Jaramillo sisters (Simona, Refugio, and Julianita) into the plaza community created one of its most tangled knots of relationships, and it was made more intricate when Simona's daughter, Encarnación, married plaza resident Reyes Naranjo and her other daughter, Francisquita, married José Inez Martínez (her first cousin, because he was Julianita's son!).

Victor Ortega's brother Reyes had a more reserved demeanor than Victor, but he commanded a great deal of respect and had a strong influence on the local political scene. "He was a big man, and he used to cross his legs and sit very comfortable for two or three hours just like that," the late Benjamín Ortega recalled. "He was also a quiet man, and very thoughtful. In fact, none of the

REYES ORTEGA
AND GENOVEVA
ARCHULETA
ORTEGA,
CA. 1910.

FELICITAS
ORTEGA AND
TOMASITA
MARTÍNEZ,
CA. 1910.

Ortega brothers talked a lot, except my father Victor—and he only talked at rallies. All those Ortegas were very bright." Reyes and his wife Genoveva Archuleta, of Sombrillo, made their home just behind José Ramón's northside dwelling. Social workers visiting Chimayó during the depression recognized Reyes Ortega's stature and named him as the patriarch of the Ortega family.

Like his father José Ramón and his grandfather Gervacio, Reyes Ortega served as a justice of the peace and was a weaver. Unlike any of his brothers, he could read and translate English, a rare talent in the early days of the century. He held a certificate from the Territory of New Mexico to teach "orthography, reading, writing, arithmetic, geography, English grammar, physiology and hygene [sic], and the history of the United States," and his children remember that he often held classes with adults in the *sala* (parlor) of his home. He maintained a passion for world affairs and was the local source for news from beyond the community, reading the *Albuquerque Tribune* every day to stay abreast of events. Reyes and Victor had a falling out that endured many years, caused primarily by a disagreement over a political issue, even though both brothers were strong Republicans. According to Grandma, the relationship didn't heal until a family member died, forcing the brothers to come together and grieve and face the folly of their antagonism. The split between these two proud men was also partly a consequence of Reyes's conversion to the Presbyterian faith, which was motivated out of a desire to send his children to the local Presbyterian school. The Catholic priests threatened Reyes and others with excommunication if they allowed their children to attend the mission school, which Reyes felt left him no choice but to give up the Catholic church—an act that Victor would never do.

All the Ortega men learned to weave from their father, José Ramón, and they made weaving a profitable business enterprise. Reyes and his brother Nicasio, who had a hard-driving businessman's grit, started the first commercial weaving enterprises in Chimayó, just outside the plaza. Their entry into the market in the early 1900s was inspired by the efforts of Sito Candelario, a Santa Fe curio shop owner who actively sought connections with weavers throughout the northern part of the state. Several other weaving businesses followed, including a highly productive, family-run shop started by Santos Ortiz just west of the plaza. Santos was also a bright and energetic businessman, but Nicasio's aggressive style and shrewd business sense—and the fact that he had several sons of a similar nature—assured his enterprise an enduring place in Chimayó. Of these early weaving ventures, his is the only one that survived. It still draws the most business of any of the local shops today. Reyes was a skilled and successful businessman, but he had no male heirs and his operation closed upon his death.

Like his brother Reyes, Rumaldo Ortega expressed his leadership in quiet ways. He apparently inherited little of his father's business acumen. His niece, Domitila Villa, remembers him as a deeply introspective Catholic and an *hermano mayor* in the local Penitente chapter. He lived on the southeast corner of the plaza, where he and his siblings had been born, until he sold his place to the

Presbyterians and moved up the road toward Centinela. Like Reyes and Nicasio, Rumaldo was an accomplished weaver, but, like all the Ortegas, Rumaldo was not without political ambitions. Documents name him as a secretary for the Territorial Legislature, reporting on meetings among representatives in Santa Fe. His role there remains unclear, but he was closely involved with state politics.

Politics and weaving were traditionally male occupations, but José Ramón's daughters were no less significant in plaza affairs than his sons. In 1921, Bonefacia organized the local Order of the Carmelite sisters, *Las Carmelitas*, a lay women's society whose special devotion is Our Lady of Mt. Carmel. This stalwart old woman was certainly one of the most remarkable people to live on the plaza in this century, and everyone who knew her remembers her well and with much respect. "Oh, Tía Bone was very sharp," Grandma remembers. "She used big words. She went to school with Ms. Clark, the first mission teacher. She tried to learn English there, going at night to study. She was a very philosophical lady, she was smart. This is what I cannot figure how all these Ortegas, all of them were so smart and so literate—they could read and write good."

Bonefacia led the community each year in their annual observance of the *Mes de María*, one of the most vivid images of plaza unity that people recall. Each year on the last day of May, Bonefacia presided as the Carmelitas, dressed in black and veiled as if in mourning, walked slowly around the plaza praying the rosary. A group of flower girls followed the solemn procession, scattering petals of the *rosas de Castilla* on the praying Carmelitas when they stopped. Even the Presbyterians came to watch this enchanting procession, though they were forbidden from participating.

Bonefacia was also famed as a hardworking and efficient *enjaradora*, or plasterer—a task reserved for women of the community—in spite of her deformed and crippled left hand. (Grandma recalls that her deformity, like all such congenital handicaps, was attributed to the negative influence of the moon during her mother's pregnancy. As another woman explained to me: "You know a lot of children are born with a hairlip? Well they had the belief that this had something to do with the moon. So, when the lady was pregnant, the mother would tie a string around her waist when the moon was bright and nice outside at night, and they'd take her outside and have the pregnant woman turn around three

TILA VILLA

120

times. And that was supposed to protect the child from the harelip and other deformities. And there aren't many people with harelip around here! Not a one!") Bonefacia's fee for plastering was one *peso* (one dollar) per day, plus meals—and she worked from dawn until dusk. "She was a very hard worker, my Tía Bone. She was never idle. She grew a big chile patch, and she only ate good foods—beans, chiles, potatoes. She raised pigs for meat. That was all, and she was so strong!"

BENIGNA
O. CHÁVEZ

And she could deliver babies, too. I was born there in the plaza in the room there in the corner, by the kitchen in Tía Bone's house, by a stove that they had there. It was Sunday at 5 P.M., and my mother had come there [to the plaza] to visit Tía Bone. She knew she was expecting a child, but she came just to visit from Río Chiquito to visit our relatives. We used to come to the plaza on Sundays to visit. And then, I was born there, and my Tía Bone delivered me, right there by the wood stove.

TERESITA
JARAMILLO

Bonefacia told the *dichos*, *refranes*, and *cuentos* (sayings and stories) that her ancestors carried over from the Old World, and she kept the family history in her memory, reciting stories for a multitude of nieces and nephews. Bonefacia also indulged in a passion for roses, cultivating the sweet *rosas de Castilla* that plaza elders remember so dearly. She was the first person in the area to grow roses, and the flower girls in the *Mes de María* procession tossed petals from her bushes as the Carmelitas passed.

Bonefacia refused her one offer of marriage, which came from a man who had murdered his wife. "Oh, one time a man asked Bonefacia to marry him, when she was already a full-grown woman, not so young. I remember when he asked her. It made Tía Bone very mad—she didn't want to marry, ever. And this man had killed his wife. She said to him—she was very brave—'How come you killed the wife you had?' And she refused to marry him. And my father and Tío Nicasio, they said, 'That Bone, she is fearless!'"

BENIGNA
O. CHÁVEZ

Bonefacia's sister Francisca married Isidoro Trujillo of Río Chiquito (Francisca's first cousin because his mother, María Antonia Ortega, was José Ramón's sister), a prominent weaving family that still operates a weaving business in

THE ORTEGAS
FROM LEFT:
SENAIDA,
NICASIO,
FRANCISQUITA,
REYES,
ESCOLÁSTICA,
VICTOR,
RUMALDO, AND
BONEFACIA,
1932.

Centinela. Escolástica was closely involved with the management of the Martínez store in Truchas. People remember Escolástica as a shrewd businesswoman and credit her in large part for the success of that well-known Truchas institution.

DAVID ORTEGA

"All the Ortegas were good business people. One of the best business ladies in the state of New Mexico was Tía Escolástica—she was the one who ran the operation in Las Truchas."

As well as leaving a legacy of grandchildren, the numerous José Ramón Ortega children also linked the Ortega clan with a wide network of families both within and outside of Chimayó. Senaida married Severiano Trujillo of Rincón, Leonides married Timoteo Martínez of Lower Chimayó, and Escolástica married Santiago Martínez of Truchas. Librada was wed to Rafael Chávez of Potrero (a grandson of Bernardo Abeyta), and Epimenia married Pedro Jaramillo. The far-flung Ortega cousins made regular trips to the plaza for visits, and these familial connections formed important links between communities. The Ortegas were

Wedding party for Benigna Ortega and Abedón Chávez, in Chimayó, 1921.

known—and often envied—in Chimayó as *riquitos* (the moderately wealthy class), and they prided themselves on their assets, earned by the sweat of their brows as well as by their wit and vision. "Yes, Victor Ortega had a little more than the others," Bersabé Naranjo Chávez explained to me. "He liked to work hard—I think that's why he built up more wealth." Victor Ortega carried his fame as a wealthy man even unto death: legend has it that he was buried in a casket that cost $5,000 and was guaranteed to last fifty years.

Signs of prosperity were also evinced by the Ortega women. Unlike other women in the area, Ortega women weren't expected to work in the fields. These proper ladies would not deign to do that kind of work. But their homemaking tasks demanded much and they didn't get off easy. After raising fourteen children, José Ramón's wife, Petrita, simply gave up one day. "They say that she was sitting at her sewing machine one day, when she stopped, put the cloth aside and said, '*De aquí no más*—from now on, no more.' And she went to bed and died soon after."

Descendants of José Ramón Ortega owned the lion's share of land in and around the plaza, in addition to several parcels in Sombrillo, La Puebla, Cuar-

STELLA
CHÁVEZ
USNER

teles, and Truchas. The Land Survey map shows that the tiny 1.64 acres inside
the plaza were divided among ten owners, and 0.81 acres, or about fifty percent,
belonged to descendants of José Ramón Ortega y Vigil. Extending back in time
to include descendants of Gervacio Ortega, the dominance of the family is even
clearer. Land outside the plaza repeats this trend, strongly supporting the idea
that the Ortega family once owned much, if not all, the land in the plaza area.

In spite of the historical precedent for the Ortega family's domination, its
hegemony in the Plaza del Cerro was not absolute. Don Reyes Naranjo, an outspoken politico of the Democratic party, also rose to prominence in the early
1900s. He lived with his wife, Encarnación (known as Chonita or Doña Chon),
just north of the unpaved road called the *Camino Real* on the east side of the
plaza and, like the Ortegas, owned extensive tracts of land in Chimayó and on
the Llano Abeyta near Truchas. The Naranjos were not originally from Chimayó.
Don Reyes's father, Jesús María Naranjo, had lived in Santo Niño, near Santa
Cruz, with his mother Pabla Ortega. (In fact, Reyes was part of the same clan
that spawned Emilio Naranjo, the reigning boss of the Democratic party today
in Río Arriba County.) When Jesús died, Pabla married Desiderio Ortega—a
brother to José Ramón Ortega y Abeyta—and moved to the west side of the
plaza. Desiderio adopted Reyes and raised him there. Reyes's sister Benigna
also came to the plaza and lived on the north side after she was married.

When Reyes Naranjo married Encarnación Ortega, a daughter of José
Ramón Ortega y Abeyta, he sealed his membership in the web of old family ties
in Chimayó. Reyes and Encarnación took up residence on the east side of the
plaza, and it was probably through his connection with the Ortega family that
Reyes came to own large tracts of land in Chimayó and at the Llano Abeyta.
The union of Juan Melquiades Ortega and Apolonita Martínez, Reyes's niece, re-
inforced the Naranjo-Ortega kin network by creating a tie between the Naranjos
and the Ortega y Vigils.

Don Reyes Naranjo joined forces with Victor Ortega as a fellow outspoken
Republican until Reyes defected to the Democratic party in the 1930s. ("My
father was a Republican for a long time. He was one of Victor Ortega's *hijitos*.
He almost worshiped him, and then he turned around and became a Democrat.

AMADA
TRUJILLO

124

But I never became a Democrat! And I never will!") The change forged bitter rivals of the two politicos. In the struggle for votes in each election, Reyes rallied the Democrats with the same forceful zeal and use of monetary rewards that Victor Ortega employed in opposition. As the chief politico of the Democratic party, Reyes sought to secure jobs and influence. The *viejitos* describe how Don Reyes spoke with great zeal at political rallies to counter the nearly indomitable politicking of Victor Ortega. Reyes and his wife raised five children at the plaza: Gaspar, Eduardo, Bersabé, Amada, and Vences. He and his family chose to take up the Presbyterian faith when the missionaries arrived in Chimayó in 1900—a decision that did little to improve Reyes's standing with the devoutly Catholic Victor.

The large Eulogio Martínez family also figured prominently in plaza affairs. Eulogio and his wife, Julianita, maintained their residence on the southeast side of the plaza. Eulogio reigned as the elder Martínez on the Plaza del Cerro through the first decades of the twentieth century, and he peers out as a grand old character in the stories people tell. Eulogio tended extensive landholdings in the area, but he came from "down below" in Lower Chimayó, a son of Teodoro Martín and María Natividad Fernandes. People say that he served in the Civil War, fighting alongside fellow Chimayosos Concepción Trujillo and Jesús Baca. Aaron Martínez, who has unraveled genealogies of several plaza families, heard that Eulogio was able to acquire his land because of the pension he received after his duty in the war.

Melita Ortega describes Eulogio as a kind and occasionally stern old man with striking blue eyes, wavy gray hair, and a finely tuned mustache: "Don Eulogio had something on one of his legs—he must have had gangrene or something [perhaps a wound from the war]. Ms. Ellsworth [a teacher at the John Hyson school] used to come help Doña Pablita put rags around his leg. He always had it bound, and for a long time he lasted that way. He'd sit out there in the patio on a chair almost all the day. And I'd go by there, and one morning I was going past and he was sitting there and I said *"Buenos días."* And he snapped back *"Buenos días dice el diablo por no mentar a Dios!*—Good day is what the devil says so as not to mention God!' And I didn't know what to say. But I learned that the old people never said just *"Buenos días,"* because they

MELITA
ORTEGA

125

WEDDING
PARTY FOR
ENCARNACIÓN
TRUJILLO AND
EULOGIA
ROYBAL, IN
SANTA CRUZ,
1905.

also want to be sure to mention God. And I never forgot Don Eulogio's scolding. When I later saw Tío Rumaldo and greeted him like Don Eulogio taught me, Rumaldo was surprised. He said, '*Mira, como tú se dices "le de Dios." Ya los de hora no dicen así.* (Look at that! You say "May God grant you a good day." People today don't talk that way anymore.)' So, I had learned my lesson from Don Eulogio."

The ceremonious, old-world Spanish that Eulogio used is typical of the speech of some *viejitos* today—especially those of Melita's age and older. The younger generations have forgotten such anachronisms, which were transported from Spain to this high-desert valley and isolated from changes for centuries. In some families, however, some of these speech patterns persist.

Eulogio was only distantly related to the longtime plaza families, but he secured a triple knot to other plaza residents when he married Julianita Jaramillo,

WEDDING

whose two sisters also married into the community. He and Julianita raised five children on the plaza: Luis, Juanita, José Inez, Nicolás, and Pablita. José Inez lived next door to them on the plaza, and Nicolás divided his father's house lengthwise to live with his wife Luisita in the section facing the plaza; the aging Eulogio lived in the outer half. Plaza residents remember Don Nicolás for his annual production of *miel de caña*, a sweet, molasseslike syrup squeezed from sorghum and prized as a rare sweet. José Inez married Francisquita Ortega, a daughter of José Ramón Ortega y Abeyta—the José Ramón Ortega who lived just outside the west side of the plaza. Nicolás chose a different path than most plaza residents when he married outside the community, to Doña Luisa Mondragón of Santa Cruz. José Inez and Francisquita lived beside the road that passed through the plaza. Sabino labeled this humble thoroughfare the *Camino Real*—the Royal Road. This dusty old track is well off the main roads today, but the name seems apt for the time when it was the plaza's only link with the representatives of the Spanish Crown in Santa Cruz and Santa Fe.

Another José Inez Martínez owned the house on the opposite side of the plaza from José Inez and Francisquita. This José Inez, known more completely as José Inez Martínez y Trujillo, was unrelated to José Inez Martínez y Jaramillo. Martínez y Trujillo married Martina Deagüero from Plaza Abajo, but he, too, was bound up in the tangle of plaza relations: he was a second cousin to the José Ramón Ortega y Vigils through his grandmother María Antonia Ortega, José Ramón Ortega y Vigil's sister. Through his grandfather Concepción Trujillo he was a cousin to the venerable Trujillo family of Río Chiquito and Centinela. José Ramón Ortega y Vigil's children referred to him as Primo José Inez. To further entangle matters, José Inez Martínez y Trujillo was also related to the Ortegas on his father's side; according to Aaron Martínez, his grandfather, Cristóbal Martínez, had married a daughter of Pedro Asencio Ortega.

It seems likely that the ownership of José Inez's plaza home, which was adjacent to Pedro Asencio's house and the *casita* that became the *oratorio*, passed to José Inez from the Pedro Asencio lineage. José Inez also owned land in Llano Abeyta that may have been an inheritance from his Ortega line. The land he owned in Río Chiquito probably came from his Trujillo side. In any case, José Inez was well-endowed with land in spite of the fact that he owned little in the plaza area.

José Inez and Martina had six children: Estevan, Sotera, Bernarda, Ersilia, Corina, and Biterbo. Only Estevan and Biterbo remained on the plaza. Estevan inherited José Inez and Martina's house and lived there with his wife, Cordelia Trujillo of Rincón (also related to the Ortegas through her grandfather, Concepción). Biterbo married Petronila Martínez and lived in her inherited house on the south side of the plaza.

Like the José Inez Martínez family, the Trujillo clan was enmeshed in the plaza family tree in several ways. The Trujillos of the plaza were related to José Inez Martínez, as described above. The link between the Ortegas and the Trujillos began when Concepción Trujillo took up residence in Río Chiquito and married his first cousin, María Antonia Ortega, José Ramón Ortega y Vigil's sister.

Although María Antonia and Concepción lived in Río Chiquito, their son Vidal grew up on the Plaza del Cerro with his grandparents, Guadalupe and

Gervacio. Vidal inherited the plaza house and had four children with Urbanita
Martínez: Pedro, Sabino (who drew the map), Julianita, and Eusebia. All of
these moved to land very near the plaza and remained in the area. Urbanita's
brother Antonio married Seferina Vigil, and they lived on the south side of the
plaza. Their daughter Petronila married Biterbo Martínez, José Inez y Trujillo's
son, and lived on the plaza until 1993—the last resident of the plaza who was
born and raised there. The Trujillos were linked again by marriage to the Ortega
family when José Ramón's daughter Francisquita (not related to the Francisquita Ortega who married José Inez Martínez y Jaramillo) married Isidoro
Trujillo, her first cousin, and moved to Centinela. Yet another bond between
these two families formed when Pedro Trujillo, Vidal's son, married Celsa
Ortega, Rumaldo Ortega's daughter.

All the family connections, though, didn't soothe some long-standing dis-
agreements over politics, such as that between Vidal and Victor Ortega. A story
related by Teresita Jaramillo evokes a comic side of the struggle for votes that
Vidal and Victor engaged:

Vidal and Victor were together until Vidal decided to go to the other party,
against Victor. One time, it was almost election day and Vidal went to Río
Chiquito to mi Padre *Concepción's house to tell him to get the voters from*
Santa Fe County together and tell them to vote for so-and-so—the ones who
were Democrats. Mi tío Vidal also told Concepción to be sure to tell them to go
to Vidal's house before they voted. So, Concepción went to talk to Tío Martín
and Tío Anastacio and the others in Río Chiquito, and he told them who to vote
for and to go to mi tío Vidal's beforehand.

So, Vidal told his wife Urbanita, "Get ready with some food, for everyone who's
coming to vote." So mi tía Urbanita hurried up and made the dinner. When they
came to Vidalito's house—they always called him Vidalito, the people from Río
Chiquito, because Vidal was very friendly with them—Vidal was careful to pass
the best plate to Anastacio, and he passed everything to Anastacio first. But
there was this fly flying around the table, and Vidal chased it away; but it came
right back, and mi tío Anastacio said, "Ah, que mosca tan traiconera!—

TERESITA
JARAMILLO

FOUR OF REYES
ORTEGA'S EIGHT
DAUGHTERS,
CA. 1919.
FROM LEFT:
MELITA,
BENIGNA,
PETRITA, AND
CANDELARIA.

What a tricky fly! You chase it away and it comes right back!" So, they had
their dinner and then they went to vote. Tío Vidal said, "Wait for me there, I'll
be right behind you."

So, they went to the voting place, and there at the door was Don Victor, on the
lookout, and he pulled them aside and said, "Come in, come in! Be sure and vote
for so-and-so and so-and-so"—the Republicans, you see. And they went in and
voted. Then along comes Vidal, and they were all standing around the patio
outside the voting place, and Vidal said, "OK, let's go in and vote." "We already
voted," Anastacio told him. "What? How could that be? Who did you vote for?"
"Well, we voted for the ones compadre Victor told us to vote for." "Ahh, what a
tricky fly!" Vidal said, and he lost all those votes that he had tried so hard to get!

See, Tío Victor was very strong willed, and after all, he was their compadre,
and they believed whatever he told them. Like they didn't know how to walk,

and he told them how. Ah, Santo Niño, can you believe that? No one could say no to mi tío Victor, see? He was muy águila—*very sharp.*

The Cruzes were another important Democratic family of the Plaza del Cerro, and they also could not escape the web of family relationships. Don Pedro Cruz and his wife Doña Maclovia lived on the north side of the plaza. Pedro's mother was Carmen Ortega, the sister of Pabla Ortega Naranjo, Reyes Naranjo's mother; this made Reyes Naranjo and Pedro Cruz first cousins. Pedro had a brother named Victoriano Cruz, who was the local public schoolteacher for a time.

Pedro Cruz's wife, Maclovia, came from near Rinconada in the Embudo area. Pedro and Maclovia had no land in the plaza area, although they did own some tracts in Los Ranchos. Pedro Cruz is remembered as an old man with intense blue eyes. Pedro and Maclovia had seven children: Doroteo, Erlinda, Carolina, Rudy, Priscilla, Delia, and Adonelia. Many of the Cruz clan inherited Pedro's blue eyes—a legacy, some say, of French blood somewhere in the lineage.

The plaza also housed a few people who were outside the kin network that tied most residents. Anastacia T. Martínez and her husband, Manuel ("Vilí") Martínez, lived on the north side of the plaza. Anastacia's familial relationships

YOUNG WOMEN
HOLDING HANDS
IN FRONT OF
THE SANTUARIO,
CA. 1910.

GRILS ON THE
PLAZA, CA.
EARLY 1900S.

remain unclear, but Manuel apparently came from "down below" in Chimayó, one of the large Martínez clan that dominates the Plaza Abajo. He was not related to Eulogio or the other Martínezes on the east side of the plaza. In a tragedy that is still all too common, Manuel Vilí was murdered at a dance in Lower Chimayó, where, the story goes, he was buying piñón nuts for his children.

Encarnación Rodríguez was another resident whose family relations remain enigmatic. She lived in the house to the north of the room that Sabino labeled as the first schoolroom on the plaza. She is remembered simply as " 'Mana Encarnación," an old woman who lived alone. I have a photograph of her sitting on the mud floor sifting wheat in her small room—an intriguing glimpse of a woman who is otherwise barely known, at least to the Chimayosos I have talked with.

Some family relationships remain deliberately vague. For example, it is widely known that certain individuals in the plaza were the undisputed offspring of a minister who served in Chimayó for a short while. The children of Ramona Martínez, the local midwife more commonly known as 'Mana Mona, had a similar fate. This remarkable woman attended countless births and bore three children herself, although the fathers of all three remain unknown, for she never married. She was nevertheless part of the plaza family: she was a granddaughter of Concepción Trujillo and María Antonia Ortega, and she also was an aunt to José Inez Martínez y Trujillo. Furthermore, one of 'Mana Mona's sons, Rafael Martínez, lived with his wife, Perfecta Jaramillo, next to the plaza *oratorio*, and Ramona's brother, Francisco, lived three rooms south of Perfecta and Rafael. One person remembers this solitary bachelor's quarters as *"el cuarto del Pancho"* because of Francisco's nickname.

In addition to these plaza residents, a number of individuals and families who were also very important in its affairs lived close to the plaza. Their presence on Sabino Trujillo's map is testimony to their relevance and importance in plaza life. Foremost among these were José Ramón Ortega y Abeyta and his wife Simona, who lived just west of the plaza. José Ramón was a *juez de paz* (justice of the peace) and an *hermano mayor* in the local Penitente Brotherhood. He was also the primary caretaker of the *oratorio* on the plaza prior to his conversion to Protestantism in the early 1900s. The Abeyta in his last name came from his mother, Francisca Abeyta, the daughter of Bernardo Abeyta of Potrero, the founder of Chimayó's Santuario. Although he and José Ramón Ortega y Vigil took pains not to call each other *"primo,"* they were probably distant cousins.

José Ramón Ortega y Abeyta's daughter, Francisquita, lived on the plaza, having married into the Martínez family, and his wife's sister, Refugio, married Victor Ortega. José Ramón's son Félix was the only person who lived outside the plaza and owned land within. Félix lived on one side of Ortega y Abeyta and an Agapito Ortega lived on the other side. Although he had the same family name as José Ramón and lived next door, Agapito was only distantly related to José Ramón. His father, José Guadalupe Ortega, was an adopted grandson of José Grabiel Ortega. The striking poverty of Agapito's life was noted by some people: "Agapito didn't have anything. He owned no property, and he slept on the mud floor of his house. He cooked only in an open fireplace, long after everyone else had wood stoves," Grandma recalls. Also nearby the plaza was the home of Vidal and Urbanita Trujillo, who owned a second house inside the plaza. This L-shaped house is better remembered as the home of Juliana and Eusebia Trujillo, Vidal Trujillo's daughters, who lived there and raised Vidal's orphaned grandchildren, Domitila and Urbanita.

A final interesting note on plaza residents is the fact that, probably to a minor degree, transient people not at all related to Chimayó people sometimes settled on the plaza. Such was the case with Manuel Silva, a traveling *maromero*, or acrobat, and all-around performer. He was from Mexico and lived on the north side of the plaza for a few years in the 1920s. Other short-term residents included Charles and Mary Barrows. Barrows (known as "El Chucka"—a local way to pronounce "Chuck") was an artist who paid his bills by working as a government-hired hunter. He trapped *zorrillos* (skunks) and other animals around Chimayó for several years. There are probably other plaza residents who came and went in a similar fashion.

The plaza was dominated by stable family clans for the most part. Most, but not all, of these owned at least some land and raised food on it. However egalitarian the community may have been in previous centuries, wealth and land ownership reflected distinct class differences by the late nineteenth and early twentieth centuries. Some people were, for all practical purposes, landless. The

EUSEBIA
TRUJILLO
HOLDING
UP TILA
TRUJILLO
[VILLA],
CA. 1923.

poverty that accompanied a lack of land became more and more common as
land was increasingly divided with successive generations so that by the twentieth
century very few people had enough to support themselves. As one area resident
put it, "There were very few people who didn't have any land, but those were
the real poor ones. They used to haul wood on burros for people. And my father
used to buy wood from them. They also used to work in the houses for others,
on the farm, or whatever."

Most people insist that the wealthier people in the plaza helped poorer
people by giving them food outright or by offering employment. Although many
lacked money and material wealth, nobody in the Plaza del Cerro suffered for
food, even in the depths of the Great Depression. The deep-rooted familial bonds
of the plaza community assured this kind of mutual aid.

Chapter Seven:
Food from the
Garden and the Llano

High on the Llano

The corn is piled high in the dispensa
And it's almost time for making the miel—
Look at Don Nicolás setting up the mill
by the ditch,
And his peones cutting the cane—
It will taste so sweet!

But Papa says we have to go in the wagon, sister,
To El Llano to cut the wheat,
And already I feel the heat of that smoky fire
Up there where the wind always blows
And we've only each other to talk to.

But soon we'll be back,
To roast piñón and shuck the corn.
We'll be tying ristras and baking apples in the horno,
And I'll find the watermelon first, I tell you,
In that great pile of chiles,
When we come back from the llano,
Loaded down with sacks of wheat.

BENIGNA
O. CHÁVEZ

"These days it's *puro* shopping (nothing but shopping), but we used to grow everything and never needed to buy so many things, like now. My father would go to Bond and Nohl's in Española once in a while to buy sugar, potatoes, coffee —just a few things. People mostly grew what they needed. Now, everything is packaged, and you know the foods from the store don't taste as good as the ones you grow yourself."

Many older Chimayosos reminisce about the days when all they needed to buy was "coffee and sugar," describing a time when people were able to survive almost entirely off of their farms and gardens. By the turn of the century, the Plaza del Cerro had been tied into a complex economic relationship with the outside world for decades and was dependent on the industrial machine in the eastern U.S. for many goods, but small-scale agriculture remained the cornerstone of Chimayó's economy. All plaza residents farmed—*ricos* and *pobres*, weavers and businessman, men and women—and everyone over the age of fifty years remembers the verdure of the plaza they cultivated. These older Chimayosos love such well-tended, "clean" land—by which they mean land that is free of weeds, trees, and organic debris—and they lament the overrun condition of most of the plaza today. They talk in glowing terms when they describe the old plaza gardens. It seems that of all the plaza memories that people hold onto, the image of children playing around cultivated gardens is the most vivid, for it emerges again and again when Chimayosos talk about the old days.

MELITA
ORTEGA

I remember how clean it was. The gardens were all hoed and watered, and the children used to play in the yards in front of the houses all the time. People used to plant corn, melons—good melons, big and sweet—and chile and onions, and peas. We used to play in the yards all the time, and people used to plant their chile and corn in the middle, but there were no trees that I remember. And there was lots of activity because of the children playing and people working on their gardens. The women used to sweep the yards every day, or the older children— girls—because boys didn't do that kind of work.

Oh, the plaza was beautiful. It was clean and everybody was in their own home, and the kids playing outside. The homes were plastered every year inside and out, cleaned out every year. There was a laughter from the kids, a lot of little kids running around and just having fun, and the people just working. The older people, if they weren't hoeing, they were plastering the houses on the outside. Every year. They did it every year. And then the gardens inside the plaza—clean, hoed, irrigated, flowers all over. They grew squash, corn, chile, pazote (Mexican tea), yerba buena *(spearmint),* cilantro. *They also planted* cebollas *(onions),* ajo *(garlic),* alberjones *(chick peas), and* habas *(cow peas) around here. In those days people had to work hard, so they had to eat good. In the summertime,* everything *was from the garden. Oh, we had corn and peas and string beans, garbanzos, carrots, and squash,* melones *(melons),* sandías *(watermelons)— and I mean* melones! *Orange and sweet. Nectarines and a lot of fruits grew in the orchards outside: apples, apricots, peaches, pears.*

AMADA TRUJILLO AND TILA VILLA

When I was growing up, almost every house in the plaza was occupied by some- body. And there were a lot of kids at that time. Many kids, of different sizes and different ages. And then the plaza was all cultivated. It was a paradise at that time—no weeds! Every piece of land was growing something for food. Later on in years, trees were planted. Before this time there were no trees, except maybe one or two on the far east side of the plaza. Oh, that place was a garden of Eden. Now it is as dead as the people who took care of it.

AMADA TRUJILLO

By all accounts, the gardens in and around the plaza made a beautiful sight, but they provided more than a bucolic backdrop for daily life: these small fields and those surrounding the plaza yielded a veritable cornucopia of food. Besides a long list of vegetable crops, people cultivated herbs such as *yerba buena* and cilantro. Some, like Juan Melquiades, grew *punche* (a local tobacco). Documents from the seventeenth century suggest that Chimayó once was also known for its grapes, but as far as anyone remembers only Victor Ortega grew grapes in the plaza, at a small enclosure in front of the store. Victor's brother Nicasio made wine from the green grapes that he tended just outside of the plaza. Around the turn of the century, the number of cultivated plants increased dramatically, for the Presbyterian Mission teachers brought a host of vegetable crops with them.

The plaza community had survived for centuries on a mix of homegrown crops and plants gathered from the wild, and many of these plants were still highly valued both as food and for medicinal purposes in the early decades of this century. Of all the wild plants collected by the Chimayosos, only piñón nuts served as a substantial food source. People from around the plaza sometimes obtained piñón nuts through trade with people who lived closer to the large stands of piñón trees, over in Pecos or up in Truchas. But they also went themselves to pick piñón.

BENIGNA
O. CHÁVEZ

We would get up very early, while it was still dark, and we'd climb in the wagon. "Here we go to get piñón!" we'd say, and we'd ride up the Cañada Ancha arroyo and climb way up to La Ceja, up on the crest of those hills there above the Cañada Ancha.

AMADA
TRUJILLO
AND BENIGNA
O. CHÁVEZ

Long ago, there weren't too many vegetables, really. In fact, vegetables were hardly known. I think the first vegetables came in when my aunt Prudence Clark [the first missionary teacher] came here. That's when people around here first saw vegetables like carrots and beets and all those things. Before that they mostly used quelites, *you know, wild spinach, what do they call it, lamb's-quarters. And another thing, there was* verdolagas, *those sour docks, that's what they had for vegetables. Those* verdolagas *are so good, kind of salty, like you had put salt on them. Later, they did grow vegetables, but before, they spread the manure from the animals on the fields and they got a lot of* quelites *and those sour docks. And those are the only vegetables I can remember. Maybe there were other people who knew about them but I didn't.*

TILA VILLA

In my times, they didn't use remedies so much, but before, they used them a lot. When we got sick, our mothers took care of us. They knew more or less what to use. When you had a cold or a sore throat, the medication for that was hot chile caribe. Eat it alone, without any other food. And it did the job, I'm telling you.

And if you had fever, they would slice potatoes and put them on your forehead and feed you apricots, or other fruit. For headaches too, they would put papas on your head.

FARM FIELDS
AND PASTURES
IN POTRERO,
CA. 1940S.

Then they used to use azogue (mercury) for stomach illness. They used to believe that stomach problems were caused by empacha, like a blockage in the stomach. And a lot of people here would come to my aunt Julianita para sobar el empacho, to massage the blockage, and you know she would stay there a long time, massaging, because it was kind of hard. And after a while, she would feed the person a little ball of that mercury. A lot of people kept mercury in bottles. And she would also turn the person around, and she would get her skin from here on the

139

back, and pull it up, and if it cracked, if it popped and snapped right back, the person got well. A lot of people came to her, but she would say, "I don't know anything about medicine or nothing. I just massage you and you get well." Maybe it was faith.

BENIGNA
O. CHÁVEZ

We'd go up in the hills to pick yerba de la cota, *which is good for curing many ailments, and* pazote *grew right around the fields here. You eat that when you eat beans, for gas. We would pick* marubio (horehound) *in the hills too—they say that is good for diabetes—and we made chewing gum from the roots of a plant we called* chíquete de pingüe (rubber bush). *Oh,* chíquete de pingüe era tan bueno! Tan bueno! *It's a plant that grows anywhere—you don't need to water it or anything. There used to be a lot of it right there, where we had the barn. First, we used to dig the plant and then cut the root, and peel it, and then we'd put the roots in a skillet and toast them a little bit. Then they were ready, and we chewed the peelings of the roots, and that was* chíquete, *what you call chewing gum. And that* chíquete de pingüe *was very good. And we used to make chewing gum from the* piñón *tree, too. We used to just chew those things that come out of the branches, and it was a very good gum. It was different from the* tremetina (pitch). *We used the stuff that wasn't sticky, and we called it* chíquete de piñón. *We also used* oshá, *and* inmortal (creeping milkweed), *and* manzanilla (chamomile), *and* yerba de la cota (Navajo tea), *and* yerba de la negrita (scarlet globemallow). Yerba de la cota *is good for the bladder, that's very good for that. For a headache, they used . . . I forgot. But the best herb was* yerba buena, *and* poléo (brook mint), *that's what they used the most.* Poléo *is similar to* yerba buena, *but* poléo *is good for fever, when you have high fever, you boil it and then you drink the juice. It's a mint. And* pazote *that was an herb a lot of people used it for stomachache.*

We got them all from the hills, except oshá—*we got that from an old man from Pojoaque who used to come to sell* remedios *that we didn't have here. He went to the mountains, and he knew what they were, and what they were good for. And then here in Chimayó, Doña Juanita Durán and Don Nicolás Baca—they were* médicos. *They used the herbs for healing. They used that* inmortal *a lot. And oh yes, I forgot to mention* coyaye *(rattlesnake weed), that was also a very good medicine and they used it a lot. For arthritis, we used to take baths with* coyaye. *We'd boil it, and then we sat on a chair, and put a big tub with* agua de coyaye, *and then we put a towel over our heads and breathed in the* coyaye. *And you know, people got well with* coyaye.

When the Presbyterian missionaries, who arrived in the valley in 1900, introduced a host of new crops and new ways of cooking food, the Chimayosos learned about the fare that midwestern Americans favored. The Chimayosos didn't forget their favorite old foods, but they integrated a new dietary regime into their kitchens—and the newcomer *gringos* incorporated chile and other foods into their meals. The mission teachers—and later, county extension agents —also taught people how to can produce. Before the teachers arrived, the women of the plaza spread apricots, cherries, peaches, and pears on tables to dry and strung apple slices on strings to make *orejones* (dried fruit slices). They sliced melons and hung them to dry on a line to make *tasajos* (strips of dried melon) and stored all their dried fruits in sacks or chests, rationing them out carefully over the winter. Sacks full of dried fruit and vegetables showed that it had been a good year, and it gave people a sense of security to see them swinging from the *vigas*, assuring them of a steady food supply through the winter. After the Chimayosos learned how to can, the sacks and chests were replaced with *trasteros* (cabinets) filled with row upon row of mason jars. Just as they had dried foodstuffs before, people canned just about everything imaginable, including beans, meat, *posole*, green chile, fruits, vegetables, jellies, and jam.

It wasn't only the good nutrition of homegrown vegetables that kept the people in Chimayó healthy; the physical labor of farming life kept Chimayosos fit and granted most a longevity that remains legendary—and for this they owed no debt to modern medicine.

There were no doctors back then, but everybody was very strong. They irrigated, they planted, and they were very healthy. And now, every day someone tells me,

GREGORITA MARTÍNEZ

141

HUSKING
CORN IN THE
PLAZA, EARLY
1900S.

*"It hurts me here, it hurts me there." It didn't used to be like this! Now they're
so lazy, they don't plant at all. They just drive up and down the road. Pero de
antes, no. People knew how to work then.*

PETRONILA
MARTÍNEZ
ORTIZ

*Yes, that's true. People worked hard, but they were very healthy. And people
lived a long time. Now everyone is sick, but back then it wasn't like that. People
were healthy because they grew their own food. The old people, they ate too
much atole, with milk—that's why they were so healthy. But now all the people
suffer—stomachache, legs hurting . . . all kinds of things.*

TERESITA
JARAMILLO

*To shuck the corn, people would get together at night, by the light of the moon
and maybe a lantern that cast a little light. I guess they had very good eyesight
then, because they always did that at night, and sometimes they finished in one
night with a whole pile of corn, and everybody would go the next night to another
person's house to start on another pile—and those were good times too! It was*

MELITA
ORTEGA

fun hearing the stories. Sometimes it was friends that helped, and later on we

would pay those who didn't have much land. Like Don Santiago and Benito Martínez, they used to come and help tie chiles at night. And Doña Perfecta, Elías's mother, and sometimes Don Luís and Doña Delfiña, our neighbors there by the ditch. Tía Bone would always come and help, and they would tell stories and adivinanzas *(riddles) and then they would hide a watermelon in the pile, so we all hurried to get to the watermelon. As soon as we got to the watermelon, we could eat it—but the piles were big! Father used to fill the* dispensa *about one-quarter or one-half full with melons. It was fun—all the stories.*

People prepared corn in a variety of ways, most of which their ancestors had learned from the Pueblo people. They roasted whole *elotes* (ears of corn) in *hornos* and dried the kernels, producing *chicos* to cook with beans. They leached the kernels with lime to make *posole* or ground them to a coarse flour for *atole* (a corn meal drink) and *chaquegüe* (a coarse, gruellike cereal). *Atole* was the only drink that pregnant women were allowed to drink, for people believed it was soothing and nutritious and that it would create a calm, stable mood for the expectant mother. Chimayosos delighted in fresh corn and anticipated the harvest eagerly each summer, but people are less talkative about the fact that

SOTERA
MARTÍNEZ
AND GENOVEVA
ORTIZ CARRYING
WATER FROM
THE DITCH,
CA. 1915.

STRINGS HUNG
WITH CARNE
SECA (DRIED
MEAT), EARLY
1900S.

143

during Prohibition some of Chimayó's corn crop was diverted for strictly non-food purposes. I hear that the local moonshine, distilled from fermented corn and called *Mula Blanca*, packed a memorable punch.

As with nearly all traditional foods produced in Chimayó, there are legends about how good the corn tortillas came out in the old days: "Your grandma's mother, Genoveva—ay, what a cook she was! She used to make blue corn tortillas on her wood stove, and I've never had tortillas *tan sabrosas* (so delicious). We would take one of those thick, hot tortillas and wrap it around fresh *chicharones* (fried pork fat) to make a *machito*. Ah, *que bueno!* I always loved to visit over there because of those *machitos*."

TERESITA
JARAMILLO

Ben Ortega also boasts about the tortillas of the old days: "The food was so good. I don't know, I guess we all say, 'They don't cook like my mother used to,' but that stove was burning all the time. In the wintertime you needed it for heat, and in the summer, she always had a little fire in there for cooking. Tortillas every day—fresh tortillas!"

Both Genoveva and Ben's mother, Refugio Jaramillo Ortega, were among the fortunate few to get a wood stove early in the century, for, as with every other modern convenience, the wealthier people acquired wood stoves first. Others kept cooking over their corner fireplaces, using simple iron *tinamaistes* (trivets) to hold the pots over the flames. In many homes, the fireplaces also remained the only source of heat well into this century. "Oh yes, Tía Bone had a corner fire-place. Everyone did. That's how they'd heat the homes—very few were starting to have wood stoves. Even at home, in the *cuartito* and in the other bedroom, we had those corner fireplaces. We always sat around the fireplace and later around the wood stove in the kitchen." "We had the corner fireplaces—four in here. There's where they use to cook, on a *tinamaiste*, an iron ring with a handle and legs. Most of the food we ate was boiled—corn and beans."

MELITA
ORTEGA

TILA VILLA

None of the gardens grown in the plaza could survive the dry summers without supplemental water, which flowed from the Acequia de los Ortegas—one of the oldest intact *acequia* systems in New Mexico. This *acequia* has watered the plaza gardens for some three hundred years. The *presa*, or diversion dam, for the Ortega ditch diverts the waters of the Río Quemado at the mouth of a deep canyon a short distance above the Chimayó Valley. The small ditch curves northward around the arid foothills to reach the plaza, which is situated strategically near the ditch and on the edge of irrigable land. A giant old cottonwood, a silver poplar, and a black locust—the largest trees around—lean over the ditch at the plaza's north wall, bearing testament to the age of this waterway. The cold water of the Ortega *acequia* supplied the plaza people with water for all their needs well into the 1950s. Besides irrigating the gardens, it slaked the thirst of people and their livestock and provided a place to wash clothing and to bathe and swim.

Most people were forced to take the risk of contracting diseases such as typhoid fever by drinking from the ditch, which could have been contaminated by human waste as well as that of livestock. ("We didn't have inside plumbing, and we didn't have outside privies or anything. So we went to the corrals. The men would go to the *milpa* and the women went to the corrals. Then the mission people built some outhouses, and people got the idea.") Most of the plaza area is well above the water table, but some people were able to dig shallow wells, which gave them a measure of protection from contaminated water. Although the Chimayosos didn't have a full understanding about the importance of clean water, they were aware that unseen contaminants in food could hurt them. There was a taboo against sharing food with strangers, manifested in a belief in witchcraft.

TILA VILLA

On Día del San Juan (St. John's Day, June 24), we'd go to San Juan Pueblo and it was also on that day that you could get in the ditch. They said that the water was holy that day. Before that day, they wouldn't let us go in the ditch to bathe. They said, "No, you have to wait until Día del San Juan." Then it was OK. And a lot of people did get in the water. Then of course, after that we were always in the ditch, all summer long. That was our swimming pool.

They'd wash pisos (rugs) in the ditch, right there in front of la casita of Tía Bone, right where there was a bridge. They used to build the fires to heat the water in big tubs. We'd heat the water in a little horno and we'd put a big can there and

MELITA ORTEGA, TILA VILLA, AND STELLA CHÁVEZ USNER

145

fill it with water and start the fire, get it going, come in and have breakfast, and then start our laundry. When there was a lot of water in the ditch, we'd rinse in the ditch, real nice, we didn't have to carry the water to the tub, empty the tub and put more water—that was a chore. Imagine how many pails of water you'd have to carry back and forth. They used homemade soap made with lye and lard. But for the homespun blankets, they used amole *(yucca) root only for washing. They would crush the root and put it in water to make suds. With that kind of soap, the blankets would not shrink and the colors wouldn't run.*

MELITA
ORTEGA

TILA VILLA

And of course we used to drink from the ditch, too—but the ditch was clean then. They didn't throw cans in it like they do now. They kept it as clean as possible. The only thing was that the animals used to step over the ditch and, you know. . . . We thought the water was cleaner farther up the ditch. And we would go up there near the road to get the water, even though it was still below some corrals. Before, my grandparents used to get water from the river. All the way from the river down a little path they had there by Petronila's—they called it the vereda. *And for babysitting, see my grandma had four kids, and she would tie each kid to the leg of the table. And she would go to get the water.*

MELITA
ORTEGA

But I got typhoid fever from the ditch. It was after my sister died in the influenza epidemic, because I remember I was about twelve. I was real sick, and my hair fell off. There was an epidemic of typhoid around here. Martha got it and so did Cande, but they didn't get it as bad as me. Their hair didn't fall out. I was so weak, and they didn't take me to the doctor. I remember that Ms. Ellsworth, the mission teacher, used to go to see me, but they didn't take me to the doctor. They knew it was typhoid fever. I wanted to get up to go to the bathroom and I couldn't. I just fell, I was so weak. And I tried and tried to yell for help, but I was so weak I couldn't even yell. I stayed in bed a long time. I was skinny, skinny. They called it the fiebre tifoidea. *It must have been around 1920 because Mother died in about 1919. I guess we got it from the water. Sometimes people died from it. One of those letters that I found among Ms. Clark's things was one she wrote to Tío Anastasio, she wrote: "I went to visit someone, and there is a typhoid fever epidemic here, and this person died from it."*

Most people drank from the ditch, but Reyes had a well right in front of the house, there where there is a big low spot there. He used cubos *(small boxes) made of wood to haul water up from the well with a pulley and a rope. It wasn't too, too deep, because we could see the water down there. And you know he dug that well by hand, just with a shovel! They were strong in those days. And 'Mano Eulogio Martínez had a well with very good water. We used to go there after our well dried up. But the mission place was the first for everything. They were the first ones to have a well with a pump, and the first ones to put water inside, and the first ones to put electricity—they had their own generator before the electric company put lines here. We used to go there for water sometimes, too.*

MELITA ORTEGA
AND STELLA
CHÁVEZ USNER

You had to be careful about what you ate and drank in those days. My aunt used to talk about people wanting to cast a spell on you. She said that one time they had gone to a velorio *and this lady gave my grandma two plums. And my grandma got them, but by the time they came home the plums were real big. And of course they didn't eat them. People were very careful about eating what other people gave them. They were very, very suspicious about that.*

TILA VILLA

We heard of two witches here in Chimayó, but I don't know if it was true. My dad never believed in that because one particular lady would bring him panocha *or whatever, and he would eat it. And Ita, who knew the history around here, would tell him, "Don't eat it." And he would say, "I don't believe in that witchcraft," and nothing happened. So I don't know if there were witches. But I do know about a lady who was really, really sick and she was nervous and crying and all that. And somebody had told her that something had happened to her like witchcraft. So she and her father went to a* curandero *in Las Vegas. And she said that this man had brought out a pan of water and had asked the lady to look in the pan and to tell him what face she saw. She looked in the water and she saw her aunt. And he told her that this aunt didn't like her and that at one time this aunt had taken her some beautiful looking vegetables. "And you ate them," the* curandero *told her. "Well, that's how one gets the spell, and I'm going to give you this, and you drink it now." So she drank it and they started home. And halfways, she got so sick, she said. Really, really sick. She got out of the car*

and she didn't know what to do. She was throwing up, throwing up balls of hair. And she got well.

People in the plaza relied on the Ortega *acequia* for water, for they were denied access to the water of the much larger ditch that cuts diagonally across the plaza gardens. This ditch presents something of an idyllic vision in the summer when the air is dry as the dust, but not a drop of its water flows onto plaza land. Most casual visitors mistake this for the plaza's original *acequia*, but a closer look shows how out of character this ditch is with the rest of the plaza: its great width and depth and the high banks of dirt along its sides make it grossly out of proportion with the tiny gardens and small rooms of the plaza. It is an industrial-grade ditch in a handmade plaza, and its water obviously couldn't flow to the gardens because most of the plaza land is higher than the level of ditch. Most old plaza residents despise this, the "District ditch," or the *"Acequia del Depósito,"* dug through the plaza in conjunction with the Santa Cruz Dam and Irrigation District project in the 1920s and 1930s. Because plaza people refused to be dragged into the expensive bond proposition arranged to finance the dam, the infamous District ditch has never provided irrigation water to the plaza or environs.

The story of the ditch makes a good example of the way that Victor Ortega, as the *patrón* of the plaza, acted to protect the interests of the community. Victor vehemently opposed construction of the dam, and he organized a group of plaza residents to speak out against it. He also vowed that no ditch associated with the dam would cross his land. Some say that the dam promoters offered to reduce his and other plaza residents' property taxes in exchange for rights of access for the District ditch, but this did not sway Victor. As a consequence, the ditch just misses his acreage on the south side of the plaza before it dives directly under the floor of the southeast corner of plaza (thereby providing a built-in air conditioner, winter and summer, for one plaza home) and traverses the interior gardens. In taking this route, the ditch engineers may simply have been following the minimum grade necessary to deliver the water efficiently to the lower valley. But some *vecinos* believe that the intrusion of the ditch in the plaza represents a bit of retribution on the part of the dam's backers against Victor and other Chimayosos who opposed its construction.

I remember Bonefacia Ortega saying that she didn't want the ditch because it would cut all the properties in the plaza in half. She said that the ditch ruined the plaza and that the people there didn't need it at all. And she was right. There are springs below Río Chiquito [the next town upstream on the creek] that keep the Río Quemado running even in the driest of years. Plaza residents always have had a good supply of water, unless the presa *washed out. That happened a lot, and one year, the Ortega* acequia *had to be abandoned for a season. But even then, plaza residents didn't use the District ditch but instead diverted water from the Cañada Ancha ditch.*

JOHN TRUJILLO

To irrigate land inside the plaza, farmers let the water from the Ortega *acequia* into the plaza through the plaza's north *callejón* (alleyway) or around the east side and through the east entrance. The *acequia* also watered most of the agricultural land surrounding the plaza. Other nearby ditches—particularly the Martínez ditch below the plaza and the Cañada Ancha ditch in Centinela and Rincón—irrigated other nearby parcels. (The Martínez ditch may in fact predate the Ortega ditch by a short time; Luis López was probably referring to the Martínez ditch when in 1706 he named as his property boundary "a ditch that the Tano Indians dug."[1])

Of all the crops grown in and around the plaza, none was more important than chile. Everyone who owned a piece of irrigable land grew chile, both inside and outside of the plaza. Chile was not only a food but also a folk medicine prescribed for colds and sore throats. For treating colds, the hotter the chile, the better, and the preparation called *chile caribe*, for which the chiles were crushed rather than ground and remain raw, was the preferred treatment. For dietary purposes, many people preferred the milder varieties, and Chimayó is best known for its mild but extremely flavorful peppers. Chimayosos watched their *huertas* (chile fields) closely, not only because they appreciated the sweet flavor and subtle physiological effects of the chiles but also because they could trade dried chiles for merchandise at mercantile stores in Española. No other crop had this kind of barter value.

MERCEDES
TRUJILLO IN
HER HUERTA
(CHILE FIELD),
1991.

MERCEDES
TRUJILLO IN
HER MILPA
(CORN FIELD),
1991.

JOHN TRUJILLO

In those days, Chimayó was very famous for its chile. I remember when all the houses used to be covered with ristras. *Beautiful. Anywhere you go, all red, this time of the year. Today, nobody wants to plant chile. We got beat by Las Cruces. But you never heard of Hatch and Las Cruces in those days. All the chile was Chimayó. Now they have plantations in Hatch and they are really producing commercially. But it's not the same. You see, the Chimayó chile is not very big. The real Chimayó chile is short and fat and crooked, and it has a better flavor than Hatch chile. My father and the other plaza people grew only those small, crooked chiles.*

BENJAMÍN
ORTEGA

Many modern retailers have capitalized on the legendary zing of Chimayó chile by marking their brands with the Chimayó name, but only a few people in the valley grow the old varieties, whose small size and thin skin make them more difficult to process and store than the new, hybridized strains of chile. Most Chimayosos agree that none of the new chiles compare in *sabor* with the fine chile peppers grown in Chimayó.

As employment dried up throughout the region during the Great Depression, chile became for many people the only means of obtaining goods from retail outlets such as the Bond and Nohl's store in Española. About 60,000 *ristras* of chile from northern New Mexico were traded through these stores in the 1930s. Bond and Nohl's shipped the chile out—either in strings or ground into powder —to destinations throughout the West on the Denver and Rio Grande Western Railroad. (Apparently, Victor Ortega was not equipped to trade his goods in the plaza general store for chile, for no one mentions trading their chile there.) People had grown to rely on Bond and Nohl's and two other retail outlets for a wide variety of wares—from food, clothing, and shoes to cooking pots and farm equipment—that only cash or chile could buy. Farmers throughout northern New Mexico were chronically in debt to the mercantile stores.[2]

Chile price varied widely from year to year and even within the same year, depending on supply and demand in distant markets and on the condition of the chiles, and some *viejitos* describe the chile harvest in the 1930s as an anxious time when everyone wondered how much chile they could produce and what price it would bring. But even in the toughest of times, chile from Chimayó and other northern New Mexico valleys brought a higher price than chile from competing areas in southern New Mexico and California—and in spite of the price difference, northern New Mexico chile sold better. Still, these prices were not high: a double *ristra* of chile five feet long (a ten-foot strand folded in half) brought at most $1 in exchange value at Bond and Nohl's.[3] In the early 1930s, the price dropped to a catastrophic 35 cents per *ristra*.[4]

The necessity of readying the chiles for market brought people together to share in the task of tying *ristras* of chile in the fall. Some families hired women to help, and everyone worked their fingers numb. The *vecinos* of the plaza tied the countless knots at night, usually indoors in a *dispensa* (storage building) or a barn, and, as with the corn, they sometimes buried a watermelon in the pile of chiles as a prize for fast tying. Many remember the excitement of this simple game and tying *ristras*, which offered entertainment and a chance for the plaza residents to visit and exchange stories and news.

That's another thing that people did to help each other. If you had a bunch of chile, they'd all come at night and help you tie it up. Family and neighbors would come from all around the plaza. My dad would hang his chile strings there, from the vigas, *and he'd have so much chile.*

BENJAMÍN
ORTEGA

I remember one year when Papa Reyes filled his dispensa *to the ceiling with chile. I was a little girl and I helped with the* ristras *for a while, but I was too little you know, so my sister Petrita and I just watched the women he had hired. They would tie the chiles together—three of them at a time—and Papa would take them and make the* ristras *and then put them on nails in the* vigas. *He had a lantern burning in there and when finally we couldn't stay awake anymore, we'd walk next door and go to bed. But we could still hear those women talking and tying* ristras *until late in the night. And when we got up in the morning, the whole* dispensa *was covered with chile* ristras. *He had a hundred* ristras *that year! Fíjate tú—just imagine!*

BENIGNA
O. CHÁVEZ

MERCEDES
TRUJILLO,
1991.

MERCEDES
TRUJILLO,
1991.

Older Chimayosos remember bringing chile *ristras* to Española in covered wagons. Bond and Nohl's store inspected *ristras* rigorously, and not all chiles were deemed good enough for barter, but there was a market for those that didn't pass muster. Chimayosos took the rejects along with other produce to trade in neighboring communities. Each year, they would load up their wagons with chile, melons, and sometimes corn and make a trip to the mountains to trade in Mora, Peñasco, Truchas, Taos, Chacón, Chamisal, and other nearby towns—anywhere they thought people might want chile.

In Mora, Chimayosos traded for *queso de cabra* (goat cheese), potatoes, and mutton. (Trade with Mora may have been facilitated by the fact that Juan Domingo Ortega, José Ramón Ortega y Vigil's brother, moved to Mora in the mid-1800s and lived out his life there. Chimayosos remained cognizant of this family connection and may have used it to make contacts in the town.) From Truchas and Peñasco, Chimayosos obtained potatoes and, if they didn't have land to grow it themselves, they also traded for wheat from the mountain villages. Valley people also sometimes exchanged their chile or fruit for firewood from the Trucheños. The men who went trading sometimes stayed away a week or more in a journey that in many ways resembled the excursions of a century earlier, when *ciboleros* from the valley rode out to the eastern plains to hunt buffalo.

BERSABÉ NARANJO CHÁVEZ

My papa would go to Mora, Chacón, Chamisal—those places—to exchange, and from there he would bring wheat, cheese, things like that. He spent a week going around because those places are very far. He went in a covered wagon, and what he brought were the things that we didn't plant here. He traded what we grew here for those things.

TILA VILLA

The way it went, they would go from house to house. You stop at this house, knock on the door, "What do you want?" the man would say. "Why don't you buy some chile, and I have some melons too?" "Well, where are you from," they'd say, standing in the door. "From Chimayó," they'd answer. "OK, you give me that and that and I'll give you a goat." "Bueno. . . ." That's the way they'd do it. And then they'd go to another house. Knock. The door barely opens. "Who is it?" "I'm selling chile and I'm from Chimayó." Bang! The door closes—slams fast. "Those bad people from Chimayó!" So at the next door, they say, "From Chimayó—from a good family!" real fast.

In the 1930s, the value of bartered goods was well established: one *almud* (sixteen pounds) of beans was worth two strings of chile while a sack of potatoes traded for one and a half *ristras*. One *fanega* (140 pounds) of wheat traded for two strings.[5] The barter system had nearly disappeared after World War I and the depression, although some Chimayosos, such as Luis Martínez, made these excursions in by wagon to Mora into the 1950s. He traded along the way and returned to the plaza as soon as his wagon was empty. An important produce trading relationship also linked many northern New Mexico villages with the cool San Luis Valley in southern Colorado. There, Chimayosos traded their famous chile for potatoes and pinto beans. But trade with the San Luis Valley stopped abruptly in 1937, when the Colorado legislature enacted laws requiring all commercial truckers to obtain Colorado licenses, carry expensive insurance, and pay a levy on all tonnage hauled. This was impossible for the small growers from the northern New Mexico villages who were accustomed to barter. For many people, the end of trading meant the end of contact with the Hispanic culture in the San Luis Valley.[6]

Chimayosos also sometimes took their produce to Santa Fe to sell. Trading adventures eased the isolation of Chimayó. Visitors from outside of Chimayó also provided contact, in the form of tourists coming to the Santuario or people from other villages coming to barter for Chimayó produce. Weavers sold both blankets and produce when they went to Santa Fe. Grandma remembers her first trading trip to Santa Fe when she was about ten years old, and she still cherishes it as one of the grandest experiences of her life:

We would leave Chimayó in the morning and ride over the hills to get to Tesuque that afternoon. We camped by the river there at a place they called "the Rancho de los Coyotes." Papa laid blankets on the ground by the cottonwood trees there and watched over me all night. It was lonely out there—there were no houses or

BENIGNA
O. CHÁVEZ

157

WASHING
WHEAT IN
THE PLAZA,
CA. 1910.

CLEANING
CHILES IN
THE PLAZA,
CA. 1910.

anything around. Very early in the morning, when it was still dark, we would get up and go up that long hill there by Tesuque. I remember the first time when we came to the top of that hill and I saw the lights of Santa Fe, all spread out below. I felt so happy, I don't know how to explain it, this feeling I had when I saw all those lights and the big town. I was just so excited to see those lights. I had never seen an electric light before. It looked like Heaven to me.

In Santa Fe, we'd go downtown and Papa brought his blankets to Sito Candelario. Then we went over by the plaza to sell the melons that we brought. We'd sit by the road there and people would come and buy the melons. One time, we were passing by some young men on the street and they shouted to my father, "You sure have a pretty daughter there." But they said it very nice, you know, not disrespectful. We stayed with Papa's friend Bonefacio and once we stayed at a hotel right there by the plaza. I remember that I was frightened by the running water in the toilet. Petrita and I thought we had dumped water on the restaurant below when we pulled the chain and flushed the toilet!

And then, Taos Indians would come here to trade in covered wagons, and the people would be cleaning the yards or husking corn or whatever, tending to the apples, and the Indians would stop right in front and come over and ask my aunt, "Do you want to trade these for the corn? For the apples?" And she said "Yeah, cuanto?" "I give you this and you give me that." And that was the trade. They usually came in the fall. We would be playing there and we would be amazed with them because of their long hair and their blankets around them, and big hats with plumas. Always from Taos, it was only the Taos Indians that came here to trade.

TILA VILLA

Occasionally, wandering *Turcos* (Gypsies) passed through town, and according to the Chimayosos who saw them, their visits often involved a great deal of one-way trading—with the *Turcos* getting the good end of the deal. The simple and trusting Chimayosos sometimes made easy prey for the seasoned wanderers. However, the *Turcos* also sometimes provided entertainment and offered cures for ailments in exchange for the food that they took from the Chimayosos.

Ooh, one time I remember—there were hardly any houses here at all in those times—none at all on the other side of the road, and they came in covered wagons, those Turcos. And they used to steal everything they could. One time this woman was making tortillas and this Gypsy came in and robbed all the tortillas and took them—right there where she was making them! And they stole chickens, they stole sheep, and anything they could get hold of. They were dressed ragged and so dirty. We were scared of them—when we knew that the Turcos were around, we were scared.

BENIGNA
O. CHÁVEZ

One time they passed by here, right in front of where my house is now. My father was outside, just looking around, like you do when you go outside in the yard, and the Turcos came passing by on the road. One of them got real close to him and she said, "What are you doing here?" She was talking to him real fast and close, and then she started touching him all over, very sly, and she got hold of his wallet and almost took it before he caught her. The Turcos did that kind of

thing. They stole money from the people, and the people couldn't defend them-
selves when the Gypsies got ahold of them. They were very clever, the way they
—how do you say?—pickpocketed people.

I don't know where they came from, but there were a lot of Turcos, not only one
family. They just slept any place—they had a camp any place they liked. If they
liked to stop some place, they stopped there and took over. There was nothing
we could do. No, we weren't too happy to see them.

TILA VILLA

Julianita told me a story about the Turcos, when they would come around in
her day. My grandma was still alive, and she suffered from stomach pains all
the time. So the Turca came, and they let her in and the Turca said "How are
you?" My grandma said, "I'm OK but today I have a stomach ache." "You do?"
"Yes." "I'll get you well. Do you want me to get you well?" And Grandma thought
for a while and then she said, "OK." So the Turca said, "Bring me twelve eggs."
In those days they had a lot of eggs. So, she brought her twelve eggs. The Turca
broke them and beat them. At that time, my father came in and he saw that the
Turcos were in the house and he had heard stories about the Turcos and all
that and he didn't like what was going on. So my dad just fell on the floor, and
was motioning like "ahhhh" and my grandma said, "You better get out Turca,
my son is getting mad, or getting a seizure. You better go away because he gets
mean when that happens." So the Turcos left.

When I was older—maybe in the 1930s or so—they still used to come around
sometimes, and sometimes if you were not at home and your door was open, they
would come in and help themselves in the kitchen. They used to go to Doña
Maclovia's on the plaza, and to a lady named Socorro over here, and for some
reason the women left the tortillas on the table—you know, they didn't have
any refrigeration, so they just left them there. And the Turcos would come and
help themselves. They would take everything. They would steal a lot and people
didn't trust them. So whenever we knew they were in town, we just didn't
answer the door.

But sometimes those Turcos *wanted to read the palm of your hand and all that kind of thing. And I guess people around here didn't believe in that and they didn't got for that. And then one time, the* Turcos *had a man with a bear, and the bear would stand up and do tricks for people. But usually, the people here would rather give them, the* Turcos, *apples or chile or whatever and let them go on their way.*

Not all the chile produced in Chimayó went to markets or into the hands of wandering Gypsies. People consumed large quantities in Chimayó, red and green, both of which were dried and stored for the winter.

The red chile, we roasted in the horno, *on the coals of the wood. We'd turn the chiles over with a big stick, a long stick. And then we kept turning them over and then we took them out with sort of a little rake, and put them in a big bucket. We roasted a lot, about two sacks full in one day. And then we peeled it and tied it and hung it outside to dry on the clothesline. That sure was good chile because it didn't lose any vitamins at all. It was so good. And then we dried it. And then we put it away in a flour sack that was not very thick so it would get air and hang it in the* dispensa *for the winter. And from there, we would get our chile.*

BENIGNA
O. CHÁVEZ

Although chile has always been Chimayó's most important trade crop—and its most prized food crop—the valley also earned a reputation for its fruit. Guadalupe Vigil de Ortega, a great-great-grandmother to Grandma and a host of plaza residents, left a small orchard to all her heirs when she died. As a consequence, dozens of Ortegas and Trujillos and others who could claim Guadalupe as a relative visited the orchard, which they called *"la tapia de mi madre* Vigila," and helped themselves to the fruit.

There were no trees inside the plaza, but small *arboleras* (orchards) grew outside, and most of these were made up of ancient apple trees. Around the turn of the century, it was rare to see a red apple anywhere in Chimayó; most people grew only the yellow *manzanas mexicanas* (Mexican apples). "Papa Reyes already had *manzanas americanas* [red Delicious apples] by the time I can

161

remember," Grandma says. Apparently, he got them from a source who lived in Sombrillo.

"My father and Don Santos Ortiz were the first ones in Chimayó who started planting the *'manzanas americanas,'* like they called them," Melita Ortega reminisces. "But isn't it funny, like Camilo Trujillo used to say, 'Why do they call everything that's little *'mexicanas'* and everything that's big *'americanas'?* Plums were the same way—they used to call the little ones *'ciruelas mexicanas.'* But the *mexicanas* are better, you know."

Impressed at first by their superior size, almost all the Chimayosos followed Reyes Ortega and Santos Ortiz in planting red Delicious apples around the plaza. Melita remembers what a hit the *manzanas americanas* were in Chimayó: "When I was in school at the mission—when I was in the grades—boys from over in Rincón used to trade me piñón, ooh, all roasted and everything, for apples. They didn't have any red Delicious apples there, and we didn't have piñón. They wanted *manzanas americanas*, but the *manzanas mexicanas* are the best. Tía Bone had a lot of those *manzanas mexicanas*. She had an *horno*, and she would bake them and peel them all by herself, and then dry them for the winter."

BENIGNA
O. CHÁVEZ

First of all, we picked a lot of apples. And after we finished roasting chiles, we'd sweep out the horno, *and then we put a big fire in the* horno, *and then we cleaned the coals away really nice, so we could put the apples in. Everybody had* hornos. *Old women and young women—everybody had* hornos. *And we plastered the mouth of the* horno *to cover it real good so it would keep the heat all night. The next day, we took off the big rock covering the opening, and the apples were already baked—so good! They were really good. We took them out with a sort of a shovel with a long handle, and started peeling apples and taking out all the seeds and everything and then we put the slices on boards to dry. And when they were dry, we put them away too in a little bag and hung them in the dispensa. We kept them there because we couldn't put them in a cupboard.*

Although apples grow well in Chimayó, they were seldom sold or traded. Perhaps this was because the market for apples was extremely limited; everyone

OLD APPLE
TREE BEHIND
THE VICTOR
ORTEGA
HOUSE, 1995.

grew apples and few needed to buy them. The fact that apple blossoms frequently freeze in the spring also hampered efforts to commercialize apples. But the *arboleras* were visited for reasons other than picking the fruit. One woman, who asked to remain unnamed, confided to me that as a young girl, she knew of young couples who had other uses for the orchard:

Our dates were in those orchards over there on the west side, by Melita's place. On the old road. That's where we used to have a date. It was different then. Oh, no, you didn't go around showing off to everybody. The boy would say, "I'm going to take care of the cows. I'm going to see how the cows are doing." But the girl knew when he was going to see her, and she would say to her parents, "I'm going to go look for eggs." And they would meet in the orchard, the arbolera behind the plaza, which they called the "tapia de mi madre Vigila." I had a date there once.

People also have sweet memories of another local crop—one that is almost forgotten as a northern New Mexico product: *caña*, or sorghum cane, also called *caña de Castilla* (Castillian cane). Every year, plaza resident Don Nicolás Martínez made *miel de caña*—a dense, molasseslike syrup extracted from the cane. Nicolás planted large fields of sorghum near the mission school, and others tended smaller amounts in the area. Nicolás cut the cane before the apple harvest, about mid-September, and stacked it in his shed. He set up his *mielero* by the Ortega ditch just outside the east side of the plaza and everyone showed up when he started squeezing *miel* from the *caña*.

BENIGNA
O. CHÁVEZ

Don Nicolás Martínez had a place near my house where he made syrup from the caña de Castilla *that he planted. By October, he had cut all the cane and hauled it in his wagon over there by the ditch, where he had made a shed. He put the cane in the shed and then took the horse and hooked it up to the* mielero *—the right kind of machine for squeezing the juice from the big stalks of cane. And he made the horse go round and round and put in pieces of cane every once in a while, and it squeezed out the juice into a big pot because a lot of juice came out. And then when it was full, he put it in another big pot and heated it until it was not too thick or too thin—until it was at just the right point. He scooped it out of there with a dipper and put it in gallon containers, and then he sold it. He must have made quite a bit because he stayed about a week making it, every day. Every fall. When he died, nobody did it anymore.*

The people liked that syrup a lot because it was natural, with a natural flavor, and so sweet! So good! We ate it with bread or tortillas, or with buñuelos *[the old name for* sopaipillas*]—oh, it was so good with* buñuelos. *That I remember very well, that I really liked that* miel. *When we saw Don Nicolás setting up his* mielero, *we'd say, "Oh,* apucha! *Let's go eat some* miel. *Oh boy, let's go!"*

Almost no one grows sorghum in the Chimayó area anymore, and the same is true for wheat, which is not well suited to the dry, hot summers of the valley. But up until 1940 or so, plaza residents planted wheat west of the plaza or in

Centinela, where large tracts of land were available. In fact, wheat was one of the most common crops grown in Chimayó during the first few decades of this century. Several plaza homeowners also owned land near Truchas and farmed wheat there. They took summer trips to El Llano de Abeyta, a large, relatively level, open area west of Truchas where several families claimed land.[7] At El Llano de Abeyta and Truchas, some also managed crops of peas, beans, corn, garbanzos, and *habas* (horse beans). Some Chimayosos also went to El Llano to farm alfalfa, but wheat was the major crop grown there.

My father hitched up his team to pull the wagon up the Cañada Ancha to the llano *to plant wheat in April or May. He returned again to the* llano *to harvest in August just before the corn was ready. I don't remember what my father paid his* peones *(laborers), but for bending over an* hoz *(a hand sickle) from dawn until dusk, I remember that Don Victor Ortega paid his* peones *just fifty cents. Meals were included.*

BERSABÉ
NARANJO
CHÁVEZ

What I remember best was when my father went up for the harvest, because most of the men who owned land up there in El Llano brought their daughters along to cook and help with the harvest, and me and Petrita went sometimes. We'd camp in a fuerte *(a log cabin) at El Llano—Papa and the* peones *and us. Father hired some of the* peones *in Truchas, and sometimes he brought* peones *with us from the valley.*

BENIGNA
O. CHÁVEZ

We just went for one week there to cut the wheat and all that. Pita and I went to cook for the men, and in the Llano Abeyta we used to cook on the fogón *because we didn't have a wood stove. In one week they finished the land—farther than from here to those garages! As far as you could see, you'd see wheat. And when it was windy, the wheat went like this. . . . So pretty! About four men went out every day to cut the wheat. And then Tía Pita and I went after we washed the dishes, we went out to help, and we sure liked it. We sure liked to cut wheat. It's hard work.*

ENCARNACIÓN
RODRÍGUEZ
SIFTING WHEAT,
EARLY 1900S.

WOMEN WIN-
NOWING WHEAT
IN THE PLAZA,
EARLY 1900S.

They brought the wheat down to Chimayó in wagons, but not every day. Only after they finished cleaning it and everything and put it in bags. Those who had wheat here in Chimayó threshed it here. But those who had wheat in El Llano, they'd thresh it there in El Llano. They'd thresh it up there with the goats, at the era—*that was a big, big area of land, shaped round, where they pressed the soil real good with water so it wouldn't be dusty or anything, just real clean just like a piece of board.*

One time, my papa took us from the fuerte *to the* era *so we wouldn't be lonely, to the* era *where they had gathered the wheat, and in the night they were sifting the wheat—they sifted it at night, you know. They used to sift it with a* criba *made out of the hide of cows with little holes punched in it. They made every-thing in those days—nothing from the store. They sifted the wheat through the* criba *and put it in the bags when it was already clean, really clean, and took it down here to Chimayó. My father made two trips sometimes, full of bags of wheat. Then he put the bags here in that* dispensa, *in the middle of the floor,*

piled up like that high. And then he took it to the miller, a little this side of La Puebla here in Chimayó where there was a man who milled wheat.

We used to go with Tío Melquiades to El Llano, and we'd stay in the fuerte—just a little room. And he would go and get the wood, and pretty soon we'd have the beans ready. We had the little fireplace. We made a little fire. And the older people would go to tend to the wheat, and the kids would stay in the fuerte and then sometimes it would get so windy, and you know that sound in the pine trees? Oooh. I hated that, when the wind came, all the kids came in the fuerte and shut the door. We thought that was a witch coming. And we would come home all black from cooking over an open fire.

THRESHING
WHEAT WITH
GOATS, CA.
1937.

TILA VILLA

167

AMADA
TRUJILLO

Those were the days when we camped out because we had to. We didn't do it for fun. And now they go out camping for the fun of it. But I don't call that fun, when you have to take up everything and get all black with smoke and then come back home and wash everything and get everything dirty. I'd rather go to a place where I can just relax.

TILA VILLA

Our wheat fields here in Chimayó were down by the arroyo. We used to thresh the wheat with goats, at the era, *there on Sabino Trujillo's land, where the community center is now. First we would help cut the wheat. And then we'd take the wheat over there, then we'd ask Don Patricio Cruz to come and thresh it with the goats. So he'd bring the goats and they'd go round and round and round. And Mr. Cruz had a whip and if they got out of line, he'd give them the whip.*

You'd stay there all day, winnowing the wheat with a pitchfork. And when everything was still and there was no wind, they would ask Santa Bárbara to send wind—they had a cute little prayer they used to say. The grown-ups would stay there and the children would finally get tired and come to the plaza. And we heard the bells on the goats, we knew they were done winnowing, and we would run to the road by the entrance to the plaza there and hold hands up like a bridge, and the goats had to go under our arms.

Then you washed the wheat and put it in front of the house there to dry. We spread the wheat out on clean pisos *(rugs), and then took it to the mills. There was a mill in Potrero and one at Prima Merced's. También* in La Cajita, *and we'd take chile there too. They'd do the corn and then the wheat and then they'd clean it real good so they could do the chile.*

Small *molinos* (gristmills) once dotted the landscape throughout northern New Mexico, including several small mills in and around Chimayó. Plaza resident Eulogio Martínez operated a *molino* in Potrero on the Santa Cruz River. Francisquito Chávez's mill also used water diverted from the Santa Cruz River while Perfecto Trujillo of Rincón sluiced the waters of the Río Quemado into his *molino* at a place called La Cajita. Still other *molinos* stood in Centinela and in Río Chiquito. A single individual usually owned each mill, but he shared access to it with his extended family and others in his community. The owners sometimes expected payment for use of the mill, usually in the form of a portion of the milled product. The small log structures housed simple, horizontal grindstone systems that ground wheat, chile, and corn. It was impossible to rid the mill-stones of the pungent residues of chile, and the wheat flour often carried a sharp edge of chile flavor. As commercial flour replaced the homegrown wheat, the mills processed only chile and most people remember them best as chile mills.

Many plaza folk used 'Mano Perfecto's *molino* at La Cajita, situated at the widening of a small box canyon about a mile east of the plaza, for many could claim relationship to this Trujillo from Rincón. The rough terrain made it impossible to build a wagon road to La Cajita, so people made the trip on foot or on horseback. At La Cajita, a ditch directed water from just above a small water-fall on the Río Quemado to an arroyo where the log building sat on a bank. The remnants of the house and the ditch are still visible, though the mill has been out of operation at least since the 1930s.

I used to like to go to La Cajita. We would fill up sacks with dried chiles and then here we go, up the cerro *to La Cajita. Sometimes we took a horse to carry the chile, but there was no road in those hills. We got the key for the* molino *from 'Mano Perfecto, my father's cousin, and we would come back with bags of chile powder.*

BENIGNA
O. CHÁVEZ

Ever the bard, El Güero Mestas composed a short poem about a *molino*. Its clever rhythm evokes the turning of the millstones.

El Molinario
por Francisco Antonio Mestas (El Güero)[8]

Del monte más alto tengo que ir a traer
Palos de molino para mi molinar

PEONES CUT-
TING WHEAT
WITH HOCES
(SICKLES),
CA. 1930S.

Del cerro más alto tengo que ir a traer
Piedras de molino para mi molinar

Del pozo más hondo tengo de sacar
Un chorro de agua para mi molinar

Tengo que ir a la otra banda del río
Maíz y trigo blanco para mi molinar

Te molinarinarita
Te molinarinare

Te molinarinaita
Te molinarinare

The poem translates:

From the highest mountain, I have to go gather
Milling sticks for my mill

From the highest hill, I have to go gather
Millstones for my mill

From the deepest well, I have to bring
A stream of water for my mill

I have to go to the other side of the river
For corn and white wheat for my mill

I will turn my little mill
I will turn it only for you

I will turn my little mill
I will turn it only for you.

Most of the ground wheat coming out of the *molinos* went into making tortillas, the staple of the Chimayó diet, but farmers always held back some of the grain for sprouting later to make *panocha*—a naturally sweet, sprouted-wheat cereal. For special occasions, the women made bread instead of tortillas, baking it outside in the adobe *hornos*.

We'd wet the wheat and put it in a burlap sack, and we would leave it behind the stove, and they would watch when the wheat was sprouting. And then they said, "It's ready, let's go." They'd make panocha. *That was the dessert for Easter.*

TILA VILLA

My aunt would make it in that bowl. She would mix it and then let it set, and then she would heat the stove—"Not too hot," she'd say and open the oven door and put her hand in there, and she could tell if it was the right temperature— she never measured anything. The panocha *stayed a long time, and it would bake real slow.*

TERESITA
JARAMILLO AND
TILA VILLA

The flour came out of the mills so good, and the tortillas were muy sabrosas. *We didn't have commercial wheat then, only the flour from the wheat they planted here. And my aunt would make stacks of tortillas that high every day. She would say, "A carpenter leaves something for people to remember him by, like Primo Hermenegildo, but not me. I make so many tortillas and they're all gone. Nobody's going to know what I did."*

TILA VILLA

We had two hornos *there, in the front, where they'd bake apples or corn to make* chicos, *and* panocha *for Easter, and the bread. A lot of times, two or three ladies would get together, and they'd say, "OK, let's bake bread today." Everybody made their own dough at home and then my aunts would heat up the* hornos *and the women would come around. They'd put in the bread and put a board over the opening.*

Not everyone who lived on the plaza owned the land or the animals necessary to make farming worthwhile. Land within the plaza was insufficient to provide for even one family, and fortunate residents additionally owned large pieces of land just outside the plaza. A short walk on the *vereda* brought them to their fields. But some residents owned very little, if any, land, and they worked other people's land, for which they often were paid only with produce.

BENJAMÍN
ORTEGA

There were so many people there that didn't have very big pieces of land, so we were able to help them out with fruits and vegetables. There was welfare, but there were not many welfare recipients around the plaza. The poor would work —except for the people who were sick. But others would help the people who were sick. They might not help them with money or anything like that but with food, clothing, something like that. There were a lot of people who were really poor, but they weren't starving. It wasn't publicized that "Mrs. so-and-so over there doesn't have any shoes." No, it was quiet, and other people might not buy them a new pair of shoes, but they'd give them a good pair of shoes that they had. There wasn't very much money, but everybody got by, even those who didn't have any land to farm.

Besides an adequate land base, successful farming also required expensive equipment, and as agriculture became more mechanized, it was difficult for most plaza people to acquire the latest technology. Some people lacked even a horse to pull a plow. One woman recalled that times were so hard that one day a man living just south of the plaza hitched his wife to a plow to get the job done: "Ah, we had a fellow down here, not too long ago. He wanted to plow this field, and he couldn't find a horse, so he hitched the wife to the plow. No kidding, he did it! And she was pulling the plow like a horse. Really. His wife was strong, and she did it. And everybody wondered, 'What's wrong with him?' But he didn't have a horse, just a wife. If you can't find anything else, it's the wife." (Some people disagree sharply that this event ever happened. As my mother says, "They were hardworking people, but they weren't barbarians!")

TILA VILLA

Motorized farming equipment didn't begin to replace beasts of burden until the 1930s and '40s, but even then the cost was prohibitive for many people. Women were rarely called on to act as draft animals, but farming did occupy both men and women from planting to harvest, and women took charge on their own when men went away to work or to fight in the Second World War. This fostered a breed of tough, hardworking women farmers in Chimayó and the other northern New Mexico communities. They worked equally hard in the home: "Men never, never helped the wife with the children or in the kitchen or anywhere. That was her job. If she went out to work with him and it was suppertime and quitting time for work, he'd come into the house and sit down. She'd go into the kitchen, cook, everybody ate, she washed dishes, and then she slept like a log. And when the men went to cut wood, it was the women's job to get up and feed them at 3 A.M. There was no question about it—the women always had to cook for the men."

BENJAMÍN ORTEGA AND TILA VILLA

173

SPINNING AND CARDING WOOL, EARLY 1900S.

CIPRIANITA CRUZ BAKING BREAD IN AN HORNO, EARLY 1900S.

The Ortega women, as a sign of their relative wealth, never worked the fields. "The women from the farms down below, they knew how to work, but the women from the Plaza del Cerro—they were too refined to work in the fields," Mercedes Trujillo recalled. "When a girl married one of the Ortegas, it was like marrying a king," added Grandma. "They were better off than others." These women enjoyed the luxury of focusing on household tasks alone: washing clothes in the ditch, preserving produce for the winter, birthing and raising children, cooking three meals a day, and cleaning house. The farming women did this while also working in the gardens every day.

Chimayosos did not live on vegetables alone. Meat was an important part of their diets, and Chimayó people celebrated their fondness for fresh meat when they butchered their pigs and held *matanzas*. Neighboring communities in the mountains, where large areas of land in community ownership had been grazed for centuries, raised livestock extensively, but Chimayó was never a ranching town. No similar Spanish land grant for grazing lands existed for Santa Cruz Valley farmers, and few Chimayó residents kept large numbers of livestock. As a result, meat was highly valued and savored when it was available. The hides of the cattle also were put to use.

They didn't have too many of anything. They just had what they needed for the family. Maybe a cow or two, and maybe some had some horses. They didn't have many cows, but they always raised some chickens and pigs—at least not until my uncle Teófilo came back to live in Chimayó. Then he had maybe about six or eight cows and Ike and I used to take care of them in the summer, take them to the pasture, down below at Los Ranchos. There were animals roaming everywhere around Chimayó, but I don't know if they took their animals to the forests then.

When they butchered a cow, they cleaned the hide real good, and they made tewas, *you know, like shoes, but soft. My Tío Nicasio and Tío Rumaldo, they*

CHIMAYÓ
MAN CUTTING
WOOD, 1955.

AMADA
TRUJILLO

BENIGNA
O. CHÁVEZ

175

wore tewas *a lot of the time. They looked liked Indians! And one time I heard someone say, "Oh, that Nicasio, he goes around like a Tewa."*

Chickens and pigs, which required little land, were the most common domestic food animals in the plaza area. Very few people enjoyed the luxury of owning milking cows, which were considered especially valuable because they provided a ready source of protein. Families relied heavily on eggs instead for protein. In the plaza area around the turn of the century, only Victor Ortega owned a milk cow; he sold milk to other residents for five cents per quart. Goat milk was much more common, sold by Patricio Cruz, who grazed his herd of one hundred or so goats on the hills and milked them at night in his corrals south of the plaza. Most of the old plaza residents grew up on Cruz's goat milk and remember the sound of the bells on his goats as they came down from the hills in the evenings. Some cattle also grazed in the hills, although the majority of people recalled their cows were kept in corrals or fenced pastures. Animals were strictly banned from the interior of the Plaza del Cerro from its earliest founding. The Cañada Ancha, which embraces several hundred acres of relatively level land and several small springs, offered the only decent grazing around. Some Chimayosos ran a few head of cattle there, as did Cordoveños (people from Córdova) and farmers from Río Chiquito. But, lacking large pastures for their animals, Chimayosos who did raise stock usually grew their own hay to feed them.

DAVID ORTEGA

Tío Victor had a lot of land, but his kids went off to school and never helped him with it. He always was working with those big horses of his, and he had to haul all their hay. Those big meadows that Modesto has, those were his and he had others over here. My dad used to have them too, over here in La Puebla, about ten acres of meadow that I guess he got from El Güero Mestas. We would have two cuttings a year of hay, and we'd feed all that hay and the hay that we got up at Las Truchas—we probably used about twenty-thirty tons of hay every year for our horses and cattle.

There may have been a day when Chimayosos maintained large herds of sheep, but only small flocks were kept in this century. My mother tells me that Manuel Chávez, who came here from Bernalillo in the early 1800s, introduced sheep to Chimayó and pastured them in the *potreros* in Potrero. (It is perhaps more than coincidental that weaving enterprises seem to have started here soon after the arrival of Manuel and his sheep.) Some say that Chimayosos Peak, a large mountain in the Sangre de Cristos (12,800 feet) was named because Chimayó herders took their sheep there for summer pasture. Others grazed on *el alto*, a level clearing on a small mesa near the Cañada Ancha arroyo; this flock provided wool for the Trujillo family of weavers in Río Chiquito and Centinela.

The plaza people built their barns and corrals outside of the plaza, fashioning them of ponderosa pine logs hauled from the mountains. Roofs of sloping, corrugated metal replaced the leaky log roofs of the old barns soon after the turn of the century. Victor Ortega's barns sat on his property outside the south side of the plaza. Rumaldo's barns and corrals were also just outside the east plaza, where the Presbyterian Church now stands, but most residents raised their barns well away from the plaza and from irrigable land, near the foothills to the east. A few of the old barns still stand, though only one retains its roof, and this is leaning closer to collapse every day.

All the tillable land inside the plaza combined could not provide much produce, and even with their animals and their gardens and fields in Chimayó and at El Llano, the plaza people could not grow all the food they needed. Shortages of food were probably common in the 1800s, when there were few alternative sources of food if crops failed. No one remembers such hard times from this century, but the late Virginia Ortega—who at 104 was the oldest person I'd known in Chimayó—told me, "I remember sometimes when there was no wheat, not a thing to eat. Then the apples froze sometimes too, and that was bad." After the railroad arrived in Española, people could get food supplies in town. As the first decades of the century passed, such trips became more frequent.

Just once in a while, my father would take the wagon to Española for groceries.
I always wanted to go with him to Española, and finally one time he let me. It

BENIGNA
O. CHÁVEZ

177

was a very cold day, in the winter, and he tried to tell me that I would be cold, but I had to have my way. He bundled me all up in blankets and put me in the back of the wagon. We went for hours and hours it seemed, crossing the icy river and passing houses only once in a while. When we got to Española, I was so stiff, he had to carry me inside and hold me by the wood stove at the store. I couldn't even move!

At Bond and Nohl's store, he bought some coffee and sugar, and a candy for me. He would go around the store and fill a box with matches and things like that, then get a gallon of kerosene at the counter. For five dollars he would fill that box to the top, and get a lot of things besides—and it would last us a long time. Then we had to get back in that wagon and go back home. Sometimes we'd stop at my grandma's house in Sombrillo, there by the river, and we'd rest and warm up.

MELITA
ORTEGA

And I remember how much one could get with five dollars. When he went he used to bring one hundred pounds of sugar, fifty pounds of lard, canned milk by the case—he believed in bringing a lot at once. Father would also buy sugar, pota-toes, coffee. But many people didn't have horses and wagons, and they'd have to buy those things from someone else who went to Española and brought it back, like Tío Victor.

Growing enough food to sustain the population was an impossible challenge, and bartering chile *ristras* or *melones* in Santa Fe provided sufficient income for only the barest survival. Making sufficient income to buy those few needed items became increasingly difficult as the twentieth century progressed through its first few decades. Meanwhile, the list of things needed grew year by year. People sought supplemental sources of income, and, although jobs were plentiful in the first twenty years of the century, they were practically nonexistent when the depression hit. The scarcity of land spurred some of the plaza people to get into commercial weaving enterprises, which provided them with a ready source of cash that didn't depend on agriculture or on leaving the region to find work. Instead, they wisely began to tap the growing tourist market.

178

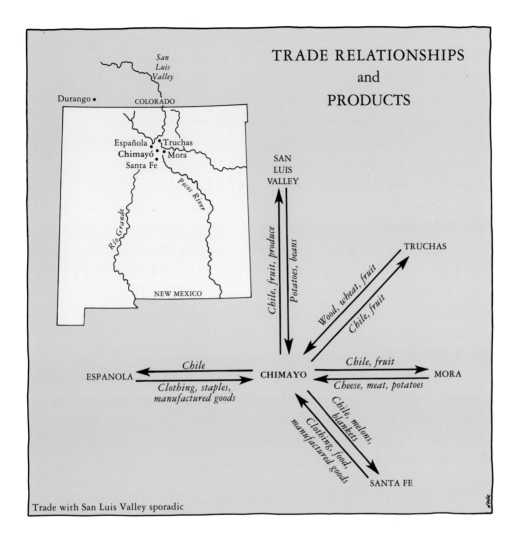

TRADE RELATIONSHIPS
and
PRODUCTS

Trade with San Luis Valley sporadic

As people's dependence on the land faded, so, too, the communal nature of the plaza began to slowly slip away.

The plaza was complete in the old days, there wasn't one building that was falling down, nothing that made it appear not so pleasing. There were no fences, and everybody stayed where they belonged, on their property—and of course if they did happen to step over the line, they didn't sue them. Now you're sued even if you look at somebody's land! People were more friendly and helpful back then,

AMADA
TRUJILLO

179

and not so much greed. I guess this is mostly greed that causes people to fence everything and all that.

BENIGNA
O. CHÁVEZ

Sí, no había cercos—*that's right, there were no fences. That I know for sure, and then there were* pisos públicos *(public rights-of-way), but later, some people were very* avarientos *(greedy people), and they put fences right into the* pisos— *and you know those weren't private pathways! Those were pathways for all the people to use to go through the plaza.*

The pathways and garden plots became pieces of private real estate even as people began to leave for the competitive world outside the plaza. It was a move that began decades earlier, when the first steam locomotive rolled into Española to the shouts of the waiting crowd. As they had begun doing in the late 1800s, men left Chimayó in search of work. Their experiences created stories of hardship and travail not soon to be forgotten in Chimayó—and left the farms and fields to become the province of neglect.

Chapter Eight:
Keeping the Faith

The Mes de María

The rosas de Castilla *and* los patitos,
Already blooming by the acequia
Nearly fill my basket;
Now we'll hurry to the hills for paintbrush
To set on the altar.

Every day the old women pray the rosary
In the oratorio,
Like the world would end if they stopped,
Looking as solemn as the Penitentes
Who sang in there last month.

But this time when the bell tolls
There will be no bloody whips.
We'll make the procession
Around the plaza,
Throwing bright petals on the ladies in black
While they pray for Mother Mary.

With the warm May sun shining
Even the Protestantes *come out to watch—*
Why are the women so somber,
Passing those beads endlessly through their hands?

BENJAMÍN
ORTEGA

Oh, my—back in those days, it was all by the book. They were all very religious people in Chimayó. The priest came there only once a year, during Lent to hear confession, but all the people would line up, with some praying while others confessed. And the children were so good! They sat there on the floor because there were no benches in the Santuario, you know—they sat there very quietly, and all the people were very reverent.

BENIGNA
O. CHÁVEZ

TILA VILLA

Mi padre Concepción—he had a cute habit that shows how religious he was. Whenever he saw my grandma getting ready to feed the family—let's say on Sunday—when the children got together and everybody was ready to eat, he'd disappear. "Well where's your papa Concepción?" "I don't know." "Well go look for your papa." And we went to the river, to the hills, everywhere. "Where is he?" You know where they would find him? In the corral, sitting on a chair, saying the rosary. That was mi padre Concepción, and that's how the old people were. Very religious.

The older people in Chimayó still share an ethic in which attention to matters of the spirit is as essential to survival as providing the basic necessities of food and shelter. All the stories from the old days and the documents that have survived the decades indicate that this tenacious religious faith was once even stronger. No personal letter began or ended without a formal declaration of faith. Villagers all over northern New Mexico lived close to a unique and mystical brand of Catholicism that emphasized the merit of suffering. Teresita Jaramillo summed it up well when she groaned, held her aching knee, and said, *"Tiene uno que sufrir para merecer; esa es lo que decían*—One has to suffer in order to earn grace. That's what they used to say." Although Catholics all over the world shared a similar doctrine, such a philosophy was especially well-suited to the harsh isolation of northern New Mexico. In the plaza early in this century, such conviction was manifested in all aspects of daily life.

Until 1900, everyone living in the plaza was Catholic, although there was no official church of any denomination in Chimayó. The nearest priest was at the parish seat in Santa Cruz, some eight miles and about two hours by wagon,

but religion played a central role in people's lives nonetheless. Plaza people maintained a small chapel, the *oratorio*, as a local place of devotion, and they took trips to Santa Cruz to baptize their young or to get married. It was also from that distant church that they summoned a priest when someone fell fatally ill and requested to receive the Last Rites. For their part, the priests at Santa Cruz endeavored to reach the area's outlying towns as often as possible, an effort hampered by the vastness of the parish. As a result, many a person in Chimayó went to his grave without a priest's blessing. Fray Alvarez of Santa Cruz had lamented this condition to his superiors in 1818. By the early 1900s things had changed little.

THE ORATORIO AND SOUTHWEST SIDE OF THE PLAZA, 1995.

183

AMADA
TRUJILLO

*Imperia's padrino (godfather) took her on a burro to baptize her in Santa Cruz.
The* madrina *(godmother) didn't go because it was a long ride. But back then, I
guess it was very urgent that they get the child baptized right away because he
went right off on his burro. Imperia used to say, "I think that my Padrino Pedro
heard something about the Imperio Romano [Roman Empire] in school or something, and so he named me Imperia. I was supposed to be named Domitila, but
he couldn't remember that by the time he got all the way to Santa Cruz, so somehow he came up with Imperia. Tell me of somebody else that's named Imperia!"*

BENIGNA
O. CHÁVEZ

*The priest didn't come when somebody died suddenly, and he didn't come when
your grandpa died. He was lying in the bed and he told me, "You better call the
priest," but I didn't have the chance to send anybody clear to Santa Cruz. And
I have that in my mind all the time, but God knows why I didn't have time. When
my mother died, it was the same way—it happened so suddenly and there was
no time to call a doctor or priest. She died of childbirth there at home, in the
back room.*

The remoteness of the plaza, and of villages throughout northern New
Mexico and southern Colorado, from the mainstream of the Catholic church
prompted people to tend to many of their religious needs themselves. The
scarcity of clergy became particularly acute in 1800, when the Franciscans were
expelled from New Mexico, leaving a void of priests. The Penitente Brotherhood
arose to fill the need, and small private chapels, or *capillas*, sprang up throughout the region to compensate for the lack of churches. Besides the plaza chapel,
there were four small community *capillas* in the Chimayó area: the Santuario and
the Capilla del Santo Niño in Potrero; the Capilla de Nuestra Señora del Carmen
in La Cuchilla; and the Capilla de Nuestra Señora de los Dolores, in Plaza Abajo.
(Several tiny chapels in the Chimayó area remained private and never became
community places.) Although the *oratorio* stayed outside the visitation circuit
of the parish priests, clergy did officiate at the other *capillas* on occasion.

The Catholic church took an immediate interest in the Santuario after its
founding, and the massive adobe chapel received the church's official blessing.

The custodian of the Santa Cruz parish paid for the wooden entrance doors, and a representative of the church from Durango, Mexico, visited there in 1818. Approval of its construction had been heartily endorsed by the parish priest of Santa Cruz, who cited the difficulty that people had in getting to mass in Santa Cruz. He urged church authorities to grant a license for mass to be given in the Santuario, which happened on special occasions before and after Bernardo's death, but the chapel remained in the ownership of the Abeyta family. Conflict over the revered shrine erupted in the late 1800s, when Bishop Lamy ordered the parish priest to seek ownership to the church from Bernardo's daughter. Lamy felt that the chapel should come under his control because it had become the site of religious celebrations sanctioned by the church. Grandma remembers Librada Ortega Chávez's version of this conflict, which dragged on for many years:

Mama Libradita—she was an Ortega, but she married one of the Chávezes, *Carmen Chávez's son, who owned the Santuario—she used to tell me how the* *people would come from all over to the Santuario. They came in wagons and* *stayed overnight there, sleeping in their covered wagons. They used to pay* *Mama Libradita to say rosaries for them. More and more people started to* *come, and miracles were happening. Then the* padres *saw that there was a* *bunch of money being made and they told the Chávezes, "You should sell that* capilla *to us." But the Chávezes didn't want to sell, and the* padre *got mad. He* *was a bad priest. And he told the people, "Don't go to that place—it's the house* *of the devil!" After that, they only said mass in the Santo Niño Chapel. I don't* *remember any masses in the Santuario until after I was grown up, in the 1920s.* *Then a gringa from Santa Fe bought the* capilla *and gave it to the church. She* *gave Patricio Chávez lots of money for it, and then she gave it to the church.*

BENIGNA
O. CHÁVEZ

It was the Spanish Colonial Arts Society in Santa Fe that had purchased the Santuario from the Chávez family in 1929, on the eve of a pending sale of the church's massive doors to a private party involved in marketing religious art. At the urging of Mary Austin, a cofounder of the society, the place was purchased and placed in the hands of the Catholic church so that its treasures would not be

185

REAR VIEW OF
THE SANTUARIO,
1934.

dispersed. Its preservation by the Spanish Colonial Arts Society and the prominence it received in the process also set the stage for the emergence of the
Santuario as a famous shrine.

The miraculous healing earth and its healing effect had been sought for
decades by visitors to the Santuario before the church acquired the building, but
the tales of wondrous healing and spiritual renewal multiplied as the number
of visitors increased with the purchase. Catholics and non-Catholics alike from
all over northern New Mexico traveled to the site. A common story attributed
to the Santuario by people of the plaza area, for whom the Santuario was less a
shrine than simply the local church, told of a supernatural occurrence involving
that most common apparition of the Hispanic world, *María Santísima*—Most
Holy Mary.

BENIGNA
O. CHÁVEZ

One time my mother's nephew Ramón, whose family lived in Santa Cruz—he was just a little boy, three or four years old—went to pick piñón, he and his mother and their family. Many people had gone there, somewhere towards Las Sierras de Pecos, and they were camping out. Very late one afternoon, they noticed that Ramón was nowhere around, so they all started looking for him. But they couldn't find him, and finally, after searching for a couple of days, they came home. And his mother was very sad—she thought he was dead out there in the mountains. They all thought for sure that a mountain lion had killed him. But then one day, I don't know how many days later, he came walking down along the river there to Potrero, all by himself. And he ended up at the Santuario with his shoes in his hands. How could he have known the way? He lived in Santa Cruz and didn't know these parts at all.

So, nobody knew who this little boy was, and they asked him, "Who is your father?" And he couldn't say it right but he said, "Quintana papa." "And your mother?" "Chelsa mama," he answered. "And how did you get here?" they asked. "A woman dressed in blue came and made me stairs and a pathway to follow," he said. And his father and mother in Santa Cruz—Demiterio and Celsa (mispronounced as "Chelsa" by the boy) Quintana—heard the story and the father rode on his horse to see, and there he found his lost son, in Potrero. And that was a miracle, you know. That was Mary who led him along the path. Ramón's mother made a vow that she would visit the Santuario every year to give thanks for the miracle, and she made her son promise to do it after she died.

Although such recountings make no explicit reference to the Santo Niño, they bear pieces of the legend of the Holy Child, who is said to roam the hills at night helping people and wearing his shoes out in the process. In fact, other renditions credit the Santo Niño for the miracle of this story.

The *oratorio* at the plaza drew its visitors from a much smaller sphere than did the Santuario and was the domain mostly of plaza Catholics. Like the Santuario, the *oratorio* originated as a private chapel in the early 1800s, although no records of a request for its building or licensing have been found. Apparently, the Catholic church never officially conferred its blessing on the *oratorio*. Much smaller in size, the *oratorio* originated as a small room in the home of Pedro Asencio Ortega, who dedicated the place to the patron saint of the plaza, San Buenaventura.

The humble *oratorio* was the nexus of the Plaza del Cerro's religious life for most of the nineteenth century and remained a focus for plaza Catholics until the 1950s, when its caretaker died and the place fell into disuse. While lacking the formal blessing of the church, it was nonetheless regarded as holy ground by plaza *vecinos*. Grandma and some other of the *viejitos* recall times early in this century when the community buried deceased young children beneath the mud floor, trusting the blessedness of the *capilla* to see the soul through to a better world in Heaven. Other people say that infants were buried inside the *oratorio* out of fear that graves would be robbed by marauding Indians.

AMADA
TRUJILLO

Bonefacia Ortega was the one in charge of the oratorio *as long as I can remember, but I know that José Ramón Ortega y Abeyta [a descendant of Pedro Asencio Ortega], my grandfather, used to take care of it before her. He was a Penitente. In fact he was one of the* hermanos mayores *(leading elders) for a long time. But when the mission teachers came, and he started attending the first church services—well, they didn't have a church then, they just gathered together wherever they could meet—then my grandfather was converted to the Protestant religion, and that's when he left and gave up the* oratorio. *He was already an older man.*

José Ramón Ortega y Abeyta was one of many pious Catholics who adopted Protestantism in the early 1900s. In his stead, Doña Bonefacia Ortega took charge of the *oratorio*. So tied to that holy place is the memory of Bonefacia that the name of one is seldom mentioned without the other. Some still refer to it as the *"oratorio de Doña Bone."* Numerous people from the plaza community assisted Bonefacia in the work of maintenance, but she took primary responsibility for the care of the place. Using the *oratorio* as her headquarters, Bonefacia led the local order of the Carmelite Sisters, a Catholic lay women's society whose special devotion is Our Lady of Mt. Carmel. The Carmelitas carried the banner of the society from the *oratorio* to the Santo Niño Church in Potrero on July 16, where mass was celebrated in honor of Nuestra Señora del Carmel. On good Friday, the Carmelitas carried the banner at the head of a procession to the arroyo, where the Penitentes would reenact the encounter of Jesus and Mary as he was being led to Calvary.

Independent of the Carmelitas, Bonefacia organized other important religious events that took place on the plaza. On July 14 each year, it was Bonefacia who orchestrated events for the feast day of the patron saint of the plaza, when the community recited the rosary in the *oratorio* and then took out the *bulto* (statue) of San Buenaventura to carry it in procession around the plaza. She was also the organizer of what was probably the most unifying social event in the plaza calendar—the *Mes de María* procession. In this solemn May ritual, a group recitation of Five Mysteries of the Rosary (each Mystery is a decade, or ten Hail Marys) was followed by a slow walk on the *pisos* of the plaza.[1] While a deeply reverent ceremony, the *Mes de María* lent an air of celebration, however subdued, to the coming of spring.

Bonefacia was a very good guide for the Mes de María. *She knew how to lead people and she used to know what to do, and what prayers to pray. And she had books, with songs to sing, with hymns. Very nice books, old books. And, oh, she kept the* oratorio *spotless—so clean! Every year, she painted it with* yeso, *and plastered the floor with* zoquete, *and washed the curtains. She kept it clean, and almost nobody went in there—just for the month of May.*

BENIGNA
O. CHÁVEZ

All the month of May we used to recite the rosary—all the month long. At night a rosary, and in the afternoon a novena. And somebody kept ringing the bell while we said the rosary. Genoveva, Anselmo's mother, and Prima Julianita, and Neria—they all used to help Tía Bone with the Mes de María. *I was small, about ten. I remember going up to the hills to pick Indian paintbrush and all the flowers that we would bring to the* oratorio. *We'd carry little bouquets in water glasses and then we'd march in before the rosary started and put them*

MELITA
ORTEGA AND
BENIGNA O.
CHÁVEZ

TILA VILLA

on the altar. That last day of May was the most fun time because all the girls would go along the ditch looking for rose petals and los patitos (sweet pea flowers) and wildflowers, and we'd get a basket and fill it with petals. Then we'd put on our best dresses and the first bell rang. We'd say, "Eeeh, allí viene la gente—there come the people! Look who's coming. What a crowd! And over there, look, there comes someone from La Cuchilla. And here we are!" It was a big deal. And then we'd go in the oratorio, and in front they'd have the resadoras, the ones that prayed the rosary, and we sat behind them, and then the rest of the people. My Aunt Eusebia was one of the resadoras in the coro—five or six ladies who sat in front in the oratorio with Bone, like the leaders. When everybody said, "Gloria al padre, gloria al hijo," we'd throw flower petals on the resadoras. And then after that they'd say, "Well, there's going to be a procession around the plaza."

DAVID ORTEGA

And everybody joined in, and the village chapel was filled to capacity. The atmosphere was so beautiful, everything was bursting out, the blossoms were out, the smell of the lilacs, irises—everything was so beautiful. At this time I think that many of the boys would go try and make their contact with the young girls, because they were a little more accessible than usual. The chapel was so very nicely kept all the time, and the bell would ring and the community would gather. It's just a beautiful impression in my memory.

TILA VILLA
AND MELITA
ORTEGA

We didn't take the santos of San Buenaventura and Santiago out on that day, but we took the Carmelita's banner out of the oratorio for the procession. The banner carriers went in the front, along with a cross, and then came the resadoras, and then the girls with the flowers, like me. And we'd start towards Petronila's house, and Ita knew very well where the first stop, second stop, third stop was. Every time that they would stop, Ita would turn around towards the people. I think one of the stops was in front of Tío Victor's. And they'd say, "Gloria al padre, gloria al hijo". . . and we would take the petals and throw them on the resadoras, and some petals would fall on the ground and leave a little pile there where they had stopped to pray. They'd pray there at Tío Victor's

THE SANTUARIO,
1917.

and then in front of Don Reyes Naranjo's and in front of Doña Maclovia's house,
and then Tío Red's, and the last misterio *was in the* oratorio. *We ended just*
right inside the oratorio for the last misterio. *They always finished the Five*
Mysteries arriving at the door of the oratorio, *where they had started. In fact, it*
seemed that the plaza was measured to say the rosary. I think the people back
then planned the plaza for saying the rosary like that! Then they went inside
and finished. It was very beautiful. And they would clean the oratorio *and close*
it until the following May.

The plaza people's ears were closely tuned to the peal of the bell on the oratorio,
for it announced the schedule of Mes de María *and many other important events*
for decades. Some elders actually recall when it was first installed in the plaza,
around 1910: "All the people pitched in with money to buy the bell, but my Tío

BENIGNA
O. CHÁVEZ

191

BENIGNA
O. CHÁVEZ

Rumaldo—he was the one who was in charge of getting it. He went around to the houses collecting money to buy it. I don't know where he bought it, but I remember him going around collecting. I was very little then—it must have been just after the turn of the century.

The *oratorio* bell also heralded the arrival of the Penitentes at the plaza when they came on their annual visit during Holy Week. The evening or night before Good Friday, they stopped at the *oratorio* to sing and pray before going on to their *morada* (meetinghouse) west of the plaza in Los Ranchos.

TILA VILLA

The Penitentes—they'd come to the oratorio *for Easter. They would visit the moradas, in Truchas, Córdova, and then the* morada *down in Los Ranchos. And there was a lot of them. For some reason I remember that they would come to the* oratorio *at twelve o'clock at night and they would be chanting there at all hours. All of them carried lanterns, and we would be asleep and hear them, and my aunt would say "Don't be scared, it's just the Penitentes that are coming to the* oratorio.*" And we'd sit out there and watch them come by here. And they would go in the* oratorio *and they would chant a lot.*

MELITA
ORTEGA

I used to be afraid of the Penitentes when they passed by our house on their way from Córdova in the late afternoon. But they came by the house there, and some of the Penitentes just had their "long distance" [long underwear] on. They didn't have any clothes—just their long distance and camisetas *[undershirts], you know. Some of them were bare from the waist up. And then they had these whips that some of them whipped on their backs. But what scared me most was that they used to put on black masks—like a black cloth tied in back of the head, with the eyes cut out, so people wouldn't recognize them. Seeing the blood running down their backs also scared me 'cause some of them hit themselves pretty hard. They came by singing or praying—singing mostly. We'd peep out the window or go out to the road to watch, but we'd see them come down the road and run inside. They prayed at the* oratorio *and then they'd go down to the* morada. *They stayed up all night I guess.*

The community of the plaza joined the Penitentes for their reenactment of *Las Tres Caídas* (the Three Falls of Christ) in the morning and then the *Estaciones* (Stations of the Cross) in the afternoon of Good Friday—rituals that continue to this day in Chimayó.

MELITA
ORTEGA AND
TILA VILLA

They'd have their crosses set up and they'd go from one place to the other, kneeling at each station. All the plaza people went to the arroyo for Las Tres Caídas. *The Penitentes came with the Christ, and they had the ladies, the Cofradías de Nuestro Padre Jesus (auxiliaries to the Penitentes), and they came from La Cuchilla. The old ladies brought the Virgin Mary, and they would meet the Penitentes with the Christ there in the arroyo and they would read from the bible, and sing very sad alabados. The two met—Christ and Mary—and he had his face covered and she was dressed in black. After the ceremony, they would open up the* morada *and people would go and adore Christ. And then everybody would go home and eat their* chile *and* torta de huevo *and beans, and* calabacitas *and* panocha, *and bread. That was Good Friday.*

The Brotherhood enjoyed strong support and wide membership in Chimayó, and members of the cult from the various *placitas* commonly visited such important local *capillas* as the plaza's *oratorio*. Chimayó was at the center of the Brotherhood's founding, and Bernardo Abeyta, the visionary from Potrero who was the inspiration behind the building of the Santuario, was an early leader in the order. In fact, some of the legends about the origins of the Santuario say that Bernardo was practicing his Penitente devotions when he discovered the crucifix that prompted him to build the shrine.

Bernardo Abeyta had close links with the Plaza del Cerro as well as the Santuario. His daughter, María Francisca, married Pedro Asencio Ortega, whose private shrine to San Buenaventura became the *oratorio*. Pedro commissioned the famed *santero* José Rafael Aragón, who had worked on the *reredos* (altar screens) at the Santuario, to paint the *reredo* in the *oratorio*. Not surprisingly, the inside of the *oratorio* bears a modest resemblance to the mysterious interior of the Santuario.

Except for the flurries of activity during the spring and in midsummer, the *oratorio* was usually quiet, but the little bell on the *oratorio*, ever the harbinger of news, sounded when someone in the community passed away.

TILA VILLA

Any time of the year other than May, if the bell tolled, everybody would go to the oratorio to find out who had passed away. "Se murió alguien—Somebody died. Let's go see who! Well, so-and-so died." "Ahh, Primo so-and-so died?" And you'd stop what you were doing and go to see. We were very nosy, you know. As children, we liked to go and touch the feet of the body, because back then, the body was laid in state right in the home. Now it's different. They take him away and you don't go see him until he's ready. Then they had the services in your house and the whole bit, with the kitchen going on and everybody sitting around eating. Just imagine—a lot of commotion. They would put a table and then sand, and then a sheet, and then the body. The sand was to keep them cool. Sometimes, they'd tie a ribbon to keep the mouth closed.

You'd go in the house and you see the corpse there and the first thing you do is kneel down and say your prayers, and when you get up, you touch his feet and then go sit down. And in those days, people really cried. And then the Penitentes would come if he was from the Brotherhood, and they'd do their rituals and singing. The next morning everybody would go to the funeral mass at the Santuario or the Santo Niño in Potrero.

BENIGNA
O. CHÁVEZ

Yes, when someone died, they would ring the oratorio bell. We didn't have telephones or anything, and we used to say, "Who died, who died!" Just by hearing the way the bell rang, we knew someone had died. All the people came out, everyone, when we heard that bell. Because we didn't have a mortuary or anything, we took care of the dead in the house where he died, where he lived. And then we used to sing. There was the dead body on the table, and there were the people singing. Outside, you could hear the men making the coffin. They covered the coffin with black cloth or gray and put crosses on the side, and inside they put a lot of very special kind of material. Very pretty, pleated on top. Very neat. They knew how to do everything. They made it wider at the top and then a little bit narrower. The family of the dead person, they would take care of the body. Some women were very good at that. They washed them real good and they shaved them, like when my father died, cousin Melquiades shaved him and then sang the alabados. *Then they put the body in a coffin the next day and took it to be buried. The priest would come and say the mass then.*

One time, we had a neighbor here, and he said that when he died he didn't want to be buried in a coffin. So they laid him on a ladder in a wagon and took him to the graveyard like that. Just like always when somebody died, we watched when they were starting to church and we joined in the procession, following the wagon up the camino *and across the river. Everybody walked, the men first and the ladies following, and we went to Potrero and the funeral and they just put him in the grave.*

TILA VILLA

The somber Easter rituals and the *Mes de María* procession primarily involved plaza residents only, and they were usually small and subdued, in keeping with the small, conservative nature of the plaza community. Their dark moods reflected the deep medieval roots of the local Catholicism, as well as the peculiarities that emerged in the isolation of northern New Mexico. However, there were many other religious gatherings in Chimayó, holidays that drew more people and had a more lighthearted air of revelry. Plaza people, like all Chimayosos, hungered for social contact, and they attended fiestas and dances from Truchas to Santa Clara Pueblo whenever they had the chance. The biggest celebration for the town of Chimayó came each July 25, *El Día del Santiago*—a celebration in honor of Saint James, the patron saint of Chimayó.

All the holidays had to do with the church—weddings, baptisms, the fiestas for the saints—those were all the celebrations that people had. But the Día del Santiago—*that was the biggest fiesta in Chimayó. People came all the way from Española in buggies for Santiago Day. They came in a big line, all those buggies. Everyone had fun, and it wasn't like now, when everybody is too lazy to come*

BENIGNA
O. CHÁVEZ

195

out. They didn't sit around—they decorated the horses and everything. Sure, it was work to get all that ready, but many times even Don Diego and Doña Serefina—they were good friends of my father—came here for the dance. All the way from Española, they came in their buggy. The people were very happy. It didn't seem like work to them.

And for that day, we prepared a feast that was really special! We baked bizcochitos, *cakes, bread, and* capirotada *(bread pudding) to eat during the day. We feasted on green chile because we had a new crop by then, and they killed some goats for meat. My Tío Longino always came from Cundiyó to sell goats and always someone would buy one and they'd tie it to a post and kill it. Then they made* burriñates—*they made those with the intestines of the goat, fried in lard. They used the milk intestines only, washing them well first. Those* burriñates *were so good!* Buenos, buenos. *And if they killed a pig, they'd save the blood and they'd cook it real good with onion and oregano, mint and fried fat, and pimientos. And ahh, those* morcillas *were so good, it wouldn't hurt you, I tell you.*

TILA VILLA

With the goat meat, they'd make a big pot of soup, and we'd eat it all because so many people came. And they took the bulto *(carved statue) of Santiago out on a horse, because you know Santiago always rides on a horse, and they'd ride through the fields with Santiago, so he could bless the crops. Many people rode along, with one person holding Santiago in his arms.*

BENIGNA
O. CHÁVEZ

And then, they had the corrida del gallo *(rooster race)—that was what the men loved. Over there by the arroyo, they'd tie a rooster to the ground and someone would come by on a horse and pick it up, and then it was a contest to see who could get that rooster away from the rider. They'd ride around and around, very fast, racing up the arroyo. It killed the rooster, but those boys loved it!*

MELITA
ORTEGA

In later years, the priests started coming to say mass for Día del Santiago, *but when I was little, there was no mass. Sometimes, they'd bring the* caballitos *(merry-go-round) for Santiago Day and set it up here, just outside the plaza.*

And the little boys and girls were so happy, riding those little horses. There was music playing, and all night long they'd play here.

We had dances on Día del Santiago, *too, wherever the person in charge of the fiesta decided to have them. One time, they built dance floors over there by Don Nicolás's* tazoleras *(hay barns) and they made a tent roof with the* camisas de carros *(canvas tops from covered wagons). Other times, they just put up a dance floor over here by Tío Nicasio's house, and they always set up stands where they sold lots of orange soda, and ice cream cones—Don Nicolás always had the ice cream stand. He also used to make a drink called* alegría, *from a wild plant. Everyone had to eat ice cream, because it was always such a hot day! Don Nicolás made the ice cream right there, and sometimes it came out too salty, but everyone bought it anyway because they just wanted to go buy something. Poor things—they liked to buy ice cream so much, and they could only get it one time a year, for* Día del Santiago.

BENIGNA
O. CHAVEZ

The next day after Día del Santiago, *it was Santa Ana Day in Truchas and sometimes we would go in the wagon. In those days the road to Truchas was a dirt road with long hills—very bad shape. Everything was fine until we'd get to this one little hill. The horses didn't want to pull the wagon and Primo José Inez would get mad and start whipping the horses. One of the horses wanted to go and the other one didn't. And finally he'd tell us, "I think you're all too heavy —get down." And we'd get down from the wagon and the horses would take the wagon up the hill and we'd walk up the hill. But coming down, he would tell us "Stay in the wagon because we're going downhill. And hang on—the horses might run away with me." A lot of people from Chimayó went up there. It was the same program as in Chimayó: mass, and then I guess they had ice cream for sale, and sodas. Then a dance at Primo Manuel Martínez's dance hall.*

TILA VILLA

And then we'd go to other feast days too, like we went to the pueblos to watch the Indian dances. We usually went with Tía Virginia and Tío Nicasio. And while there, Tío Nicasio would buy a watermelon and my aunts would get bread and chorizo and we'd go to the river and eat there. Very good tasting. Nice and cool under the trees after watching the Indians dancing. Everybody from all over the plaza would go. And then Santa Clara [Pueblo] Day. Then we'd go with Tío Melquiades. Same thing. Because he had a lot of melons by then and he would take melons in a wagon and us, all his kids. And he would sell the melons to the people.

On the day of mi Señora del Carmen—*that was who the capilla in* Cuchilla *was dedicated to*—*the ladies from La Cuchilla, and men also, and kids, would come in procession from La Cuchilla to the* oratorio, *and in the* oratorio *they would meet with people from the plaza. And from here we would all walk to Río Chiquito, and the men would go on to the* presa *to bless the Cañada Ancha* acequia. *The women would stay at Tía Genara's in Río Chiquito, and she would serve cookies and sodas to everybody. Then when the men came back, we would come in procession back to Chimayó. And leading the procession was a little boy with a drum: Dumdadarumdumdumdumdum. . . . Whenever we heard that coming, we go out there and join the procession back to the plaza. That was in the summertime too.*

Plaza residents were also drawn to events in the nearby *placitas*. In the wintertime, the monotony of long nights and cold days was broken by celebrations in La Cuchilla that featured dances by the Matachines. This dance, which originated in Spain, was introduced in Mexico by early Hispanics and later modified to include aspects of Aztec rituals and to dramatize the clash of Hispanic and Mexican cultures.[2] The dance is traditionally performed on August 10, but for some reason it was shifted to Christmastime in Chimayó.

BENIGNA
O. CHÁVEZ

We used to also go to see the Matachines dance. They danced there in La Cuchilla on Christmas. Oh, they were big doings. Besides the dances, they had sort of like entertainment there. They had a special man dressed as a clown, dressed different, and he used to tease the children and the pretty women and say a lot of jokes.

APOLONIO
MEDINA
AND ELENA
QUINTANA
MEDINA,
MUSICIANS,
EARLY 1900S.

WEDDING
PORTRAIT,
EARLY 1900S.

First, they had mass and then Matachines danced in the churchyard. They danced so pretty! With ribbons all hanging and a cap with ribbons, too. People came from all around here. And the Matachines were from here too, but they knew how to dance—almost like the Indians, to a violin and guitar. They used to play the guitar a lot in those times, not only for the Matachines but for all the dances. Almost everybody knew how to play the guitar. For wedding dances, and they sang verses to the bride and the groom, telling them with very nice verses how beautiful they looked and all that. All about the bride, that she was dressed like a queen, and, oh, they sure sang nice about the bride. The Matachines usually danced in La Cuchilla, but one time they danced in the Plaza Abajo, by the Nuestra Señora de los Dolores Church.

Chimayosos also held social dances that, by all descriptions, usually were very controlled, formal affairs. Alcohol was prohibited and a master of ceremonies, the *bastonero*, carefully monitored behavior. The music was often provided by local musicians, who played traditional favorites on violins and guitar. The young people loved the social atmosphere of the dances and sometimes walked miles to attend. As far as anyone remembers, there were no dances in the plaza. Besides the fact that no room in the plaza would hold a crowd, such rambunctious affairs were probably contrary to the quiet sensibilities of plaza folk.

BENIGNA
O. CHÁVEZ

Most of the time, the dances were in Primo Manuel Vigil's dance hall in Potrero. We used to have to walk there, and everyone had to carry their own chair. I remember one time when we went with my father, and we had to cross the river, you know, to get to Potrero. There was no bridge then, and the water was very high, and my father took the chairs and put them in the water and we crossed from one to the other. Then he came across and picked up the chairs behind him. Another time, father carried my chair and Primo Nicolás took two chairs.

MELITA
ORTEGA

At the dance, the men used to stand. Just the ladies sat on one side, and the girls on the other. And the boys would say, "¿Venga a bailar? Quiere bailar?" And we would stand up right away.

For most of three hundred years, life in Chimayó had been defined by the Catholic calendar. But in 1900, the Catholic dominance of plaza religious activities came to an end. The first Presbyterian missionaries, Juan and Juanita Quintana, began to spread the word of Protestantism in Chimayó in 1898, and in 1900 a Presbyterian mission school was established in a single room on the Plaza del Cerro.

The first mission teacher was Miss Prudence Clark of Eden Prairie, Minnesota. "La Miss Clark," as she became known in Chimayó, did not choose Chimayó; in a sense, Chimayó chose her. Although she had applied to the Woman's Board of Home Missions to teach specifically at a mission school in New Mexico, it was by chance that the board, meeting in St. Louis, received a joint petition from people in Chimayó and Córdova (then called Quemado) requesting a school that same year. The long-isolated Catholics of the area had been inspired to write the petition by the evangelist Juan Quintana. Chimayó was chosen as the better location for a mission.[3]

No bureaucratic inertia slowed the process of getting Prudence Clark out to her assigned post. The petition, the application from Miss Clark, and the opening of the first classroom all took place in 1900. Miss Clark held class in a room across the plaza from her residence, a single room that belonged to Doroteo and Carmelita Cruz. When class started in September, only five students showed up, but by the end of the school year forty-seven crowded into the tiny room. The space barely fit the students and left no room for the teacher's chair.[4]

Prudence Clark came to Chimayó ignorant of Spanish at a time when no one locally used English. It is doubtful that she realized what she was getting into when she and her ailing sister, Jane, left Eden Prairie on the train. A Minnesota newspaper announced their departure, reporting that Chimayó had a "delightful climate" and that the vegetation was "decidedly tropical." The report went on to declare that the Misses Clark would have a "comfortably furnished cottage with few luxuries besides the necessary piano."[5] Compared to Minneapolis, Chimayó's weather is indeed balmy, but if Prudence Clark entertained illusions of the tropical paradise and cozy cottage touted in the newspaper, those visions were certainly dashed when she was delivered to the plaza. There, the sisters moved in to a small, mud-plastered room heated only by wood, with no running water or electricity. The roof leaked and the most outstanding thing about the vegetation around the plaza was its scarcity.

Prudence Clark cut a classic figure, the archetype of the turn-of-the-century schoolmarm, and she set about her task with astounding dedication. She taught young and old, tended to the sick, cared for her tuberculosis-stricken sister, oversaw the development of a church and schoolhouse, and with her hard work won over most of the Chimayó community. She sang songs at the "necessary piano," in English, of course. To the great fortune of posterity, she also carried a camera, and with an eye that only an outsider could bring, she documented many aspects of life in and around the plaza. *"Mi comadre la* Miss Clark" is still remembered fondly today, fifty-six years after her death.

The students of the new Presbyterian school were not long cramped in their quarters on the plaza. In 1901, the Presbyterians built a new school just outside the plaza. The students marched to the new, two-room schoolhouse singing "America" and "Praise God from Whom All Blessings Flow."[6] Clark promptly moved herself and her sister into the new-fashioned building and took up residence in a curtained-off portion of a schoolroom, glad to escape the leaky adobe

on the plaza. The schoolhouse—dedicated to John Hyson, the father of a mission teacher in Ranchos de Taos—featured a bell donated by a woman in Minneapolis. This bell created some competition for the one on the *oratorio*. The tolling of the mission carillon did more than call children to their classroom. Like the *oratorio* bell, it sang out its peals for more momentous occasions, including funerals and weddings, and it rang in 1910 when Halley's Comet lit up the sky over Chimayó and terrified the local residents.

The whole plaza came out to see that comet. It was a star with a tail—a big star with a big tail. The tail started out sort of narrow and then it got a little bit wider. It was there in the west, of the same color as the stars, like the sun or the moon. But one night, the tail was very big. Very late, like about midnight, the tail got huge, and it was almost touching the earth, and Miss Ellsworth [the mission teacher] rang the bell to get everyone up, to alert everyone to what was happening. And the people came out to see what was happening because it was strange for the bell to be ringing at those hours. The comet looked like it was going to burn up the earth. Everything to the west was lit up red, very red, like

PRUDENCE
CLARK ON A
BURRO IN FRONT
OF THE JOHN
HYSON SCHOOL-
HOUSE, CA. 1910.

a fire, and Miss Ellsworth thought it was going to burn the fields, but it didn't. It went away and by morning it wasn't so big and in a few days we didn't see it anymore. But you know, it was a sign that something was going to happen— and then the world war started a few years later, in 1917. So, it was a sign!

The tones of the new bell drove home for the Catholics of the plaza the fact that theirs was no longer the only creed in town. It must have been a discordant and bitter reminder for some, like Bonefacia Ortega, who grumbled that the *Protestantes* were *herejes* (heretics). The Presbyterians brought with them a radical new viewpoint on religion and life, going so far as to encourage people to read the bible—a practice that the Catholics had never allowed. Suggestions that there might be an alternative to Catholicism and the worldview it espoused caused quite a stir in the plaza, striking deep into the marrow of the restrained, traditional community. Those who chose to convert in the first few decades of this century did not have an easy time.

MELITA
ORTEGA

The first one to bring a bible to the plaza was Agapito Ortega—and he didn't dare let his bible be seen. He carried it in a sack of grain so no one would notice. At first, he and the other new Presbyterians really suffered persecutions. Like I remember when Primo Sabino joined the church. One day—it happened to be on a Sunday—I was at Tía Bone's after Doña Maclovia walked over to her house, and Doña Maclovia said, "Sabes qué? Que el Sabino se hizo Protestante —You know what? Sabino became a Protestant!" And Tía Bone had a fit! She had a fit! "Pero, qué tiene ese Sabino, tonto!—What's wrong with that Sabino, so foolish!" And she started saying all kinds of things.

And another time, Tío Teófilo was passing the plaza on his way to Sunday school. The men would sit in the solana *by the wall on Sunday mornings to visit, and they mocked him when he passed. "Allí va Teófilo con su Biblia?—Oh, so there goes Teófilo with his bible?" They didn't throw rocks at him but they did at others. But I don't blame the people. I blame the priests, who used to tell people all sorts of things about the Protestants. I heard that they even had a bonfire and made them burn the bibles that the missionaries gave them—right here in Chimayó, in La Cuchilla, or down below in Santa Cruz. The priests told the people that they didn't understand the bible anyway, and the poor people did what the priests told them.*

The furtive Presbyterians held their first communion services in secret in the John Hyson school. The year was 1902 and four people attended: Prudence and Jenny Clark, Juan Quintana, and an anonymous townsperson.[7] Evangelical services continued in the schoolhouse, and within a year church officials arrived to consider whether to found a church in Chimayó. Besides the two visiting church administrators, only the Misses Clark, Juan and Juanita Quintana and their son, Elías, and plaza resident Victoriano Cruz were in attendance, but in spite of the meager turnout the decision was made to build a church in Chimayó. The Presbyterians purchased land for the church from Rumaldo Ortega—who, ironically, was a devout Catholic and respected Penitente—in 1922, but it wasn't until 1933 that the church was completed. Meanwhile, the growing Presbyterian congregation continued to meet in the schoolhouse.[8]

The religious division in the community wrought by the Presbyterians divided families and created enmity for years to come. No longer was the *Mes de María* procession an event for the whole community. Some of the Carmelitas tried to keep the *herejes* away.

One time I was trying to watch the Carmelitas and the procession and Doña Bone said, "Go away, we don't want any Protestants!" But there was a cousin of mine there, and she was a Carmelita, and she said, "Oh, let her stay."

AMADA TRUJILLO

My mother was expelled from the Carmelitas because when she sent her kids to the mission school. But you know, the missionaries knew a lot about nursing, and they were nice to the people, so naturally the people grew to like them. And people used to go to the missionaries when they got sick, or the teachers used to come to their houses, and people liked them and found out that they weren't so bad.

JOHN TRUJILLO

MELITA ORTEGA

The open attitude of the Presbyterian missionaries and their evangelical Christianity attracted many Chimayosos, but it was the schooling that they offered that won many more over. Those who were concerned about their children's future in the rapidly changing world outside of Chimayó saw that education was a key to success, and they leapt at the chance to send their kids to the mission school. They recognized that the Presbyterians represented many aspects of the Protestant American society that was growing to dominate even the more remote Hispanic villages. Many people embraced the new faith in the same way that they embraced the emerging political and economic order.

Father liked to go to the mission, he liked the teachers and got along with them. He even read the bible a lot. His sister, Tía Bone, didn't like it when we joined the church. She was really mad for some time. She didn't come over to the house or anything. But father told her that he didn't care, so why should she?

MELITA ORTEGA

My parents, they put me in the mission school and I came to stay at the plaza at my Tía Bone's house. But then the priests started saying, "Take your children out

TERESITA JARAMILLO

CHILDREN
PRAYING IN THE
JOHN HYSON
SCHOOL, EARLY
1900S.

PEARL ENGLISH
AND PRUDENCE
CLARK, CA.
1906.

BENIGNA
O. CHÁVEZ

of the Protestant school and put them in the public school, or we'll excommunicate you." And it scared my father and mother, and they put me in the public school.

We liked those mission teachers because those teachers that they hired there at the public school, they were not good at all. They didn't teach us anything. We lost our time there, and it was all because the priests said that the parents that sent their children to the Presbyterian school—they were going to Hell. And many people believed the priests. They just obeyed them because they told them they were going to put them out of the church. But after a while, some people got wise, and they began putting their children in the Presbyterian school, and we learned a lot there, but not in the public schools. Later the teachers at the public school were better.

DAVID ORTEGA

Some families stuck to their guns and never sent their children to the mission school. "My father, he was one of them. Of all my four brothers and sisters, we never attended the Presbyterian school. Father was a very hard-set man in his ways, of conviction. He was a very hardworking man, and managed to give us a private school education, all of us."

206

PRUDENCE
CLARK WITH
HER FIRST
STUDENTS, AT
THE SCHOOL-
ROOM ON THE
PLAZA, 1901.

The mission teachers and preachers were the first dedicated emissaries from the outside world to come to Chimayó. They carried their culture with them, including medicines, healthcare, food-preparation techniques, and better standards of sanitation. The effects of this missionizing effort have been deep and long-lasting, changing much more than habits and life-style. The plaza people remember each mission teacher well.

Miss Clark was my first mission teacher. She was the first Anglo missionary to come here. The Quintanas came before, but they were just lay preachers. La Miss Clark didn't know a single word of Spanish when she came. It was difficult for her and the others who came. They really had to learn Spanish. Pearl English

AMADA
TRUJILLO

207

came after her. There wasn't one person here who knew English. Miss Clark married my uncle Teófilo Ortega, and he became a lay preacher later, and they left Chimayó to preach. But they came back to Chimayó.

Prudence grew quickly to love life in Chimayó, as attested to by some of the letters she wrote from her new home. Her teaching style, developed during her tenure as a teacher in Minnesota, was based on discipline and consistency. The first to come to her for schooling varied in age from six to middle-aged. A particularly striking student from her first class, Teófilo Ortega, courted and wed her several years after his graduation. It may not have been an accident that she was standing near Teófilo in the picture of the first class, taken outside the tiny adobe room on the plaza where class met. They lived together in Chimayó until Prudence's death in 1939, traveling together to missionize in Truchas, the Jémez Mountains, and elsewhere before settling in Chimayó. They are buried side by side in the Presbyterian cemetery east of the plaza.

Prudence and Teófilo started something of a tradition among the mission teachers who came to Chimayó. The next mission teacher after Miss Clark, Pearl English (whom people called "La Miss Pell"), came to Chimayó in 1906 and later married Chimayó resident Anastacio J. Trujillo. Later teachers also got hitched to local men: Ruth Renick married Louis Sandoval and Evelyn Frey ("La Miss Fry") married Atilano Ortiz. The teachers already were well accepted because of the education, healthcare, and religion that they brought to Chimayó, but their marriages served further to integrate the missionaries into the community.

It seems that the missionaries were extremely fond of their fold in Chimayó, but not all shared a glowing assessment of the local population. One missionary wrote: "Here [in Chimayó] live some families who are descendants of the famous old Spanish Señors, but who have married and intermarried until the cultures and mental powers of their ancestors have been lost, and, at the foot of these wonderful mountains, we often find unspeakable squalor and ignorance."[9] Perhaps some of the missionaries married into the community to save what they perceived to be a dwindling gene pool.

If it hadn't been for the mission school, we wouldn't know a thing. We had desks and slates, but we didn't have any paper like now. We used to spit on our slates to clean them—but we were happy drawing on those slates. And we had imagination, I'm telling you. We were not so dumb, we were bright, naturally bright. We knew how to draw.

BENIGNA
O. CHÁVEZ

Everyone was happy when the mission school came. Even some married men went to learn English—some that were older than Miss Clark. They were bigger than she was, with their hats on and so forth. They wanted to learn English. Primo Severo was one of those, and Prima Teresita, Prima Alfonsa, and mi Prima Neria learned English from her.

MELITA
ORTEGA

People used to walk a long way in those days, just to come to school. That's how badly they wanted to learn. Primo Ramón Quintana, our first cousin, he came all the way from La Puebla to board here with my father and mother so he could go to school here [at the mission]. Oh, he was in love with Miss Clark and it's a wonder that he didn't marry her. But Tío [Teófilo] was Miss Clark's pupil. And then he married her. And I remember that José Bond Martínez and his sister Esther—they used to walk from down there where Leopoldo's is now. About three or four miles each way, they'd walk every day.

HAROLD
MARTÍNEZ

La Miss Clark, she was good at helping people with their ills. She knew quite a bit about medicine. They didn't have doctors around here until I don't know when. There were one or two doctors in Española, but people hardly ever went to them, they just took care of themselves the best they could, with the médicos and herbs and all that. One woman that lived in Rincón was kind of a médica. And midwives, there was one living here in the plaza.

AMADA
TRUJILLO

The day my mother died, even the midwives and the mission teachers couldn't help. That was a sad day. I remember Father hitching the horses to the buggy to go for the midwife, Doña Juanita Durán from Rincón. That was the first time that she had attended my mother because all the times before, Doña Ramona

MELITA
ORTEGA
AND BENIGNA
O. CHÁVEZ

PRUDENCE
CLARK PLAY-
ING WITH
CHILDREN IN
THE PLAZA,
CA. 1901.

BOYS PLAYING
MARBLES IN
THE PLAZA,
CA. 1901.

(who everybody called 'Mana Mona) that used to live here in the plaza—she was the one that used to go. But 'Mana Mona wasn't here then, so they had to go for Juanita Durán.

I went to the kitchen and I was sitting there on a chair right there by the stove, just waiting for someone to tell me what was going on. They used to put a rope on the vigas like a swing, so that the mothers would hold onto that to lift them-selves up, so they could push. The mother sort of kneeled down. I could hear Mother groaning and hanging on to that rope, from way over there in the kitchen. My sister was there, walking back and forth in the kitchen. And then Father came out of the bedroom, looking real pale and troubled, and he just told us he was going to take Doña Juanita back home in the wagon. They had a mass for Mama at the Santuario a few days later. I remember because they baptized Mama's baby the same day that they had her mass, in the Santuario.

The Presbyterian mission teachers couldn't work miracles, and in fact the new preachers decried the mysticism of Catholicism as practiced in Chimayó, with its attendant belief in supernatural powers. One mission teacher wrote: "These poor people have been warped spiritually by a religion that has . . . deteriorated into idolatry. . . . Countless people are seen bowing to a . . . doll which, at Easter time, is paraded through the plaza. . . ."[10] They also disdained the numerous celebrations that took place in association with Catholic holidays, and they especially frowned upon the dances, where young men and women shamelessly embraced each other in public—even though all dances were carefully chaperoned and couples didn't dare to talk to each other while dancing.

The Protestants then didn't believe in dances. Couples were only allowed to visit one another in their houses, with the parents there. We had our social time in the John Hyson school. We had what they called "a social." We'd play games and they'd serve refreshments, and that was it. Sometimes, we used to meet somewhere secretly, but the Protestants were definitely against dancing.

AMADA
TRUJILLO

Many of the Catholics in the community were also banned from attending dances, not out of fear of moral degeneration but for safety. Festive gatherings, whether associated with religious holidays or not, were all too often a focus for violence. Although the plaza community was relatively free of violent disturbances, the larger community was far from tranquil. Altercations were common, and Chimayó suffered from a reputation as a violent town, although plaza residents insist the violence rarely erupted in their neighborhood.

Oooh, there were more bad people then than now! Yes, Chimayó was the worst place, it had the fame of the matadores *(killers). Really, really, "los matadores Chimayosos—the killer Chimayosos," they used to say in Santa Cruz, "nothing but killers up there." They would even kill a person for the water rights. Mostly from Plaza Abajo. But there weren't any killings here, by the people up here around the plaza. No it was* allá abajo—*down below. And the violence ran in families. There's a place down there that they used to call the "pueblo de los leones." The lion's den.*

BENIGNA
O. CHÁVEZ

AMADA
TRUJILLO

It's no wonder that devout Catholics and Presbyterians alike learned to avoid the dances and that the plaza people declined to host dances in their community. The admonitions of Bone and the Presbyterian teachers and preachers had a positive effect. The strong sense of community in the plaza, where people treated each other as family, no doubt lessened the chances for violence. But perhaps the plaza community's close adherence to religious tradition also cultivated an outlook that discouraged such outbreaks. Events like the *Mes de María* or the annual visitation of the Penitentes served as a reminder that matters of the spirit had more than passing value. They had sustained the plaza through times of great violence before. The addition of the Presbyterian's religious tenets, while they did create some discord, only strengthened the moral certitude of the community. Religion and life remained closely intertwined, and the ringing of the bells, whether on the *oratorio* or at the Presbyterian church, meant something profound that all the *vecinos* of the plaza could understand. The Presbyterians succeeded in converting nearly a quarter of the people in the plaza area, and two branches of the Christian faith remain strong in Chimayó today.

Chapter Nine:
Para Ganar Dinero

Riding the Chile Line Home

The conductor calls out "Embudo Station—
Next stop Ess-pan-nola!"
And I know Papa will be waiting with the wagon,
Pacing the platform in his overalls
Smelling of wool and chile.

The sunny hills by the muddy río
Warm me from that Durango chill,
Where the smoky sky stains our clothes
Hanging frozen outside the clapboard shack—
That's not a home!

Long ago Papa taught me to weave
On the old loom there in the dispensa *beside*
boxes of wool,
And I can show you too,
And we won't have to ride this old train anymore
Para ganar dinero.

The economic boom initiated by the Denver and Rio Grande Railroad in 1880 picked up steam after the turn of the twentieth century. Rail transportation fostered continued growth of agriculture and resource-extraction industries and linked the northern New Mexico Territory more closely with the United States. Presented with the opportunity for cash income, Chimayó and other villages of northern New Mexico prospered as never before. Men who did not want to become entrapped in the *partido* system of sheep raising—a kind of share-cropping arrangement that was practically the only source of wages before the railroad arrived—could now find wage labor outside of the area in farming, mining, and ranching. Employment opportunities became available to just about any man who wanted to work, and just about all young men seized the opportunity.

TERESITA
JARAMILLO

Everyone went to work outside of Chimayó. The men worked in many different places—Durango, Silverton, lots of places. Ledey-ville [Leadville]. Wherever they could find it. I lived in Durango for a year and ten months while my husband worked in "la smelda" [ore smelter]. That was very hard work, and he didn't even earn much, really. He didn't get anything worthwhile. Eee! He came home from work all covered with black from the smelter. And like the other men, he got sick from working there—they said their stomachs would ache and the smoke hurt their lungs. He would push little carts filled with ore, and then they'd put it on a burro. He and Don Clemente—they used to compete to see who could finish loading the cart first, and they were killing themselves working so hard. My husband worked there in la smelda *for eight years. Eee, eight years!*

Prosperity did not come without hardship. Although seasonal excursions for work often turned into adventures that families recount fondly, most of the accounts describe hard and sometimes dangerous jobs in strange, faraway lands. In most families, the men left each fall after harvesting and worked through the long winter months before returning home in the spring. Some took their wives and families with them, but most went alone and sent back cash. As many as ten thousand villagers from the upper and middle Río Grande valleys migrated annually for jobs outside the region. [1]

214

Most people from here, they used to go work out of here, like in the mines in Colorado, Utah, and Arizona. My father worked in Globe, Arizona, in the mines, and in Bingham, Utah. They used to go to Colorado by jumping trains. Once he was in Colorado, this guy jumped, and he missed the train and he was killed. They'd ride on top or underneath the flatcars. Or on top of a load of lumber—however they could get on.

CAMILO
TRUJILLO

There was no Social Security in those days, no nothing, and my Tía Epimenia was left alone and without support when her husband died. And my husband Severo, he was only nine years old when his father Pedro died—on the thirteenth of October, it was. So, then they were struggling to survive, and he went to work. First, mi tatita *gave him a burro, and Epimenia tried to teach him and his brother how to bring wood from the hills for sale. But they couldn't get the wood loaded right and it fell off again and again and it was a lot of work anyway, so they decided there must be a better way to make a living.*

TERESITA
JARAMILLO

One day this man came from Chama [about seventy miles northwest of Chimayó] to see Mama. He was the boss of a ranch owned by some gringos up there. It was a big place and they needed lots of peones, *see? "How are you making a living?" He asked Mama. "Well, I work for Don Victor sometimes." "Well, I think it would be good if you sent your son to work to earn some money," he said. "How about if I take him with me?" And at that time, Severo was only twelve years old! His family had a lot of land here in Chimayó, but it was very bad land, and they couldn't live with just that. So off he went to Chama with this boss man.*

And up there, he had to plant beets and cabbage and potatoes and everything, there in Chama. And he really had to work, you know! After a while, Pula and some others from Chimayó told Severo, "We're going to get out of here, and you'll have to stay here alone with the manager, and he's a cruel boss. So, you better come with us. Don't be afraid—it will be better if you come with us, because if you don't, you'll have to work twice as hard." And that was true. That

215

boss was very hard on the boys, and he only paid them five pesos for a month. So Severo and the other boys came on horses from Chama, but they wouldn't let Severo ride on the horse, so he had to walk. They left from Chama, and when they came to Embudo, they left Severo to come by himself. Then one day here in Chimayó, someone was watching the arroyo and here comes a person falling down and getting up, falling down and getting up—and it was Severo! His feet were all beat up and bleeding and he didn't have any shoes, and some-one went out to help him. He walked all that way from Embudo and found his way home. "Ahh, thank goodness that you came back!" his mother said. That was his first experience going away for work, and all he had to show was five pesos. They paid him twenty-five centavos per day—no, sixteen centavos!

Severo's hardship was worse than most Chimayosos faced when they left in search of wages, but many endured personal tribulations. The Plaza del Cerro community as a whole nonetheless benefited greatly from the exodus. An average of 250 to 300 men worked away from Chimayó for at least half of each year and were paid an average monthly wage of $35 to $50.[2] The influx of cash helped create something of a golden era for many Chimayó residents in the first few decades of the century. The period 1900 to about 1930 is the time people speak of with pride and fondness when all the plaza houses were inhabited and main-tained, the garden space in the middle was carefully tended, and Victor Ortega's general store carried on a brisk business, relying on the railroad to deliver goods from the eastern U.S. Pitched roofs made with imported, corrugated steel announced the relative wealth of those who could add them to their houses, and a few auto-mobiles appeared on Chimayó's dusty roads. Were it not for the cash flowing into the plaza from employment away, it is doubtful that the old people would remember the plaza as fondly as they do.

The regional economic expansion created some jobs in New Mexico, such as the mines in Terrero and Raton, but these opportunities were limited and most New Mexicans had to leave the state to find work. Chimayosos went as far as Wyoming and Utah to work on sheep ranches. Others traveled to work in the western mines. A favorite destination for employment was Durango, Colorado. Durango was popular for Chimayosos partly because of the influence of Juan

Chávez, a powerful Chimayó *patrón* whose mother, Libradita Ortega, was a daughter of José Ramón Ortega y Vigil. Juan owned a boardinghouse and store (the Santa Fe Grocery) across from the train station in Durango and personally aided newly arrived laborers from Chimayó in finding work. The newcomers were happy to see someone from back home, and Juan provided them loans and kept their paychecks until they were ready to return to Chimayó. Like his Tío Victor back in Chimayó, Juan mediated between the Chimayosos and the Anglo business community, into which he was closely integrated, and augmented his personal wealth considerably in the process. There developed in Durango a small and variable community of *compadres* from Chimayó. Most returned to Chimayó each year and moved home permanently when they could afford to, but some remained and made Colorado their new home.

A letter from Nicasio Ortega to his parents on the plaza conveys a sense of his search for work while revealing much about the manner of relating that was probably typical of the day. The letter is dated "Abril 25 de 1896" from Silverton, Colorado:

Señor Don Jose Ramon Ortega y Señora Doña María Petrita Mestas de Ortega, my very dear parents, it will make me very happy if when these poorly written letters find themselves in your hands, they find you in the good company of my brothers and sisters. My health has been good, thanks to the All Powerful. I find myself here with my companions . . . and we are without work, but we have hopes to start work the 27th on a tailings pile [bordo] that they're working here. The salary they're paying is $2 per day. I also should mention that we worked for a few days at some other tailings, but we left because we didn't like the wages. At the same time we heard that there was a lot of work here [in Silverton], and we found out that it was true, and also they're going to open the first of May, so we find that we can find work, and not just for now. And answer my letter as soon as possible so I'll know how you are.[3]

The mass departure for employment ensnared most of Chimayó's young men, but some from the plaza found new ways to bring in cash without leaving the valley. Victor Ortega set up his mercantile store on the plaza in 1907. Ledgers

217

REYES ORTEGA
AT HIS LOOM
WITH GRAND-
SON ROBERT
CHÁVEZ, 1940.

from Don Victor's business indicate that everyone in the plaza community relied on him for small purchases of both staple and "emergency" items that didn't justify a trip all the way to Española. Salt, coffee, and sugar topped the list of items sold, but Victor also dispensed potatoes, tobacco, crackers, bacon, eggs, lard, corn flakes, rice, and sundry items such as oil (kerosene), matches, candles, socks, twine, candy, Doan's pills, and miscellaneous small hardware items. Running tabs were kept of the debts people owed him, and occasionally an account was marked "no more credit."[4]

Ortega's store was typical of many that opened in the early decades of the century—a total of eleven in the Chimayó area by 1935.[5] "They had everything in those stores—all that the people wanted. But they didn't have pizzas." "What I remember best is the candy. He had penny bars, nickel bars, and those Jolly Jacks—those were my favorite."

MERCEDES
TRUJILLO

CAMILO
TRUJILLO

Reyes Ortega never left Chimayó but instead continued farming and began selling his weavings on the side. After his stint working in Silverton and Durango in the late 1800s, Nicasio Ortega followed suit, and early in the 1900s the brothers established weaving shops just outside the plaza and became deeply involved in developing the local weaving industry. Gradually, a family tradition was transformed into a viable economic enterprise. Although there were many weaving retailers in Chimayó (at least six by 1935), the plaza area soon became the most active center for marketing local weavings.

Correspondence and ledgers from Reyes Ortega's business indicate that by the 1930s, he was selling blankets to private individuals and retailers all over the country. However, his first outlet, and for a long time his primary one, was with Sito Candelario in Santa Fe.

BENIGNA
O. CHÁVEZ

My father [Reyes] started to sell his weavings to Sito Candelario when I was very little, right after the turn of the century. He got interested in that, and he would get orders from Sito and then take the blankets to him in Santa Fe. Sito gave him the wool, and he wove it into blankets. Pretty soon, he asked other people here to weave for him, so he could keep up with the orders. I went one time in the wagon to Santa Fe to deliver some blankets for him. And he sold to other people, too, whoever made an order. Whenever he or Nicasio got a big order, they would get together and put all their weavers together to make the order. They helped each other out with the business.

DAVID ORTEGA

I don't know how the other people started, but my father [Nicasio] got his first contract from some people in California who wanted to buy a certain amount of production—more than he could produce. So what he did, he just started hiring weavers, or contracting weavers—some of his own family—and then he started setting them up with looms and wool and all that. And in order to secure his money he arranged to make the shipments through the bank in Española. I guess the buyers would deposit the money in the bank, and he would supply the order right away. He didn't want to risk it. And that's how he got started, and then pretty soon the demand took off. In those years the Santa Fe Railroad was one of the best outlets. It used to have all the different stops where they had Indian stores. And the Chimayó weaving was very desirable.

It was going on in Santa Fe too, because of this guy Sito Candelario, who almost everybody would work for—everybody, except for my father, my father never worked for Sito, because he was himself independent. Sito Candelario would do what we're doing today, and he would be the distributor, the retailer. And then came in Julius Gans in Santa Fe, about 1915—he set up shop and kept going the same way as we're doing today, selling blankets, and my father just kept doing his own size and capacity. And others came along, but there was nobody who knew the business like Sito Candelario. In order to dispose of what we produced in those days, we had to wholesale, we had to ship the product to people for resale.

The weaving business didn't grow by chance or luck nor did people come and "discover" the weavers in Chimayó. People such as Sito Candelario, Julius Gans, and, before them, Jake Gold kept a steady correspondence going with retailers involved with railroad tourist trade and retail outlets in distant cities. Letters poured in to Candelario's curio shop in Santa Fe requesting particular colors and designs and rejecting others. Candelario worked directly with the weavers in Chimayó, endeavoring to develop styles of woven goods that would sell to his clientele, which included curio dealers across the Southwest and throughout the country. The Fred Harvey Company—a pioneering retail operation with outlets along the Santa Fe Railroad—also purchased many blankets for resale and no doubt had a role in shaping styles after 1900. These merchants were indispensable to most Chimayó weavers, whose isolation and lack of capital and retail experience prevented their successful entry into the market.[6] In the early decades of the century, tourists had to come by horseback or wagon if they wanted to purchase a Chimayó weaving direct from the weaver.

With deliberate guidance from the merchants, weavers here and elsewhere in New Mexico changed their style and adapted to new materials readily. This change had begun in the late 1800s with dealers such as Jake Gold. The emphasis shifted from utility in the Hispanic home to portability for the tourist. The *conga*, a kind of small *sarape*, was taken up and transformed into a small weaving type marketed as furniture scarves and pillow tops. Gold may also have introduced cotton warps to weavers long accustomed to woolen warps. By the early 1900s, most had switched from hand-spun and hand-dyed materials to commercial wool.[7]

The Fred Harvey Company was the first to use "Chimayó" to describe its New Mexican weavings, and the term was appropriated to deliberately confuse buyers by suggesting that Chimayó weavings were produced by Indian artisans. To confuse matters even more, the Chimayó weavings sometimes were marketed as products of Pueblos Indians, and promotional literature, as well as some scholarly work, was replete with references to "Chimayó Indians" or "Chimayó Indian blankets." At the same time, Chimayó weavings were sometimes labeled as the products of Mexicans or "Native Mexican Chimayos."

The northern New Mexico weavings labeled as "Chimayó" competed with Navajo weavings for tourist dollars, and soon each became specialized for different markets. The Hispanic product was lighter in weight and proved more suitable for use as a seat cover or a blanket while the Navajos continued to produce heavy woolen rugs. Because Hispanic crafts were not as highly regarded by the tourists, they usually brought a lower price than comparably sized Navajo weavings. Whereas a 4 x 5–foot Navajo rug sold for as much as $25 in 1905, a slightly larger (42" x 80") Hispanic weaving brought the retailer only $10.

Responding to demands from a diverse clientele, the designs on Chimayó weavings in the first two decades of the twentieth century included thunderbirds (an image from Great Lakes Indian groups), Oriental swastikas, various logos and initials, and bow-and-arrow designs similar to those being produced by Navajo weavers. The weavers produced whatever the client ordered. On blankets not specifically ordered, designs on Chimayó weavings remained relatively simple and similar to those from earlier eras. Although many weavings were marketed as "Chimayó" weavings, a distinctive design style from Chimayó had yet to emerge.

In the midst of accelerating economic growth, New Mexico finally was granted statehood in 1912. Eastern politicians had been loath to admit this poor state with its predominant Hispanic population into the union, but sixty years of effort finally came to fruition, as did the long-standing ties between plaza Republicans and the capitol in Santa Fe. Victor Ortega traveled to Santa Fe as a delegate to the constitutional convention and helped draft that first charter for the new state.

World War I added a new dimension to the changes taking place. The same train that had carried so many men away for work carried young soldiers away to serve in the war. In 1917 and 1918, eight thousand soldiers and their equipment moved out of northern New Mexico on the Denver and Rio Grande Western Railroad—the famous "Chile Line"—which ran between Santa Fe and Antonito, Colorado, with connections on to other lines.[8] Remarkably, no soldier from the plaza area died in World War I. "In the first war, I was very young, a very pretty young girl, seventeen years old. And when they started to take boys from here, we were really worried, especially those that had sweethearts going.

We sang one song over and over then, 'Over there, Over there . . .' while they were gone. But then, they all came back—they didn't kill a single man from here. And when they came back, they had a big party for them, with parades, and they played the guitar and violin everything, and made speeches. I was teaching school in La Cuchilla, and I took all my students there to the celebration, and one of the veterans—his name was Canuto—he gave a talk about what it was like. They talked a lot and sang songs about the war." After the war, the great epidemic of influenza swept through New Mexico, claiming thousands of lives. The plaza community, already blessed once, considered itself blessed again, for no one in town died from the dread illness.

Experiences in eastern cities and in Europe exposed many Chimayosos to a world that they had not previously known or imagined, and returning soldiers possessed new material expectations and ideas about the life-styles they wanted. The rewards of the highly materialistic, industrializing outside world primed them with desires for higher-wage employment and for comfortable living situations near the conveniences of cities.

The economic impact of the First World War was generally positive for northern New Mexico. Following the war, the weaving industry in New Mexico began to expand, fueled in part by the newfound American fascination with southwestern arts and crafts and with the still-rural conditions in New Mexico. Because of Americans' increased leisure time, tourism, which had been slowly developing during the previous decades, became a major component of the New Mexico economy. Numerous weaving enterprises sprang up in Chimayó, most of them continuing to focus on wholesale arrangements with distributors in Santa Fe. Men began to turn to weaving as they grew disillusioned or ran out of work elsewhere. Severo Jaramillo's story describes a typical pattern for families that knew weaving as a family craft.

When he was fifteen years old, my husband went to work in Durango. I think my Tío Severiano helped him—he helped him a lot. Sabes como? And he was there for seven years, and then he came back here to plant here again, and to weave, in 1919. And then we spent the money fast to fix the house and to buy seeds to

TERESITA
JARAMILLO

223

*sow, and then came the fall. He said, "We aren't making money or nothing. We
aren't getting anything." And he went back to Durango in November 1919, and
he was there until March. And he came back in the spring to plant. We planted
only to eat—we had no place to sell produce. And then he said he was going to
Ledeyville, because* la smelda *shut down. He went to Leadville for four months,
and when he came back I said, "Ooh, it's better if we start to weave. Weaving you
can make money and you can be in your house." And he went to look for wool
and got it from Sito Candelario. And then we didn't go looking for work anymore.*

In the years before and after the war, major forces came into play that
strongly influenced the indigenous arts of New Mexico. A group of idealistic
easterners, many of whom were artists and writers, relocated to New Mexico
in search of refuge from urban life and in pursuit of what they believed was
America's true vernacular. In 1915 the Taos Society of Artists was formed, in 1917
the Museum of Fine Arts opened in Santa Fe, and, most important to Chimayó
arts, in 1925 the Spanish Colonial Arts Society was established to promote Hispanic arts and crafts. The society led a backlash against the commercial wares
that they felt devalued the traditional forms, and it attempted to revitalize the
earlier, hand-spun weavings. Leaders in the group found the commercialized
Chimayó weavings to be degenerate, inferior products. They worked with retailers
to stimulate tourism in a new direction, emphasizing production of "traditional"
products, which, although entailing more labor and generating less profit, greatly
increased the value of the Chimayó weavers' wares.[9]

About the same time that the Spanish Colonial Arts Society began promoting
traditional Hispanic weaving, automobile travel reached Chimayó. First as part
of organized tours and later in their own automobiles, tourists began visiting
Chimayó in numbers, coming to see "Mexican settlers" and to "watch the weaving of colorful blankets on 100-year-old foot looms."[10] The rough dirt road to
Chimayó continued on to the mountain villages of Truchas and Trampas, where
weavers were brought into the loop that tourism stimulated. In Chimayó, a handful of weavers opened retail outlets to meet the increased trade. Severo Jaramillo,
Nicasio Ortega, and Reyes Ortega continued to operate their weaving businesses,

and they were joined by Ursulo Ortiz, a nonweaver who sold weavings at his gas station/grocery store, and E. D. Trujillo. Using the new roads and automobiles, some of these entrepreneurs traveled to distant curio shops and other retail outlets to market their weavings. New woven products, including Chimayó jackets and purses (originally conceived by Santa Fe businessman Julius Gans), became part of the arsenal for enticing the new wave of tourists.[11] In spite of the efforts of the Spanish Colonial Arts Society, items designed for tourist tastes continued to proliferate.

The first car in Chimayó—that belonged to Eusebio Martínez. I was about seventeen years old, maybe a little younger. My Tía Bone, she paid ten cents for a ride, she was so excited. Everyone came to see the car, and it amazed them because it didn't have any horses. My father bought his car a little later, about 1923, and it was just after Nicasio bought his. Pretty soon, lots of cars were coming to Chimayó, and my father started selling blankets right there in the sala. He had the blankets piled high.

BENIGNA
O. CHÁVEZ

It was also in the 1920s that a distinctive design system appeared on Chimayó weavings. Some credit Antonio Mier, a Mexican who moved to Santa Fe in the first decade of the twentieth century, with inspiring this dramatically different style. A highly skilled weaver, he may have taken on apprentices from Chimayó, who in turn took the design ideas back to their families. The design that emerged from his influence blended traditional Saltillo, Río Grande, and commercial "Chimayó" elements into a distinctive style of Hispanic weaving, although it represented a local expression of a regional trend in blanket design.[12] This blanket style was recognized as something particular to northern New Mexico, and especially Chimayó, and it became a popular local product.

In addition to stimulating tourism, changes following World War I also significantly expanded markets for agricultural products produced in the Santa Cruz Valley. Farmers with large landholdings in the lower valley were particularly encouraged to bring more acreage into production. To meet the increased demand for water, they formed the Santa Cruz Irrigation District in the 1920s with the purpose of building a dam on the Santa Cruz River above Chimayó. Residents of the Plaza del Cerro, however, were suspicious of the motivations of the dam builders and opposed the idea. Seventy-five Chimayó residents, led by Victor Ortega, were on hand to object to the formation of the district and because of their protest were not served by the impounded waters.[13]

Work on the dam didn't begin until 1926, and it wasn't completed until 1931, although the dedication took place on a chilly February day in 1929. Besides John Bloch and others who had pushed for construction of the dam, dignitaries such as New Mexico Governor Dillon, state and federal legislators (including the newly elected Bronson Cutting, a liberal Republican who owned the *Santa Fe New Mexican*), the state land commissioner, and many others drove up the rough dirt road to attend the ceremonies. In all, some two thousand people showed up, and the U.S. Indian School band played music. After ceremonially breaking a bottle of water against the dam and joking about the much-talked-about "one quart"—a cryptic reference to the failing policies of Prohibition—the governor and other speakers voiced their high hopes for the dam. In reporting the event, the *New Mexican* briefly mentioned rumors that the cost of the dam might "prove a hardship to a number of native farmers in that region," but lost in the under-statement was the fact that the project already had bankrupted three contractors.[14]

Its organizers heralded the dam as a boon for the valley, but it soon became little more than a weight for landowners who were strapped for funds. The advent of the Great Depression in 1929 left many of them totally unable to pay the tax they had agreed to, and they faced the necessity of giving up the land that had been in their families for generations. Critics of the dam pointed out that the corporations set up to take over lands where taxes were in default were owned by the same people who had initiated the dam project, cynically suggesting that a land-grabbing conspiracy was afoot.

In the end, irrigated acreage did not expand to the level predicted, and growers never realized the visions of a robust agricultural industry in the valley based on "that great delicacy, chile, used as a relish with meat all over the world."[15] It was a pivotal moment of failure for the Santa Cruz Valley, for it rep-

WEAVER IN
THE GANS
STORE IN
SANTA FE,
CA. 1920S.

resented the last effort to create a viable farming enterprise in the area. While
critics pointed fingers at those who lobbied for the dam, the agricultural failure
was really owed more to the depression, a national catastrophe that left countless
local ventures in ruin. Bound to the vagaries of the market economy, the short-
lived prosperity of New Mexico's northern villages ended with the crash. Those
who in the past explored opportunities for seasonal work away from home could
do nothing but remain in the villages and struggle to grow some food on the
strained land base while seeking federal relief funds. In the Plaza del Cerro,
Victor Ortega's store stayed full of men, who sat and talked politics while listening to the news on the radio.

By 1934, only twenty men from Chimayó could find employment as laborers, at an average monthly wage of $9.60. Health workers visiting the area
claimed that malnutrition among Chimayó children ran rampant and that health

conditions were poor. They compared the economic well-being of families in the area to that of tenant families in the rural South. After a considerable lag time, federal relief funds flowed into the region. In the late 1930s, one hundred and fifteen heads of families in Chimayó received FERA work relief, and twenty-eight received direct aid.[16]

The highest concentration of relief cases was in the poorest agricultural land in the area, along the badlands on the north side of the valley. The New Deal programs that eventually came to the villagers' aid were tailored specifically for the northern New Mexico region, which eastern social ideologues saw as the perfect testing ground for creating a utopian, rural society freed from the failed capitalism of the East. In the small Hispanic and Indian villages, where a sense of community was still strong and where people still lived close to the land, the newcomers saw a living model of the communistic, agrarian society they longed for. To encourage this vision, New Deal programs channeled in the Hispanic villages focused on agriculture and on arts-and-crafts revivals rather than on new kinds of industry. The programs aimed to help the villages regain a measure of economic independence while restoring the degraded fertility of the land. At the same time, surplus foodstuffs were also delivered to villages, including Chimayó. There was a special emphasis on weaving and woodcarving. Schools were established to train Hispanics to weave "traditional"-style products.[17] The weavers of Chimayó, who were already well established in their trade, didn't rely on relief funds to build their businesses or on training programs to teach them how to weave, but their markets expanded because of the new attention given to their craft.

Some people were able to find work in the highly coveted Works Progress Administration projects in the area.

CAMILO
TRUJILLO

My father used to work for the CCC [Civilian Conservation Corps] and for the WPA. He was a blasting man. He worked on the road to Hyde Park [above Santa Fe]. And then another WPA project was in Española, there where the Big Rock is, there was nothing but swamps. They dug a big trench there, to get rid of those swamps. And they used to say that the people in the WPA didn't

228

work—they just leaned on their shovels. They weren't in any hurry. And one time a guy died on the job, and no one noticed until the end of the day, when he just stayed there leaning on his shovel.

The statistics paint a grim picture of the depression years in Chimayó, but the people of the plaza do not recall it as an especially hopeless time. Few here received relief, and most people remember that things changed little with the advent of the depression. They remember neighbors helping each other out with food and they say that life went on much as it always had, although cash was very scarce. Food, derived in large measure from local gardens, was adequate. "There was no malnutrition among the children here! They were all hearty and healthy. There was not a single case of rickets or other diseases that come from malnutrition."

STELLA
CHÁVEZ
USNER

We didn't feel the depression, but there were a few families that did. So what we did was to help the ones that didn't have anything. Whenever somebody would die, we would take a big pan filled with jars of fruit, corn, peas to the house. So we helped those that didn't have. There weren't many people around here who needed help, maybe someplace else they did. But usually everyone was fine here in the plaza.

TILA VILLA

I remember a story about a man that had a big family, and he didn't have a job, and for some reason he couldn't work on the farm or do anything. So what he did was, at night he would go to the neighbor's and help himself to the corn or whatever, and the people would get up and go to the farm and notice that they were missing chiles or whatever. One day the neighbor decided he was going to find out who was taking his corn. Eventually, he followed fallen ears to the house of the man who was stealing the corn, but he never mentioned anything to the man or his family. Finally, the man passed away, and after his funeral his wife carried out his wish that she thank the people there for the produce her husband had taken. But no one got mad or anything. That's a lot of patience—but people did have patience in those days, and love and care. They were always helping others.

229

Researchers who visited Chimayó during the depression, while noting the grim statistics for the region in general, did not fail to notice the relative well-being of the Plaza del Cerro, which they identified as the heart of Chimayó. "The people of Chimayó are shrewd and hardworking . . . and their thrift and industry are proverbial in the region. . . . [They are] the Spanish American go-getters. Very proud are they of the fact that the Chimayosos never loaf, and of the fact that the products of this pleasant valley have been justly famous among the natives of New Mexico since the reconquest (1692), and among the natives of Colorado and Arizona since before the coming of the railroad."[18]

Chimayó's interest in national politics came to a peak during the depression when people became acutely aware that national politics affected their lives directly. No longer could they claim, as Alejandro Read had boasted to José Ramón Ortega in the 1890s, that national politics were of little importance. The Republican dominance of politics in northern New Mexico came to an end with the trend nationally, but the tenacious Ortegas never let go of the old guard. They and other plaza people would huddle around radios to monitor the progress of the presidential elections, counting the votes carefully.

CAMILO
TRUJILLO

One time, I think it was 1936 when Roosevelt and Landon were running against each other—they were listening to the radio because they didn't have TVs but they had radios, you know, and the Ortegas always had radios. They were there listening and they heard that Roosevelt was two million votes ahead of Landon. And then Bonefacia Ortega pops up and she says, "Oh, pero todavía no cuentan los votos de La Cuchilla!—Oh, but they haven't counted the votes from La Cuchilla yet!" She thought Landon was going to catch up.

During the depression, Victor lost his contract for the post office, and it was moved down the road outside the plaza. This may have indicated a loss of power for Victor or a general decline in his business. Meanwhile, the weaving industry faltered but didn't fail. The shops were able to employ numerous Chimayosos, albeit at very low wages. At the outset of the depression, the leading Hispanic blanket dealers signed an agreement to fix prices in an effort to avoid attempts to undersell each other.[19] They realized that a price war would be costly to all their businesses. The dealers also asked Victor Ortega to intervene on their behalf when the governor proposed a weaving program for inmates at the penitentiary. Victor wrote to his friend Thomas Catron to pressure the governor. They limped along, supplying blankets to the wholesalers and retailers in Santa Fe, who in turn advertised to maintain growth in the tourist industry in New Mexico. These outlets continued to embellish stereotypes of a rural paradise in New Mexico with postcards and brochures that touted the artistic skills of Indians and the novelty of their wares. A steady flow of tourists coming to Chimayó continued to provide the weavers with small retail opportunities.

Weaving gave many families an alternative source of income during the depression. Unfortunately, the pay was extremely low for all but those who owned businesses. The nature of a craft based on a nonindustrial mode of production made it almost impossible to make a living wage, for mechanized textile factories could always outprice the hand weavers of Chimayó for textiles. Furthermore, the tourist industry promoted the concept of cheap, native crafts rather than expensive fine art. Critics of the New Deal social programs of the era point out that the emphasis on craft production hampered the villagers' ability to develop more practical skills and industries. In short, they charge, the wholesale promotion of the "quaint villages" of New Mexico and their traditional products trapped them in their preindustrial state and left many people in a condition of poverty—where many remain today.

In any case, as the weaving industry developed most weavers in Chimayó practiced their craft on the side as they struggled to find other employment with more substantial financial possibilities. In many families, the women took up weaving—traditionally a male task—while the men sought work away. The Ortega brothers, Severo Jaramillo, and E. D. Trujillo, among others, made a decent living by marketing the work of many weavers, although their fortunes waxed and waned in relation to fickle demand. These successful families worked to sustain a market for weavings, yet they often became targets of resentment. Like Victor Ortega and other entrepreneurs had done before, the weaving vendors managed to find a way to participate in the new economic order when most others struggled on the margins that the new order created. Such differences in material well-being became especially evident during the depression.

As the aggressive new economic order of American-style capitalism closed its grip on northern New Mexico, it impinged on traditional culture in the Chimayó Valley in many ways. Older Chimayosos comment that the change from a farming to a labor economy did much to diminish the sense of community. No longer did people gather to help each other tie chiles or husk corn. *Para ganar dinero* —to earn money—men were taken out of the family and community for a big part of each year, and women were forced to take on even more work than they had performed in the traditional farming family.

In the early 1900s, Chimayó had been primarily a farming community, and, with few exceptions, everyone was on relatively equal economic ground. Although some people enjoyed a greater land wealth than others, even the *ricos* such as Victor Ortega worked the land and participated in community agricultural activities, such as the threshing of wheat. Almost everyone had to leave town to labor for income, but those who didn't formed a new kind of merchant class in Chimayó. The vigorously expanding cash economy widened these differences in the first two decades of the century, and they only intensified when the depression left migrant workers destitute. The new economic order of the depression years split the community along party lines, with the old-guard Republicans holding to their standard while the working class of disenfranchised migrant labor defected to the swelling ranks of the Democrats. This set the stage for envy and resentment, which was further exacerbated by the close political ties between some plaza Republicans and well-placed Anglo politicians in Santa Fe.

While World War II delivered the region from the throes of depression-era poverty, the political and economic split in the community remained. The economic recovery came as a great relief for the job-hungry workers, but it also added more stresses to the structure of the plaza community. After the war, the people leaving for work stopped coming back.

Chapter Ten:
Moving Away

Resting in the Shade

Compadre, *let's sit down here in the shade*
And share some sandía.
It's too hot to work
And besides,
We're old men now and getting tired.

So many years, old friend,
We've watched this plaza change,
But now the young ones are gone,
And each year we bury more of our vecinos
In the camposanto *by the arroyo.*

Look over there at the gardens—
No one to plant them and they've gone to weeds,
And over there by the ditch washing clothes,
Your sister is looking tired and worn.

You know, compadre, *soon we will join*
All of our parientes *from this old plaza in* El Cielo,
And we'll sit in the shade just like today
And talk about old times.

By the time the U.S. entered World War II in 1941, Chimayó and the Plaza del Cerro had weathered many changes. Two and a half centuries had elapsed since Hispanics began building their adobe homes here. Droughts, floods, revolutions, invasions, and epidemics all whittled at the community without lasting effect, but the war years were a watershed for the plaza. Besides an emigration of young men enlisted for the military, many others left Chimayó to take advantage of war-related employment. One of the principal destinations was the San Francisco Bay area, where word had it that unskilled laborers could land jobs in the naval shipyards. A number of families from around the plaza left for San Francisco, where they tasted urban life and formed a small subcommunity of *compadres* in the city. The San Francisco era brought these people thoroughly into the modern world, and though most of them returned to Chimayó, their perspective had modernized. Many also brought back spouses, augmenting the flow of Anglos into the Chimayó community that had begun with the Presbyterian missionaries.

DAVID ORTEGA

Wars change communities pretty quickly. When those boys came back from the first war, things started changing a lot. But things didn't change as much as they did after the second war. There were more changes, more time was spent on education and travel after that.

AMADA
TRUJILLO

We went to San Francisco. Sabino left here, he and other men, it was during the wartime. And then he went to the shipbuilding business. He, Pedro, Juan Trujillo, and Félix Ortega were about the first ones that went to San Francisco to work, in 1942. About November or December. And I left to join him in January of '43. So he worked in the shipyards. A lot of people from here worked in the ship-yards. They heard that there were jobs there, so they were going.

I liked San Francisco all right. My husband said one time, "Let's sell our place in Chimayó and move here." And I said "No, if you want to be here fifteen, twenty years, OK, but we're going back to Chimayó to spend the rest of our lives." And so we came home. Later on he had the bug to stay there again, so I told him, "What am I going to do if you die and leave me there in San Francisco?" I had

*acquaintances there, but it wasn't like the folks here in Chimayó. Here, I knew
that people would take care of me.*

*When everybody went to San Francisco, to the shipyards, I was little and I
stayed here. I was the favorite sobrina of Tío Reyes, and I would see him out
there plowing his fields or hoeing all by himself. And I would bring him water
and sit with him while he had a drink. He was already old, and there was no
one to help him. And my aunts would go by on the road, and he would say, "I
don't care if everybody else goes to California, but don't let her go."*

TILA VILLA

*And I guess since then—since the '40s—the plaza started to deteriorate. 'Cause
everybody went to San Francisco to work in the shipyards, and they weren't
here to plaster. Then, after the war, well, the old people died and the youngsters
went to school and had to leave to find work. For example, Tío Victor had three
sons, and they all went to private school in Santa Fe and then they stayed to
work there. They opened a cantina, and then Ben [Ortega] got into politics,
and they didn't have any reason to live in the plaza anymore.*

TERESITA
JARAMILLO

*And then of course as the young people came home, they started finding jobs
outside of Chimayó. That left the older people to take care of the land. And they
did as long as they were able to, but they were too old. And the time now has
come when every able-bodied person is away from the plaza, so it's all weeds
now. And some of it is crumbling.*

AMADA
TRUJILLO

Los Alamos Scientific Laboratory became the most significant employer in
the region after World War II. "The Lab," and the secret city founded to house
scientists producing the world's first nuclear weapons, acted as magnets for Hispanics in search of work. People within a large radius of the new town flocked
to the Lab. As in all previous employment booms, the Hispanics landed the
positions at the low end of the salary scale, but by local standards they still rated
as well-paying jobs. Countless valley residents found work building the town
itself, in the homes of the scientists, or at the Laboratory, where they labored in

construction or acted as technicians on expensive and complex projects. This dramatic leap took some Hispanics from a life tending gardens in Chimayó to work in one of the most sophisticated scientific ventures of the day. The confluence of Anglos and Hispanics at Los Alamos resulted in many new marriages between the two cultures. Scores of newcomers settled into the nearby Hispanic villages while some valley folk moved to live in Los Alamos.

Before the war, an older generation of Chimayosos had continued to farm both inside and outside the plaza. For the young people returning from overseas or from jobs in U.S. cities, it was clear that farming as a livelihood was over for good. Although the interior garden space was cared for into the 1950s, more and more buildings fell into disuse as working people moved away from Chimayó or to larger landholdings outside the plaza. There, many continued to farm, and Chimayó still enjoys a reputation for its agricultural products, but after World War II the labor in the fields was relegated to the status of a pastime. A milestone in this change was marked in 1944, when Don Nicolás Martínez set up his mill, harvested his fields of sorghum, and squeezed *miel de caña* for the last time.

New roads and changing traffic patterns that came with the postwar growth of New Mexico had a lasting effect on the plaza. The plaza had straddled the main road from Española to Truchas and the Santuario, and the mercantile stores operated there by Victor Ortega and Eduardo Naranjo relied on the traffic. Chimayó's first paved road, State Road 76, which was built just after the war, bypassed the plaza. Equipped with the automobiles that their jobs allowed them to purchase, people found it easier to drive to Española for goods than to patronize the small plaza establishments. Shops and mercantile establishments nearer the new highway, including the weaving shops belonging to Nicasio Ortega, Severo Jaramillo, and John Trujillo, fared better than the isolated plaza.

Adding to the drain on the plaza population, many of the older residents of the plaza passed away in the years after the war. Reyes Ortega collapsed in 1944, leaving a loom with a half-finished blanket and no male heirs to take over his weaving business. Victor Ortega died in 1948, and his sons all remained in Santa Fe, leaving his plaza mercantile store to collect dust and cobwebs. The old man of civil war fame, Eulogio Martínez, had passed on before the war (in 1933), and his son José Inez and their neighbor on the north side of the plaza, Don Pedro

Cruz, joined him in the war years or shortly thereafter. Doroteo Cruz inherited his father's house and remained there into the 1970s, and Don Reyes Naranjo lived in his house until his death in 1968 while his sons continued to operate the small store they had started in the 1930s. But families that stayed in the plaza were the exception; the average age of plaza residents grew higher by the year.

The community that gathered to bury Bonefacia Ortega in 1953 included few children. The ringing of the bell on "her" *oratorio* announced the passing of one of the plaza's most esteemed *vecinos*. Bone's house, too, was to remain vacant for many years after her death. The story was the same on the west side of the plaza. José Inez Martínez y Trujillo left his land to his son, Estevan, who raised a family there with his wife Cordelia. Eventually they moved to a bigger piece of José Inez's land to the west of the plaza. When Rafael Martínez died, his house was sold and left uninhabited.

This slow process of attrition left parts of the plaza neglected, especially the row on the southwestern quadrant. Few people commented on this decline until the late 1950s, when it came to the attention of architects and historians, most of whom were from outside of Chimayó. Chimayosos who had moved away were not wont to look back to the small parcels of land and tiny houses. In the postwar growth of middle-class America, everyone was scrambling for a piece of the American Dream, and Chimayó's old plaza held no promise for the future. Ironically, just as the young Chimayosos by necessity began looking forward to a future away from the old adobes, the world outside began to look backward to the old adobes as remnants of previous eras worthy of preservation.

One of the first to write about the plaza was geographer Stephen F. deBorhegyi, who lived in Chimayó in the early 1950s and published a historical study of Chimayó in 1954, complete with sketch maps of the plaza. (While in Chimayó, deBorhegyi also gathered data for his definitive studies of the Santuario in Potrero.) Of the thirty-seven houses he mapped in the plaza, he believed that sixteen were "abandoned" at that time (although some weren't vacant at all but served as storage buildings for plaza residents). He gathered piles of data on the Chimayó community and interviewed many old people during his stay in Chimayó.[1]

The Spanish Colonial Arts Society also took a great interest in Chimayó. The rescue of the Santuario in 1929 became the best-known project undertaken

A NEW ROOF
AND PLASTER
AT RUMALDO
ORTEGA'S
HOUSE ON
THE PLAZA,
CA. 1915.

in Chimayó by this group, but the organization also showed concern for the *oratorio* on the old plaza. When the roof began to leak and fall apart in 1954, the society funded the restoration work that kept the *oratorio* standing, marking the first time that plaza people had turned to outside help to take care of the hallowed *capilla*.

While outside attention on the aged buildings of the plaza increased, Chimayó residents occupied themselves with projects designed to bring the town into the present and prepare it for the future. The first community well for the plaza went in in 1958, and a group formed to address other basic needs of Chimayó residents as it planned community improvements in the late 1950s. Restoration of the plaza was not among their goals, as David Ortega's recollections make clear.

DAVID ORTEGA   *In about 1958, with the technical direction and cooperation of the county extension service, we organized a Chimayó Community Development Association, and I was named the chairman, and I kept that post for twelve years. During that time we had a good organization, and we were instrumental in getting this road [State Road 520] built and paved, getting the natural gas here, starting a fire department. And we had a recreation center that was very good. And then I quit,*

I was so tired, and my business was getting big, and I was getting old and tired, and I wanted somebody else to take over and nobody made it work. It fizzled out.

The Chimayó Community Development Association's focus on modernizing Chimayó didn't reflect any ignorance about the plaza and its condition. Priorities for the community stayed in a more practical realm, but the locals kept a vigilant eye on the old plaza. In 1962, David Ortega and others in the community were shocked to discover that Santa Fe County records failed to identify ownership of the *oratorio*. After nearly 150 years of continuous care by the community, ownership of the chapel was in a legal limbo because surveyors overlooked it in 1925. Perhaps the communal nature of the *oratorio* stopped anyone from claiming ownership, and the surveyors simply passed it over. Acting quickly, Ortega, who had been in charge of the *oratorio* since his Tía Bonefacia's death, arranged for the property to be transferred to the Archdiocese of Santa Fe, which he believed was Bonefacia's intention before she died. By 1963, the transfer to church ownership

239

via a patent was complete, at a cost to the church of $50. The church, however, took little interest in the *oratorio*, where priests had rarely set foot. For all practical purposes, responsibility for its upkeep remained in the hands of the Ortega family. No one else in the community seemed ready or able to help, and so the *oratorio* became known as the Ortega family chapel.

Other unused buildings on the plaza were less fortunate than the *oratorio*. Most lacked a benefactor with the vigilance and financial resources to provide for maintenance. Organizations like the Spanish Colonial Arts Society did not, as a rule, take an interest in structures that did not contain examples of colonial art. With old people dying and younger people away or too busy to help, roofs in need of repair stayed leaky. Cracks in walls stayed unpatched, and buildings began to crumble. These processes wore at the plaza but at the same time intensified the interest of people drawn to them as historical artifacts.

The completion of a second major highway in 1965—the "new" highway from Nambé, which followed the old wagon route—opened up Chimayó to even easier access. The concurrent opening of the Rancho de Chimayó restaurant added incentive for visitors to drive up to Chimayó from Santa Fe, and tourists flocked here as never before. Some took the time to make a side trip to the old plaza, and they were taken aback by the "authentic" nature of the buildings— a quality that derived mostly from the neglect that the buildings had endured. Architects and historians also visited the plaza in increasing numbers, and soon they came with classes in tow to marvel at the ancient structures and to produce detailed drawings of the place. Pictures of the southwest side of the plaza—the part that was least maintained—served in publications covering architecture of the Southwest to illustrate "the best preserved example of a traditional fortified Spanish village" and also recognized it as a repository of diverse architectural styles from the colonial period through the early 1900s.[2]

The hoopla about the Plaza del Cerro paralleled the continuing expansion of tourist industries in New Mexico in the 1960s. Countless brochures and travel articles spouted the wonders of New Mexico, and none neglected to mention Chimayó, labeled since 1925 as the "Lourdes of America" because of the annual Easter pilgrimage to the Santuario. The new highway from Nambé created a better route for pilgrims, giving people miles of open space to traverse rather than the busy highway from Española, and religious tourism was on the rise. The mounting interest accompanied a national concern for historical sites that resulted in passage of the National Historic Preservation Act in 1966.

By 1970, the old plaza was as popular for its "oldness" as Don Victor's store had once been for the new things it offered. Seeing great value in "preserving" the plaza, the State Planning Office in 1971 nominated the Plaza del Cerro for the National Register of Historic Places, as provided in the National Historic Preservation Act. The nomination noted that, if restored, the plaza would offer "out-of-state visitors . . . the chance to walk through an example of eighteenth-century village planning," and added, "so few places in the Southwest remain from this period in such entirety." Other documents concerning the plaza noted that federal funds could be available for restoration, suggesting that the federal Economic Development Administration might offer assistance "if restoration will stimulate tourist traffic and create jobs."[3]

The statements made by state officials convey the prevailing sentiment of those interested in preserving the plaza at that time: that it should be maintained as a historic site for tourists to visit. In July of 1972, the National Park Service entered the Plaza del Cerro in the register. Back in New Mexico, E. Boyd of the State Planning Office had already drawn up plans for preserving the plaza. Her emphasis fell on maintaining the large and small architectural details that together made the plaza valuable to historians: *raja* ceilings (ceilings made of rough, handmade lath), hand-adzed beams and lintels, adobe floors, examples of early plastering techniques, corner fireplaces, Greek Revival door and window trim, and a *soterano* (a small storage cellar with a wooden lid and leather hinges). The old storefront and the *torreón* behind it were special items of concern.[4]

Boyd's plan for preservation went on to offer detailed suggestions for ways to maintain the plaza's historic stature. She recommended that the state negotiate with property owners for removing structures not "architecturally valuable" and for replacing outhouses with indoor plumbing—adding that "public restrooms might be installed in one of the unoccupied houses." Envisioning a local tourist attraction in full detail, the plan suggested that one building "might house a snack

DOORWAY IN
THE ABAN-
DONED HOME
OF RAFAEL
AND PERFECTA
MARTÍNEZ,
1991.

bar . . . offering *tacos, empañadas* [*sic*], *bizcochitos*, and other traditional, locally made foods." To stock these stores, the plan proposed tapping the labor of "housewives who do not go out to work . . . [to] prepare jams and jellies from the indigenous wild plum." With regard to educational opportunities, the plan states that "educational exhibits housed within existing buildings could be very convincing . . . [including] an early New Mexican interior with fireplace, an old-style weaving room (a live one with working weavers would be preferable), and an exhibit of old farm tools." Other than these vague suggestions that Chimayó residents might be employed in the revised plaza, the only time the plan mentions the local people comes when it recommends that the "owners" be prodded to change their homes to match the historical styles that the state deemed worthy of preservation. Clearly, this was not a plan by or for the Chimayosos who would be most affected by it.

While the state plans were being written and nomination for the register of historic places churned its way through the bureaucracy, interest in renovating the Plaza del Cerro also came from the private sector. About 1970, residents of Chimayó formed the Chimayó Historical Sites Committee and hatched a strategy for the plaza. Working with Robert McKinney, owner of the daily *Santa Fe New Mexican*, the committee unveiled a plan "for the purpose of planning restoration of the old Buildings [*sic*] surrounding the plaza."5

We had had several opportunities to restore the Chimayó plaza. One of the offers came from Robert McKinney and his daughter Robin McKinney—they were good friends of mine, and Robin was very much interested in the preservation of the oratorio. *So we invited everybody in the plaza and had a* posole *dinner at the parish hall, and Mr. McKinney told us that he wanted to restore at least the west side of the plaza, where the* oratorio *is and all those old houses are. He proposed that a corporation be formed of these owners, there were four owners. And according to the size of the property they had, that would be the size of the shares of that corporation each would get. He would then be given title to these properties —and this would all be done legally. He would restore them at no cost to anybody, and then he would transfer back the titles to these owners, with them being fixed—water, sewer, everything. Once McKinney fixed them up, the owners could*

DAVID ORTEGA

use the properties for whatever they wanted to, like commercial or whatever. But the people didn't like that. They couldn't believe it, they couldn't see it— they just couldn't trust anybody. And there it is.

The other opportunity that came about involved the Ford Foundation. The full Ford Foundation Board of Trustees was here in Chimayó and we had a date with them. And I got to meet one of the big shots, all of them, but the girl that disperses the money got interested in the Chimayó plaza. I showed it to her and told her how beautiful it would be to fix it up. And she says, "You can do it, we can get you the money." So I got people together to try and get them to apply for it—and there was no interest whatsoever. And so it goes with this place.

These two efforts at preservation had at least some representation from inside the Chimayó community, and yet still they failed. While the Chimayosos who had conceived and promoted the plans believed the ideas to represent a safe, no-strings-attached way to keep up the plaza, other plaza people found the schemes suspect because they feared losing control over their properties. Furthermore, the Chimayosos didn't trust any money coming from outside of their own ranks. They feared that any attempt to restore the plaza would increase outside interest and investment and eventually cause the locals to lose an invaluable piece of their cultural past. They pointed to Santa Fe, where the original inhabitants long ago lost their tenure in the old part of town and now live on the fringes of a world-famous and ever more abstract tourist mecca.

On the other side of the argument, some Chimayó natives saw the restoration attempts as an opportunity to conserve something of the roots of their culture. For them, a restored plaza would rekindle pride in the community and its past and perhaps help to mend some of the tears in the cultural fabric—tears that even then threatened to undermine the basic integrity of Chimayó. To these people, bringing tourists' attention to the plaza would not be a bad thing and could help people here by bringing tourist dollars into the town.

On a more subtle level, the debates about the Plaza del Cerro had very little to do with tourism or "outside" funding versus "local control." Attempts to fix up the plaza buildings failed in large part because of a fracture in the community rooted in the early part of the century—or perhaps even earlier—when the plaza became politically and economically divided. On the surface, it's hard to see this split, for many people from both political parties and from alienated family clans supported restoration attempts. A similar diversity opposed the plans. But the sharpest conflict did reflect the old wounds, and old rivals had squared off in the debate. In general, the descendants of the old plaza *patrones* —primarily the Ortega businessmen—were most outspoken in their support of the restoration efforts. The descendants of their Democratic rivals raised the most vocal opposition to any kind of renovation. The enmity between these groups had simmered for decades in the plaza, and the call for unified support of renovation plans merely catalyzed its awakening. At the base of the opponents' resistance to the plans was the envy and suspicion of those in favor, for, like the *patrones* of old, among the advocates were businessmen with outside political connections. Cooperation under these circumstances proved impossible.

Amid the controversy, a tragedy struck at the heart of the plaza in the fall of 1971. Under the cover of darkness, thieves broke into the *oratorio* and stole the *bultos* of San Buenaventura and San Antonio. Using a ladder to climb on the roof, they also made off with the bell. They probably sold the artifacts to unscrupulous dealers in folk art—the same circles that routinely robbed prehistoric ruins and disposed of the spoils on the lucrative black market. Never in its history had the little chapel been so violated. The loss stunned those who cared for the place and struck a death knell that darkened the hopes of the Historical Sites Committee.

Not long after the *oratorio* was burglarized, thieves struck at Victor Ortega's mercantile store, which had rested in peaceful abandonment for many years. These enterprising burglars carted off the two hundred pairs of old button-up shoes left over on the shelves, all of which Victor's son Ben had already agreed to sell to Buster Brown shoes to be used for promotional purposes. A few weeks later, Ben Ortega noticed that a few people in Chimayó sported the old shoes about town. The robbers apparently had unloaded some of their goods on the local populace. Sadly, they also took old photographs from the walls, among them the only image in the family of Petra Mestas Ortega.

Things stayed pretty quiet on the old plaza for several years after the flurry of restoration attempts and burglaries. Small-scale maintenance and some renovation took place in the 1970s, most notably on the abandoned adobes on the southwestern corner of the plaza. There, a person from outside Chimayó settled and slowly repaired some *casitas*—the old "cuarto de Pancho" and the house that the first Presbyterian schoolteachers rented—remodeling them into a residence with few changes to their exterior appearance. Arturo Jaramillo, the owner of the Rancho de Chimayó, bought the old adobe by the road that had belonged to José Inez Martínez and his son Estevan and repaired it with new plaster, doors, and windows. (The building soon fell prey to vandals, who stole the doors, broke the windows, and covered the walls with graffiti.) In the early 1980s, David Ortega initiated a complete reconditioning of Bonefacia Ortega's residence, and his son Andrew established an art gallery there in 1983. The life span of the gallery in this location was short, however, as Andrew realized, as so many before him had, that the plaza was too far from the main thoroughfare to sustain business. A family moved onto some property inside the plaza and built a house there—establishing the first residents inside the plaza since Luisita Ortega died and left her tiny house in the 1930s.

Controversy erupted full force in the plaza again in 1986, when filmmaker Robert Redford proposed filming *The Milagro Beanfield War* there. The production company contacted the State Planning Office and agreed to consult with the state historic preservation officer and a state archaeologist concerning alterations to the plaza, for Milagro Productions planned to "reconstruct" the Plaza del Cerro. "We're trying to help the local people and pump some money into a desperately depressed area," production manager David Wisnievitz said. Wisnievitz had talked with property owners on the Plaza del Cerro—and reported that "all of them were very excited about us being there."[6]

The first intimations of a challenge to Redford's plans arose at a public meeting, where production company officials assured some forty Chimayó residents that disruptions would be kept to a minimum and that the three temporary buildings to be erected in the plaza would be removed after the filming. They promised that the plaza would be left in better condition than the moviemakers found it. Wisnievitz assured residents that they would be compensated in a "monetary fashion" but cautioned that the sum that Milagro Productions could offer would be small because industry financiers had been less than optimistic

about the revenue-generating potential of the film. He claimed that investors felt that "nobody is interested in making a film about a bunch of Mexicans, but we're going to prove them wrong." (Hastily, he added that he had some Mexican blood in his lineage.) Amid the generally supportive comments and high hopes that it would stimulate interest in restoring the plaza, plaza landowner Harold Martínez objected to the noise and traffic that the filming would entail. At this early stage, Martínez's protest seemed a minor annoyance. The only other sour note came when Wisnievitz announced that there would be an unarmed guard posted at the site around-the-clock, and a Chimayó resident quipped, "Who's going to guard the guard? How long have you been in northern New Mexico?"[7]

As negotiations with plaza residents continued, Martínez refused to cooperate. New Mexico Governor Tony Anaya, former Governor David Cargo, and other elected officials met with Martínez in an effort to persuade him to change his mind, but none could budge him. "I just didn't think it was fair that the

TERESITA TRUJILLO JARAMILLO, 1991.

VIRGINIA TRUJILLO ORTEGA, 1989.

247

people who actually lived in the plaza weren't polled about their feelings," Martínez explained. "It wasn't so much what they planned to do as how they were going about doing it. And then I was made a scapegoat, but I wasn't the only one against that movie." Increasing offers of cash also failed to persuade Martínez and the others in opposition—offers that were by this time in the thousands of dollars. Exasperated but determined, Wisnievitz proclaimed "we don't need him," and the production company found a way to construct their sets to avoid the northern part of the plaza where Martínez's property lay. The first phases of the plaza cleanup were to begin in a few days.[8]

But the filming of *Milagro* was not to happen. Martínez rallied the support of a few other residents, among them individuals who lived on the south side of the plaza. "We're not going to let them [film here] just because it's a neat little movie," one plaza *vecino* huffed. The protesters succeeded in obtaining a restraining order to halt construction until the dispute could be settled, and faced with a deadline to start filming—and receiving a generous welcome from the town of Truchas—Milagro Productions elected to give up on the plaza location.[9]

The *Milagro* debacle touched sensitive nerves and left in its wake a bitterly divided community. Those who had welcomed the prospects of a cleaned-up and revitalized plaza were deeply disillusioned by the stubbornness of their neighbors while the minority who defeated the movie basked in their victory and in the media attention it gave to some long-standing grievances about "outside" meddling in Chimayó's affairs. "I am pleased [because] the plaza will survive a little longer now that it isn't the center of all this attention," one of the quieter members of the opposition said.[10]

Among the most disgruntled was Ben Ortega, Victor Ortega's son and the owner of his old mercantile store and residence. At the time, Ben, who lived in Santa Fe most of his life, was debating whether to sell the old family property or to fix it up and develop it into a business, such as a bed-and-breakfast. "I had already done all the groundwork. We knew what we'd have to invest to make it work. My son is a developer and we had the plans and everything. But then to see everything ready to go on something so simple as a film, and then have the whole thing fall apart over such a silly goddam thing! And actually, that's what made me sell my place. I got so discouraged about the place."

Ben's absence from Chimayó for so long perhaps made him oblivious to the old enmities that were still seething in the plaza. In disgust, he sold his store and residence—the most opulent on the plaza, the home of the plaza *patrón*, and the site of the old *torreón*—to some people from outside of Chimayó. The news of the sale shocked many in Chimayó, for some had been negotiating with him to keep the property in local ownership. In many ways, this property could be called the most historically significant site on the plaza, and its sale, combined with the burglaries of the *oratorio* and the mercantile store and the rejection of the movie deal, further demoralized many people who were hoping to see the plaza renovated by local hands.

Tranquil times and slow decay once again settled on most of the plaza, and no comparable conflict has arisen to date. Some homes have new residents, including Gervacio Ortega's house, which was repaired to become the home of his great-great-grandsons, but even with the few new residents architectural changes in the plaza in the last decade of the twentieth century have been small, although not insignificant. Bonefacia's small adobe *dispensa* on the northeast corner of the plaza collapsed on a winter night in 1990, an important loss because it contained some of the last original *raja* ceilings and old-style corner fireplaces in the plaza. The roofs of two buildings on the southwest side—long ago the residences of Rafael and Perfecta Martínez—fell in, and a resident who had long rented the old Cruz adobe on the north side left, leaving it to start its slow decline. By 1990, most of the architectural details noted by E. Boyd in the 1970s had vanished from the plaza.

Fortunately, the fears of the Chimayó people about Don Victor's property proved unfounded. The new owners began a renovation project that no one could quibble about, for it returned some of the old grandeur to the boarded-up buildings. The owners' intentions of starting a business there developed slowly and seemed to reflect a sensitivity to history and to other property owners.

Chimayó came into the media limelight again in 1991, when a spectacular mass murder made national news. Once again Chimayó's image was tarnished, and the tragedy seemed to confirm to many that Chimayó was a violent and crime-ridden town. The killings, as with most in the past, took place down the valley from the plaza. Much less attention was focused on Chimayó in the fall of 1993 when people from inside and outside Chimayó cooperated to acquire and

Alejandro
Ortiz and
Petronila
Martínez
Ortiz, 1990.

Harold
Martínez,
1990.

install a new bell in the vacant belfry of the *oratorio*. The task of finding a bell
to fit the small weathered belfry had proved vexing, but finally the replacement
arrived, and dozens of people showed up for the dedication. It was a remarkable
gathering, attracting a long list of old *vecinos* whom locally are regarded as the
dignitaries of Chimayó. This small event seemed to suspend the rivalries and
bitterness between factions.

My grandma was there, ninety-five years old and still smiling from the
car where she sat for fear of walking on the uneven ground. Grandma's cousin
Teresita Jaramillo, only one year younger than Grandma, smiled back from the
car where she stayed. Teresita's sister Mercedes, a sprightly eighty-six, took a
seat on the worn wooden bench that was retrieved from the *oratorio* and placed
in the sun. These sisters had been among the Carmelitas in decades gone by.
Grandma's younger sister Melita Ortega long ago converted to join the Presby-

MELITA
ORTEGA AND
BENIGNA O.
CHÁVEZ, 1991.

MERCEDES
TRUJILLO,
BENIGNA O.
CHÁVEZ,
AND MELITA
ORTEGA, 1991.

terian church, but it didn't stop her from coming out for the momentous occasion
—just as "heretic" Presbyterians used to turn out to watch the *Mes de María*
procession long ago. Amada Trujillo, the daughter of old Victor Ortega's political
rival, Reyes Naranjo, added her diminutive figure to the cast of *viejitas*.

The younger ranks that came to the plaza that day included David
Ortega, who had been maintaining the *oratorio* since his Tía Bonefacia's death.
He stood alongside Tila Villa and my mother, who were once flower girls for the
Mes de María ceremonies. Josephine Martínez, who was raised in her grandfather
Don Victor's home on the plaza, was there, as was Elsie Miranda, the daughter
of old Juan Melquiades Ortega, a plaza resident and renowned weaver who had
recently died at 102 years of age. Lawrence Martínez walked over to represent his
mother Petronila—the last person living on the plaza who had been born there.

The distinguished cast of characters included a host of other people, some
new to Chimayó, some descendants of old Chimayosos. And there were people
from the Smithsonian Institution and the Spanish Colonial Arts Society, and
others from Santa Fe who just liked the old plaza. As had happened in the past
when the *oratorio* needed help, a community of generous souls had assembled
to give their support.

Father Casimiro Roca, the priest at the Santuario for forty years, blessed
the bell and cast holy water. David Ortega related his memories of how the old
bell used to sound and what it meant to the plaza, and I gave a short presenta-
tion on the history of the *oratorio*, listing the names of people who had contributed to its upkeep over the decades since Pedro Asencio Ortega first dedicated
the place to San Buenaventura. Finally, Father Roca rang the bell. Faces lit up,
and people marveled aloud at how it sounded remarkably like the original. As
the sound echoed over the plaza, I reflected on a comment that a friend had made
the day before. He said that the plaza's darkest moment must have come the
night the bell was stolen. Now, as people took turns ringing the bell, it seemed
that a tiny spark of new life filled the Plaza del Cerro.

But the most poignant moment for me came later, when people were beginning to leave. Teresita gathered up her strength and, against the admonitions of
her sister and grandson, determined that she would go inside the *oratorio*. She

hobbled up to the door of the old chapel and we helped her into its dark interior. She gasped and exclaimed, *"Madre María!"* when she saw the whitewashed walls, the wooden chandeliers, and the simple altar screen that she knew so well as a Carmelita. She had not set foot in the *oratorio* since Bonefacia had died and the Carmelitas had stopped meeting there forty years previously. She sat on a bench with her head bowed and prayed aloud, asking for blessings for all the deceased Carmelitas who had shared this place. Her voice rang in the quiet room as it had so long ago, recounting a litany of names of people long gone, and I knew that her faith had not diminished in all those years. Outside, the bell rang in the quiet of the old plaza as it had when Teresita and my grandma were young and played here. The small group that was gathered outside looked up and smiled, and it seemed that their faith, too, had endured.

Perhaps that small event was a turning point, the start of a new concern for the old plaza. Within a year, a new organization formed, the Chimayó Cultural Preservation Association, with the goal of preserving historic sites in Chimayó, not expressly for the benefit of tourists from outside of Chimayó but primarily for the sake of the community. Just a year and a few months after the bell rang, the committee was busy replacing the roof on the *oratorio*, aided by volunteers from the plaza, among them individuals from both of the old plaza factions. For the first time in years, a group of plaza people came together to perform *Las Posadas* that Christmas, filling the *oratorio* with candlelight and song.

Old enmities seem to be forgotten in the common ground of the *oratorio*, where there is no single owner. Everyone seems to recognize collective good in that small room. If people are to take care of the plaza, this spirit of cooperation would have to be extended outward to other buildings. Such cooperation is surely warranted, for if my discussions with the *viejitos* and all my research of documents have shown me one thing, it is that the Plaza del Cerro embodies a large part of the heritage of all Chimayosos. Whether they live here or not—and whether they own property here or not—countless people can trace their ancestry to one of the plaza's many large families, and most can claim an ancestor who worked laying the adobes of the original buildings. As one person put it, "If we used to get together to tie chiles, why not to clean up and repair the old

plaza? If we don't do it, somebody else will buy it out from under us and do it for us—and they won't understand what it means to us."

I think many people in Chimayó shared a feeling that day, one that my grandma expressed when we returned home from the *oratorio* after ringing the bell. Warmed by the goodwill that focused on that small event, she sat at her kitchen table and exclaimed *"Ojalá que compongan la plaza!*—How wonderful if they fix up the plaza!" On the other hand, others would agree with the sentiment I overheard some time later at the post office after a number of residents gathered to do some maintenance work on the *oratorio*. Not knowing that I was behind him in line, a *vecino* from the plaza told the postmaster, "I'm not going to help out with that project, no way. I'm not going to help those people get richer. You know that is what it's all about, don't you, *hijita?*"

The fate of the last remnants of the Plaza del Cerro hinges on the resolution, if one ever comes, of this perennial conflict.

Notes

A Note about Sources

Copies of most of the primary documents cited can be found in the Borrego-Ortega Papers at the New Mexico State Records Center and Archives in Santa Fe. The bulk of this collection comes from my family's private collection. Wherever I have used the original papers, I refer to them as the Chávez-Usner Collection to distinguish them from the copies in the archives.

Although in some cases quotations were derived from unrecorded interviews, most of the personal communications used in this book can be found in the Plaza del Cerro tapes at the Center for Regional Studies at the University of New Mexico in Albuquerque. Each tape includes a written log summarizing its contents; all are available for research use.

Many people who contributed information for this book are not quoted directly, but their statements were invaluable nonetheless. In some instances, I have combined comments from two or more people into one quotation, in which case I name all the people contributing.

Introduction

1. In Spanish, the name Victor normally is spelled with an accent over the "i," but people in the plaza area pronounce this name with the accent on the last syllable. Since this pronunciation requires no written accent, I have omitted an accent from the name throughout this book. Unless noted, all other names are spelled consistently with the spelling given in Francisco Sisneros and Joe H. Torres, *Nombres: Nombres de Pila in Nuevo México: Spanish Given Names in New Mexico* (Bernalillo: Las Campanas Publications, 1982).

Chapter 1: From the Hills

1. John Peabody Harrington, "Old Indian Geographical Names around Santa Fe, New Mexico," *American Anthropologist*, n.s. 22 (1920): 341–359; see specifically page 346. See also John Peabody Harrington, "The Ethnogeography of the Tewa Indians," in *The Twenty-Ninth Annual Report of the Bureau of American Ethnology to the Smithsonian Institution*, 1907–1908 (Washington, D.C.: The Smithsonian Institution, 1908), 341–343.

2. Stephen F. deBorhegyi, "The Miraculous Shrines of Our Lord of Esquipulas in Guatemala and Chimayó, New Mexico," *El Palacio* 60, 3 (March 1953): 89, footnote.

3. Stanley, F. *El Potrero de Chimayó* (limited-edition booklet published by the author, 1969), 4. Stanley gives no source for his definition.

4. Alfonso Ortiz, *The Tewa World: Space, Time, Being, and Becoming in a Pueblo Society* (Chicago: University of Chicago Press, 1969), 19.

5. Ibid., 19.

6. Barry S. Kues and Spencer G. Lucas, "Summary of the Paleontology of the Santa Fe Group (Mio-Pliocene), North-Central New Mexico," in Raymond V. Ingersoll, ed., *Guidebook to Santa Fe County* (Albuquerque: New Mexico Geological Society Guidebook, 30th Field Conference, 1979), 239.

7. Chávez-Usner Collection, 17 August 1880.

Chapter 2: Donde Vivian los Indios

1. William J. Mayer-Oakes, *Cultural Resource Inventory, Santa Cruz Reservoir, New Mexico, Volume II: Archaeological Resources* (unpublished manuscript on file in the Laboratory of Anthropology, Santa Fe, no date), 35–41.
2. Harrington, "The Ethnogeography," 255.
3. Harry P. Mera, "A Survey of the Biscuitware Area in Northern New Mexico," Technical Series Bulletin Number 6 (Santa Fe: Laboratory of Anthropology, 1934).
4. Stephen F. deBorhegyi, "The Evolution of a Landscape," *Landscape* 1 (1954): 26.
5. Records of these and other finds in the Santa Cruz Valley are maintained in the Laboratory of Anthropology in Santa Fe.
6. Stewart Peckham, "Highway Salvage Archaeology, Number LA 3319, a Fragmentary Site Near Española, New Mexico" (unpublished report on file in the Laboratory of Anthropology, Santa Fe, 1956).

Chapter 3: Scraps of Paper

1. Chávez-Usner Collection, 10 September 1706.
2. Myra Ellen Jenkins, "Settlement of the Jurisdiction of La Cañada," in Myra Ellen Jenkins and John O. Baxter, "Settlement and Irrigation in the Santa Cruz and Quemado Watersheds" (unpublished report on file in the Office of the State Engineers, Santa Fe, May 1986), 1.
3. Fray Angélico Chávez, *Origins of New Mexico Families*, rev. ed. (Museum of New Mexico Press, 1992), 58. See also Ralph Emerson Twitchell, *The Spanish Archives of New Mexico*, Vol. 2 (Cedar Rapids: The Torch Press, 1914), 25.
4. For a summary of the Pueblo Revolt and the reconquest, see J. Manuel Espinosa, *The Pueblo Indian Revolt of 1696* (Norman: University of Oklahoma Press, 1988); and J. Manuel Espinosa, *Crusaders of the Río Grande* (Chicago: University of Chicago Press, 1942).
5. Jenkins, "Settlement," 2.
6. Letter of Padre José Arbizu, 10 March 1696, translated in Espinosa, *The Pueblo Indian Revolt*, 178.
7. Luis Granillo to Governor Vargas, 21 March 1695, from microfilm court transcription, "The Settlement of the Villa Nueva of Santa Cruz," in "The Spanish Archives of New Mexico," Series 1 (Santa Fe: New Mexico State Records Center and Archives, no date), Document #882, Roll 50, Frame 955; also appears in Twitchell, *The Spanish Archives*, Vol. 1, 241–265.
8. Boyd Pratt and David Snow, *The North-Central Regional Overview* (Santa Fe: State Historic Preservation Division, 1988), 57.

9. Letter from Fray José Arbizu to Fray Francisco de Vargas, 9 March 1696, in Espinosa, *The Pueblo Revolt*, 170.
10. Letter from Arbizu to Fray Vargas, 10 March 1696, in Espinosa, *The Pueblo Revolt*, 177.
11. Arbizu to Fray Vargas, 9 March 1696, in Espinosa, *The Pueblo Revolt*, 170.
12. Fray Vargas to the Commissary General, 21 July 1696, in Espinosa, *The Pueblo Revolt*, 243.
13. Harrington, "The Ethnogeography," 256. Tewa informants told Harrington that the Santa Cruz Valley had been inhabited by Tewas, who fled to Hano to aid the Hopis in their fight against "the Navaho [sic] and Mexicans." It seems likely that the informants were referring to Tano people.
14. Espinosa, *Crusaders*, 303.
15. Ibid., 226.
16. Granillo to Vargas, "The Settlement," Frame 956.
17. Chávez-Usner Collection, 7 January 1712.
18. Ibid., 23 October 1758.
19. Ibid., 18 April 1766.
20. Ibid., 12 February 1776.
21. Miscellaneous papers in the Chávez-Usner Collection; also summarized in Myra Ellen Jenkins, "Irrigation in the Chimayó Cañada," in Jenkins and Baxter, "Settlement and Irrigation," 71.

Chapter 4: Para la Defensa Otra Vez

1. Twitchell, *The Spanish Archives*, Vol. 1, 213; see also E. Boyd, *Historic Preservation: A Plan for New Mexico* (Santa Fe: New Mexico State Planning Office, 1971), 80.
2. Twitchell, *The Spanish Archives*, 213; see also Boyd, *Historic Preservation*, 80.
3. Archives of the Archdiocese of Santa Fe, Santa Cruz Marriages, cited in Victor Dan Jaramillo, "La Casa del Patrón" (unpublished manuscript loaned by the author, no date), 3.
4. Twitchell, *The Spanish Archives*, Vol. 2, 252; see also "The Spanish Archives of New Mexico," Series 1, Document #666, Roll 10, Frame 712; "*San buena bentura*" [sic] also appears on a 1752 land sale from Luis López to Grabiel Ortega (Chávez-Usner Collection, 23 October 1758).
5. David H. Snow, "Rural Hispanic Community Organization of Northern New Mexico: An Historical Perspective," in Paul Kutsche, ed., *The Survival of Spanish American Villages* (Colorado Springs: Colorado College, 1979), 47. See also Atanasio Domínguez, *The Missions of New Mexico, 1776*, translated and annotated by Eleanor B. Adams and Fray Angélico Chávez (Albuquerque: University of New Mexico Press, 1956), 83, 99.
6. Archives of the Archdiocese of Santa Fe, Santa Cruz Baptisms, cited in Jaramillo, "La Casa del Patrón," 4.

7. Marc Simmons, "Settlement Patterns and Village Plans in Colonial New Mexico," *Journal of the West* 8 (1969): 17.

8. Domínguez, *The Missions*, 83

9. Interview with Chimayó resident David Ortega; not recorded.

10. Twitchell, *The Spanish Archives*, Vol. 2, 252.

11. Ibid., 252; see also John O. Baxter "Irrigation in the Las Truchas Area," in Jenkins and Baxter, "Settlement and Irrigation." 91.

12. Alfred B. Thomas, "Governor Mendinueta's Proposals for the Defense of New Mexico, 1772–1778." *New Mexico Historical Review* 6 (1931): 29–30.

13. Ibid., 33.

14. Simmons, "Settlement Patterns," 18.

15. Chávez-Usner Collection, 9 April 1806.

16. Zelia Nuttall, "Royal Ordinances Concerning the Laying Out of New Towns," *Hispanic American Historical Review* 5 (May 1922): 249–255.

17. Alicia V. Tjarks, "Demographic, Ethnic, and Occupational Structure of New Mexico, 1790," *The Americas* 35 (1978): 58.

18. Susan A. Roberts and Calvin A. Roberts, *New Mexico* (Albuquerque: University of New Mexico Press, 1988), 90. In spite of the vaccine, smallpox continued to be a scourge to some populations. See John Kessell, *Kiva, Cross, and Crown* (Albuquerque: University of New Mexico Press, 1987), 455–456.

19. Chávez-Usner Collection, 25 March 1803.

20. Marcial Ortega Papers, 5 May 1826, 30 August 1861. The original documents have been lost, but translated summaries and photocopies of the originals are available in the Myra Ellen Jenkins Collection at the Center of Southwest Studies, Fort Lewis College, Durango, Colorado.

21. Ibid., 9 April 1806.

22. Ibid., 7 July 1827.

23. Tjarks, "Demographic, Ethnic," 86.

24. Suzanne Baizerman, "Textiles, Traditions, and Tourist Art: Hispanic Weaving in Northern New Mexico" (Ph.D. thesis, University of Minnesota, 1987), 39.

25. Marta Weigle, *Hispanic Villages of Northern New Mexico* (Santa Fe: The Lightning Tree Press, 1975), 100.

CHAPTER 5: FROM INSURGENTS TO PATRIOTS

1. Ward Allan Minge, "Efectos del País: A History of Weaving Along the Río Grande," in Nora Fisher, ed., *Spanish Textile Tradition of New Mexico and Colorado* (Santa Fe: Museum of New Mexico Press, 1979), 22–28.

2. Richard L. Nostrand, *The Hispano Homeland* (Norman: University of Oklahoma Press, 1992), 132.

3. The most thorough treatment of this rebellion was written by Janet Lecompte, *Rebellion in Río Arriba*, 1837 (Albuquerque: University of New Mexico Press, 1985). Much of the information here comes from Lecompte's work.

4. Ibid., 149.

5. Ibid., 148.

6. Weigle, *Hispanic Villages*, 35, 224.

7. Baizerman, "Textiles, Traditions," 47–49.

8. Joe Ben Wheat, "Río Grande, Pueblo, and Navajo Weavers: Cross-Cultural Influence," in Fisher, *Spanish Textile Tradition*, 36.

9. Adjutant General Records, New Mexico State Records Center and Archives, Santa Fe. An absence of enlistment records does not preclude service in the war. Some men were not properly enlisted and others used names different than their common names.

10. Document (photocopy) provided by David Ortega of Chimayó.

11. Marc Simmons, "Who Ordered That Retreat?" *Santa Fe Reporter*, 13–19 April 1994, 19.

12. John A. Gjevre, *Chili Line: The Narrow Trail to Santa Fe* (Española: Rio Grande Sun Press, 1969), 18.

13. Poem recited by Petrita Ortega and recorded by Melita Ortega.

14. Esquipulas is often misspelled by placing an accent over the "i," but this reflects a repetition of a typesetting error made in deBorhegyi's seminal paper on the Santuario. "The Miraculous Shrines."

15. Inventory of the Santuario in 1818 by Don Juan Bautista Ladrón del Niño de Guevara, cited in E. Boyd, *Popular Arts of Spanish New Mexico* (Santa Fe: Museum of New Mexico Press, 1974), 68–76. The numbers presented here represent the total of two lists of goods identified in the inventory—one set of goods "for the chapel" and the other "things which have been brought to sell with Don Juan Vigil"; see also Minge, "Efectos del País," 20.

16. Boyd, *Popular Arts*, 76.

17. Marta Weigle, *Brothers of Light, Brothers of Blood: The Penitentes of the Southwest* (Santa Fe: Ancient City Press, 1976), 50.

18. Petition of Bernardo Abeyta on behalf of the residents of Potrero, 15 November 1813 (Miscellaneous Church Records, Folder 1, New Mexico State Records Center and Archives, Santa Fe); also shown and translated in deBorhegyi, "The Miraculous Shrines," 92–93.

19. deBorhegyi, "The Miraculous Shrines," 84.

20. Letter from Fray Sebastian Alvarez to the acting Vicar General of the Diocese, Don Augstín San

Vicente Fernández, 16 November 1813 (Miscellaneous Church Records, Folder 17, New Mexico State Records Center and Archives, Santa Fe).

21. deBorhegyi, "The Miraculous Shrines."

22. José Rafael Aragón has often been misidentified as Miguel Aragón; see, for example, Charles D. Carroll, "Miguel Aragón, a Great Santero," *El Palacio* L, 3 (March 1943). This confusion resulted from a mix-up in the names as remembered by residents of Córdova. Miguel was a son of José Rafael; a signature on the back of one of José Rafael's works has clarified the confusion.

23. Although it is not among the Chávez-Usner Collection, this document is on file with the Borrego-Ortega Papers in the New Mexico State Records Center and Archives in Santa Fe.

24. This document is in the private collection of Melita Ortega of Chimayó; it has not been archived.

25. Chávez-Usner Collection, 13 November 1890.

26. Chávez-Usner Collection, 11 October 1868.

27. Baizerman, "Textiles, Traditions," 63–70.

28. Chávez-Usner Collection, 11 October (year illegible) and 10 October 1868.

29. José Ramón's commission from the governor is in the Chávez-Usner Collection, 22 November 1876.

30. Chávez-Usner Collection, 23 November 1887.

31. Ibid., 22 September 1888.

32. Ibid., 20 November 1886.

33. Ibid., 22 November 1892.

Chapter 6: A Plaza of Primos

1. Chávez-Usner Collection, 30 May 1889.

2. This story is recorded in Weigle, *Hispanic Villages*, 90.

3. I can find no evidence of a genealogical link between Gervacio and Grabiel, but the lineage from Grabiel to Gervacio and then to José Ramón is so entrenched in the oral history of the plaza that I have decided it has a basis in fact.

4. For a thorough—and very critical—discussion of the Santa Cruz dam project, see Hugh G. Calkins, "Village Livelihood in the Upper Río Grande Area, and A Note on the Level of Village Livelihood in the Upper Río Grande Area," Regional Bulletin No. 44, Conservation Economics Series No. 17 (Washington, D.C.: U.S. Department of Agriculture, Soil Conservation Service, 1937), 10; see also Weigle, *Hispanic Villages*, 95.

5. I have not found any documentary evidence to support this idea, but the county boundary change is evident in many documents.

Chapter 7: Food from Garden and Llano

1. Chávez-Usner Collection, 10 September 1706.

2. For a discussion of chile in northern New Mexico during the Great Depression see Weigle, *Hispanic Villages*, 223–234.

3. Ibid., 232.

4. Ibid., 89.

5. Ibid., 86.

6. Ibid., 230.

7. A total of fifty people from Chimayó owned land in El Llano in 1935; thirty to forty owned land in the Rosario Grant of Truchas; see Weigle, *Hispanic Villages*, 94.

8. From Melita Ortega's collection of papers.

Chapter 8: Keeping the Faith

1. Jaramillo, "La Casa del Patrón," 13.

2. Rubén Cobos, *A Dictionary of New Mexico and Southern Colorado Spanish* (Santa Fe: Museum of New Mexico Press, 1983), 108.

3. Ruth K. Barber and Edith H. Agnew, *Sowers Went Forth: The Story of the Presbyterian Mission in New Mexico and Southern Colorado* (Albuquerque: Menaul Historical Library of the Southwest, 1981), 72.

4. Ibid., 73.

5. Newspaper clipping on file with the Prudence Clark Collection of photographs in the Menaul Historical Library of the Southwest in Albuquerque (no date).

6. Carolyn Atkins, ed., *Los Tres Campos (The Three Fields): A History of Protestant Evangelists in Chimayó, Córdova, and Truchas, New Mexico* (Albuquerque: Menaul Historical Library of the Southwest, 1978), 38.

7. Barber and Agnew, *Sowers Went Forth*, 73. This date differs from that given in Atkins, *Los Tres Compos*, which is January 14, 1903.

8. Atkins, *Los Tres Campos*, 39.

9. Olga E. Hoff, "The Life of a Recent Graduate from an Eastern College as Maestra in a New Mexico Plaza," *Home Mission Monthly* (November 1914), 12–13.

10. Ibid., 13.

Chapter 9: Para Ganar Dinero

1. Suzanne Forrest, *The Preservation of the Village: New Mexico's Hispanics and the New Deal* (Albuquerque: University of New Mexico Press, 1989), 79.

2. Weigle, *Hispanic Villages*, 92.

3. Chávez-Usner Collection, 25 April 1896.

4. Ledgers from Victor's store were obtained from Dan Jaramillo of Chimayó.

5. Weigle, *Hispanic Villages*, 91.

6. Baizerman, "Textiles, Traditions," 62–67.

7. Much of the information here is taken from Baizerman, "Textiles, Traditions."
8. Gjevre, *Chili Line*, 18.
9. Baizerman, "Textiles, Traditions," 16, 103.
10. Ibid., 122.
11. Ibid., 123–131.
12. Ibid., 181.
13. Calkins, "Village Livelihood," 5.
14. The *Santa Fe New Mexican*, 18 February 1929; Weigle, *Hispanic Villages*, 95.
15. The *Santa Fe New Mexican*, 18 February 1929.
16. Weigle, *Hispanic Villages*, 90; Calkins, "Village Livelihood," 29.
17. Forrest, *The Preservation of the Village*, 65.
18. Weigle, *Hispanic Villages*, 33–34, 85–86.
19. Baizerman, "Textiles, Traditions," 126–127.

CHAPTER 10: MOVING AWAY

1. deBorhegyi, "The Evolution of a Landscape."
2. Bainbridge Bunting and John P. Conron, "The Architecture of Northern New Mexico," *New Mexico Architecture* (September–October 1966), 35; see also Boyd, *Historic Preservation*, 81.
3. Boyd, *Historic Preservation* 81; see also a memorandum from Melvin B. Jaschke, 18 May 1967, on file with other papers related to the Plaza del Cerro in the State Historic Preservation Office in Santa Fe.
4. Boyd, *Historic Preservation*, 82–86.
5. Announcement by the Chimayó Historic Sites Committee, on file in the State Historic Preservation Office in Santa Fe.
6. *Río Grande Sun*, 15 May 1986.
7. Ibid., 29 May 1988.
8. The *Santa Fe New Mexican*, 5 June 1986.
9. Ibid., 6 June 1986; *Albuquerque Journal*, 7 June 1986.
10. *Albuquerque Journal*, 7 June 1986.

PHOTO CREDITS

Don J. Usner photographs: 7, 11, 15, 34, 35, 39, 50, 58(B), 86, 95(A), 98, 99, 150, 151, 154, 155, 163, 183, 239, 242, 247, 250, 251, 254.

Laura Gilpin photographs, from Amon Carter Museum, Fort Worth: 23, "Erosions Near Chimayó, 1951," Safety neg., Acc. #P1979.223.879; 87, "Chi-mayó [Set made for Post Cards] May 1939," Nitrate neg., Acc. #P1979.208.1363; 87, "Chimayó and Figures, 1945," Safety neg., Acc. #P1979.208.748; 90, "Chimayó [Set made for Post Cards] May 1939," Nitrate neg., Acc. #P1979.208.1357; 91, "Chimayó (For Taylor Museum), July 1934," Nitrate neg., Acc. #P1979.208.1340; 102, "Chimayó Weavers," 8 x 10 nitrate neg., Acc. #P1979.202.241; 186, "Chimayó (For Taylor Museum), July 1934," Nitrate neg., Acc. #P1979.208.1345; 218, "Chimayó Weavers, May 1940" 8 x 10 nitrate neg., Acc. #P1979.202.240; 219, "Chimayó Weavers, [Ignacio Ortega], July 1947," Safety neg., Acc. #P1979.202.217. From Museum of International Folk Art, E. Boyd Files: 95(B).

Prudence Clark photographs, courtesy of the Menaul Historical Library Collection: 51, 58, 115, 142, 143, 158, 166(B), 174, 199(A), 202(A), 203, 206, 207, 210.

Prudence Clark photographs courtesy of Melita Ortega: 131, 199(B), 202(B), 206(A).

Other photographers: 11, Rosanna Hall photograph courtesy of Amada Trujillo; 55, Jesse Nusbaum, MNM; 175, Art Taylor, Museum of International Folk Art, E. Boyd Files; 191, Odd Halseth, Museum of International Folk Art, E. Boyd Files.

Unknown photographers: 63, MNM Neg. #59316; 94, MNM Neg. #29067; 114, MNM; 227, MNM Neg. #6918; 139, 170, Museum of International Folk Art, E. Boyd Files; 106, 122, Courtesy of Mercedes Trujillo; 118(A), 123, 130, Courtesy of Benigna Ortega Chávez; 118(B), 166(A), Courtesy of Melita Ortega; 107, Courtesy of Amada Naranjo Trujillo; 111, Courtesy of Helen Jaramillo Córdova; 126–27, Courtesy of John Trujillo; 134, 238, Courtesy of Domitila Villa; 167, Courtesy of Luis Sandoval.

Index